The

Theological

Truth

By:

William Rundle

Copyright © 2025, 2026 by William Rundle

All rights reserved.

No part of this publication may be reproduced, stored in a retrieval system, or transmitted in any form or by any means—electronic, mechanical, photocopying, recording, or otherwise—without the prior written permission of the publisher, except by a reviewer who may quote brief passages in a review or scholarly analysis.

Published by William Rundle

Printed in the United States of America

ISBN: 979-8-218-92015-9

Revised Edition, 5.5 x 8.5 inches

Scripture quotations are taken from the King James Version (KJV) of the Bible.

Scripture quotations marked "NIV" are taken from the Holy Bible, New International Version®, NIV®. Copyright © 1973, 1978, 1984, 2011 by Biblica, Inc.®

Used by permission. All rights reserved.

Cover design by William Rundle

Interior design by William Rundle

Table of Contents

Introduction 1
Chapter 1: Is There a Higher Power? 3
Chapter 2: Who Is the Higher Power? 13
Chapter 3: Divine Inspiration 32
    Scientific Facts 33
    Archaeology 41
    Fulfilled Prophecies 59
Chapter 4: Authority 186
    Islam 187
    Is Jesus the Messiah? 198
Chapter 5: The Apostasy 229
    The Trinity Fallacy 235
    Is the Soul Immortal? 286
    Lucifer 306
    Satan 318
    The Devil 350
    Heaven 369
Chapter 6: The Future 379
    Resurrection 382
    Judgment 384
    Marriage Supper of the Lamb 393
    Elijah's Mission 398
    Armageddon 401
    March of the Rainbow Angel 474
    The Kingdom 489
Chapter 7: Righteousness 515
Chapter 8: Resolution 544

Introduction

If there is a higher power, why haven't they revealed themselves to us—or have they? And what's the purpose of life if we all die anyway? These are just a few of the questions that I attempt to answer in this book.

I often find myself debating with people online about such questions, and those conversations have deepened my knowledge and pursuit of the truth. They've also inspired me to write down what I've learned so it can be accessible to any who are interested. For I believe it would be foolish of me to conceal the enlightenment I've gained through studying these life-changing, eye-opening topics and not continue the work of certain pioneers before me.

This book was written to help those who are searching for answers find the truth. Through logical and systematic theology, I hope this helps more people understand that the answers they seek have been present all along, not hidden.

Chapter 1: Is There a Higher Power?

There has always been a belief in gods or a god throughout the long history of civilization. There have been many different gods that various groups have claimed are real. But are they really?

For the vast majority of these deities, there is no logical evidence to support their existence, especially those that people would build. Idols that were made out of gold, wood, stone, and other materials could not have possessed any power before the builders, as they were nothing more than inanimate objects.

Chapter 1: *Is There a Higher Power?*

Well, where did everything come from then? Can nothing make anything? It sounds ridiculous, but it is what atheists believe.

Atheists do not believe in a higher power; instead, they believe that the whole universe came into existence by pure chance. Many believe that there was originally one cell that, over time, continued to expand, eventually giving rise to the life we know and see now.

However, where would that one cell have come from? Moreover, if it just appeared out of nowhere, the likelihood of it transforming into the universe we have now is essentially impossible.

> The complexity of life is not merely a question of large numbers, but of precise arrangements and functional interdependencies. The probability of even a simple protein forming by

Chapter 1: *Is There a Higher Power?*

chance alone is so small as to be indistinguishable from zero.[1]

If even a single protein has essentially a zero percent chance of forming on its own, then how did the entire universe?

An Oxford physicist named Dr. Roger Penrose calculated that the odds of the universe forming by chance are 1 in 10^10^123. This number is so high that it cannot even be written down! The amount of zeros following the 1 is so large that if every atom in the universe wrote a zero every billionth of a second, it still would not finish. That is how desperate atheists are to not believe in a higher power.

---

[1] Walter L. Bradley, Charles B. Thaxton, and Roger L. Olsen, *The Mystery of Life's Origin: Reassessing Current Theories* (New York: Philosophical Library, 1984), 130.

Chapter 1: *Is There a Higher Power?*

When we examine the theory of evolution more closely, we see that not all evolutionists agree on every aspect. Two main branches of evolution are macroevolution and microevolution. Macroevolution refers to the occurrence of significant evolutionary changes within entire taxonomic groups over extended periods of time. Microevolution refers to the gradual changes within a species over shorter periods. Microevolution is well-documented and observable, whereas the same cannot be said about macroevolution.

The different races of humans are a great example. Those who live closer to the equator will have darker skin than those who live further from the equator. Let's say there were two brothers. One decided to live in Ireland, and the other decided to live in Sudan. In just a few generations, their descendants

Chapter 1: *Is There a Higher Power?*

would be related, but they would look a lot different from each other.

There have been experiments conducted on lizards and fish, where they were placed in different habitats and temperatures. Over time, they adapted and changed to better fit into their new environments. However, they're still lizards; they're still fish. We have never observed an animal transform into a completely different species, which is what macroevolution is.

Some people believe in theistic evolution. The belief is that there is a creator who created life and allowed it to evolve over billions of years.

This belief does not make much sense. Why would a creator create life just for it to change? Why not just make the final product?

Chapter 1: *Is There a Higher Power?*

It is even harder to deny the existence of a creator when examining the complexity and order of the universe. The universe is full of mind-blowing intricacies that all function together in seemingly perfect order.

We live on a planet called Earth, which orbits the Sun in our solar system and floats in space. Earth is home to millions of animal species that work together to maintain balance in several different ecosystems. Every single living thing has a purpose.

Organisms known as producers yield their food. Examples include trees, grass, algae, and seaweed. Other organisms, called consumers, are creatures that eat plants or animals to obtain their energy. Examples include humans, deer, lions, mice, and hawks. Organisms such as earthworms, termites, millipedes, bacteria, and fungi are decomposers, which

Chapter 1: *Is There a Higher Power?*

means they break down dead organisms to release nutrients, leading to the growth of new organisms. All of these living things rely on each other in one way or another.

Organisms can live on Earth because Earth contains the right temperature, hospitable land, plenty of water sources that provide lush vegetation, gravity to pull us all down so we are not floating, and oxygen so we can breathe.

There is also a large ball of fire that provides ample light for us and for plants, which need it to live and thrive. If it were any closer, we'd all cook to death, and if it were farther away, we'd all freeze. However, it just so happens that it is in the perfect place to help sustain life on Earth.

Chapter 1: *Is There a Higher Power?*

But what happens when the Sun goes down? Well, that's when the Moon and stars appear to provide light, so it's not utter darkness.

Phytoplankton is one of the most important organisms in the world due to the incredible amount of oxygen it produces. They are microscopic algae that are found in oceans, lakes, and rivers.

Even these minuscule organisms have a complex, intricate cellular structure made up of a nucleus, cell wall, and chloroplasts. The nucleus contains the organism's genetic material and controls cellular activity. The cell wall provides structure to the cell and is composed of several different components.

Chloroplasts enable plants to perform Photosynthesis, which provides oxygen. Chloroplasts also contain several different components, such as the lumen, stroma, thylakoids, and stroma lamellae.

Chapter 1: *Is There a Higher Power?*

Considering that even one of the smallest of organisms is this intricately built, one would be a fool to believe that the entire universe somehow formed itself from nothing without any errors occurring in the "evolutionary process."

Sir Isaac Newton, one of the most renowned scientists of all time, had this to say about atheism:

> Atheism is so senseless & odious to mankind that it never had many professors. Can it be by accident that all birds beasts & men have their right side & left side alike shaped (except in their bowels) & just two eyes & no more on either side the face & just two ears on either side the head & a nose with two holes & no more between the eyes & one mouth under the nose & either two fore legs or two wings or two

Chapter 1: *Is There a Higher Power?*

arms on the shoulders & two legs on the hips one on either side & no more?[2]

The overwhelming evidence of intelligent design in the universe is undeniable. If anyone rejects that there is a higher power and instead convinces themselves that everything somehow came into existence by accident, they are lying to themselves, especially when considering how improbable and extraordinary the existence of life truly is.

Atheists do not want the responsibility to live with morals. They would rather believe in the scientific impossibility that nothing created everything so they can feel free to pursue their fleshly desires.

---

[2] Isaac Newton, *Memoirs of the Life, Writings, and Discoveries of Sir Isaac Newton*, ed. David Brewster (Edinburgh: Thomas Constable and Co., 1855), 2:354.

Chapter 2: Who Is the Higher Power?

Now that we have established the existence of a higher power, the question arises as to who this higher power is. The Bible, the most popular and influential book of all time, claims to have the answer, so let's see what it has to say.

The Bible tells us that there is one God who is the creator and sustainer of the universe (Genesis 1, Deuteronomy 6:4). He created everything in a literal six days, including mankind (Genesis 1:26, 31), which contradicts the belief of theistic evolution. This God revealed His name to be "Yahweh" (YHWH), which probably means "I am" or "I will be" (Exodus 3:14).

Chapter 2: *Who Is the Higher Power?*

Although we have free will, this God gave several commands on what we should and should not do.

This has caused many people to believe that the God of the Bible is an evil narcissist, so let's see if there is any truth to this claim.

One reason why people claim the God of the Bible is a narcissist is because He constantly commands people to fear and serve Him:

(Unless otherwise noted, all Scripture quotations are from the King James Version.)

> And now, Israel, what doth the LORD thy God require of thee, but to fear the LORD thy God, to walk in all his ways, and to love him, and to serve the LORD thy God with all thy heart and with all thy soul, to keep the commandments of

Chapter 2: *Who Is the Higher Power?*

the LORD, and his statutes, which I command thee this day for thy good? (Deuteronomy 10:12–13)

Let all the earth fear the LORD: Let all the inhabitants of the world stand in awe of him. (Psalm 33:8)

Now, if this was a human saying these things, trying to exalt themselves, then obviously, we should label them as an egomaniac. But this is the supposed creator of the universe! He didn't have to make anything, but He decided to create this planet designed for humans to thrive on, gave us free will, and gave us dominion over all the animals (Genesis 1:26). As far as I'm concerned, He would deserve to be worshiped,

Chapter 2: *Who Is the Higher Power?*

praised, and feared for just as He gave us life, He can just as easily take it away.

Imagine you're the all-powerful creator and sustainer of the universe, and you decide to share your glory and create a place for people who are made in your image to inhabit. But the people constantly chase after their selfish desires, mock you, and even make up their own gods that they worship instead of you. Do you think you would accept that? Of course not.

God wants us to fear Him because it not only rightfully glorifies Him but it also helps us:

> The fear of the LORD *is* the beginning of wisdom: A good understanding have all they that do *his commandments:* His praise endureth for ever. (Psalm 111:10)

Chapter 2: *Who Is the Higher Power?*

In fear of the LORD *is* strong confidence: And his children shall have a place of refuge.

(Proverbs 14:26)

Slavery

Another popular claim made by critics is that the God of the Bible is in favor of slavery. Here are some verses that are used to support this:

> If thou buy an Hebrew servant, six years shall he serve: and in the seventh he shall go out free for nothing. (Exodus 21:2)

> Both thy bondmen, and the bondmaids, which thou shalt have, *shall be* of the heathen that are round about you; of them shall ye buy

Chapter 2: *Who Is the Higher Power?*

bondmen and bondmaids. Moreover of the children of the strangers that do sojourn among you, of them shall ye buy, and of their families that *are* with you, which they begat in your land: and they shall be your possession. (Leviticus 25:44–45)

Servants, be obedient to them that are *your* masters according to the flesh, with fear and trembling, in singleness of your heart, as unto Christ. (Ephesians 6:5)

Exhort servants to be obedient unto their own masters, *and* to please *them* well in all things; not answering again; not purloining, but shewing all good fidelity; that they may adorn

Chapter 2: *Who Is the Higher Power?*

the doctrine of God our Saviour in all things.
(Titus 2:9–10)

This opinion may seem confusing since God freed the Israelites from slavery in the Book of Exodus. We need to take a closer look, and try to conclude whether or not the God of the Bible is in fact in favor of slavery.

An essential detail to point out is that the slavery spoken of in these verses is not what we would typically picture when we think of slavery. They were not slaves in chains getting whipped; they were servants. Rabbi Joseph Hertz wrote:

> Slavery as permitted by the Torah was quite different from Greek and Roman slavery, or even the cruel system in some modern

countries down to our own times. In Hebrew law, the slave was not a thing, but a human being; he was not the chattel of a master who had unlimited power over him. In the Hebrew language, there is only one word for slave and servant. Brutal treatment of any slave, whether Hebrew or heathen, secured his immediate liberty.[3]

These servants were not treated as property; rather, their humanity was respected by their masters. Servants could also be hired (Leviticus 25:40), so at times it was the person's choice to become a servant.

Contrary to popular belief, a Gentile getting bought by a Hebrew back then was actually a great

---

[3] J. H. Hertz, *The Pentateuch and Haftorahs: Hebrew Text, English Translation and Commentary* (London: Soncino Press, 1936), 426.

Chapter 2: *Who Is the Higher Power?*

blessing. A prime example of this is Abraham's servant, Eliezer. In Genesis 15, Abraham voiced his concerns to God about his inheritance because he had no children and was old:

> And Abram said, Lord GOD, what wilt thou give me, seeing I go childless, and the steward of my house *is* this Eliezer of Damascus? And Abram said, Behold, to me thou hast given no seed: and, lo, one born in my house is mine heir. (Genesis 15:2–3)

Abraham (his name was still Abram at this point) said that if he were to die childless, then his servant Eliezer would inherit his possessions. Eliezer was from Damascus, which is located in modern-day Syria, so he likely never heard about God until he

Chapter 2: *Who Is the Higher Power?*

entered Abraham's service. The fact that before Abraham had a son, his foreign servant was first in line for his inheritance doesn't sound like slavery to me.

Later on, in Genesis chapter 24, Abraham sends Eliezer to find a wife for his son Isaac. After he set out, he prayed to God to help him find the right woman:

> And he said, O LORD God of my master Abraham, I pray thee, send me good speed this day, and shew me kindness unto my master Abraham. Behold, I stand *here* by the well of water; and the daughters of the men of the city come out to draw water: and let it come to pass, that the damsel to whom I shall say, Let down thy pitcher, I pray thee, that I may drink; and she shall say, Drink, and I will give thy camels drink also: *let the same be* she *that* thou hast

Chapter 2: *Who Is the Higher Power?*

appointed for thy servant Isaac; and thereby shall I know that thou hast shewed kindness unto my master. (Genesis 24:12–14)

God answered Eliezer's prayer, and Rebekah, the daughter of Bethuel, fulfilled the sign that Eliezer had requested.

And the man bowed down his head, and worshipped the LORD. And he said, Blessed *be* the LORD God of my master Abraham, who hath not left destitute my master of his mercy and his truth: I *being* in the way, the LORD led me to the house of my master's brethren. (Genesis 24:26–27)

Chapter 2: *Who Is the Higher Power?*

After coming into Abraham's service, Eliezer, who was from Damascus, converted to worship the LORD, which most likely would not have happened if he had stayed in Damascus. (We will explore later in this book whether the God of the Bible is real or not, which would make or break this case.)

> Thou shalt not deliver unto his master the servant which is escaped from his master unto thee: he shall dwell with thee, *even* among you, in that place which he shall choose in one of thy gates, where it liketh him best: thou shalt not oppress him. (Deuteronomy 23:15–16)

This law protects the safety of a servant if they were to run away from their master. Why would a

Chapter 2: *Who Is the Higher Power?*

servant run away from their master? If their master was mistreating them.

So if a servant was being oppressed or abused by their master, which is what we imagine when we think of slavery, the law allows them to escape, and they would be well protected. All of the Hebrew laws concerning slavery favored the servants.

The God of the Bible is not a God who wants people to be oppressed and mistreated, but rather to gain a mindset filled with obedience to help them on the path towards righteousness:

> Let every soul be subject unto the higher powers. For there is no power but of God: the powers that be are ordained of God. (Romans 13:1)

Chapter 2: *Who Is the Higher Power?*

Cruelty?

Another claim skeptics make is that the God of the Bible is evil because He murders innocents. Here are some verses that are commonly used to support this claim:

> And every living substance was destroyed which was upon the face of the ground, both man, and cattle, and the creeping things, and the fowl of the heaven; and they were destroyed from the earth: and Noah only remained *alive*, and they that *were* with him in the ark. (Genesis 7:23)

Chapter 2: *Who Is the Higher Power?*

And it came to pass, that at midnight the LORD smote all the firstborn in the land of Egypt, from the firstborn of Pharaoh that sat on his throne unto the firstborn of the captive that *was* in the dungeon; and all the firstborn of cattle. And Pharaoh rose up in the night, he, and all his servants, and all the Egyptians; and there was a great cry in Egypt; for *there was* not a house where *there was* not one dead. (Exodus 12:29–30)

Now go and smite Amalek, and utterly destroy all that they have, and spare them not; but slay both man and woman, infant and suckling, ox and sheep, camel and ass. (1 Samuel 15:3)

Chapter 2: *Who Is the Higher Power?*

These verses may seem harsh. However, it's essential to understand the reason why God carried these out: they were acts of judgment. God says that He does not delight in the death of the wicked:

> Say unto them, *As* I live, saith the Lord GOD, I have no pleasure in the death of the wicked; but that the wicked turn from his way and live: turn ye, turn ye from your evil ways; for why will ye die, O house of Israel? (Ezekiel 33:11)

It is made clear in the Scriptures that God did not create people so we could follow our own selfish desires without a care in the world. He commanded us to pursue righteousness (Exodus 20:1–17, Deuteronomy 28).

Chapter 2: *Who Is the Higher Power?*

When the flood occurred, Noah was the only righteous person on the earth, and the rest of humanity was sinning greatly. They were defiling themselves, exalting themselves, and engaging in all of the hedonistic pleasures that the world had to offer without any concern for their creator. The flood was a judgment on mankind for their immorality and disregard for the LORD.

God brought judgments upon Egypt for enslaving His people, Israel. Nine plagues passed by, but Pharaoh still hardened his heart and would not let them go. The final plague resulted in the death of every firstborn in Egypt, excluding the Israelites, who were spared by putting sheep's blood on the doorframes of their houses (Exodus 12). The Egyptians also worshiped several false, made-up gods and were

Chapter 2: *Who Is the Higher Power?*

overall a very sinful nation, so why would God owe them anything?

There is this common misconception that God owes us something. He doesn't owe anyone anything! Job understood this principle when he said: "Naked came I out of my mother's womb, and naked shall I return thither: the LORD gave, and the LORD hath taken away; blessed be the name of the LORD." (Job 1:21)

God also commanded the Israelites that when they attack a nation, they are to destroy everything. This was because the nations were very sinful, and something the Israelites would often tend to do was get influenced by the corrupt ways of these surrounding peoples.

For example, in 1 Samuel 8, the Israelites voiced their complaints to the prophet Samuel about

Chapter 2: *Who Is the Higher Power?*

wanting a human king who would lead them into battle, just like the other nations had. They rejected God as their king and wanted a human king instead.

These other nations worshiped idols (Deuteronomy 12:2–3). Some would even sacrifice their children to them (Deuteronomy 12:31), so it makes perfect sense why God would want to punish those wicked people for their sins as well as remove those influences from the presence of His people who were to be a holy nation separate from the world (Exodus 19:6).

After analyzing the biblical texts, I believe we can conclude that the God of the Bible is not an evil deity but a just creator who cares for us and wants us to love Him and follow His righteous commands.

Chapter 3: Divine Inspiration

Why should we even believe what the Bible says? Why should we follow some book written by men thousands of years ago? 2 Timothy 3:16 tells us that the Bible, although written by men, is inspired by God. How can we prove that the Bible is the inspired work of the creator of the universe?

Firstly, the chances of ancient texts written thousands of years ago being preserved and continuously transcribed to form the most influential book of all time are slim to none. Surely, if there were an all-powerful being who wanted His inspired word to get passed down through the centuries, it would happen.

Chapter 3: *Divine Inspiration*

The Bible also exhibits incredible consistency, as it contains thousands of cross-references. For a book written by different men at different times without any divine inspiration, this would be extraordinarily impressive.

Scientific Facts

Contrary to popular belief, the Bible contains scientific facts that were recorded several years before the technology to verify them existed.

In the Book of Job, it says that the earth is floating in space: "He stretcheth out the north over the empty place, *And* hangeth the earth upon nothing." (Job 26:7)

Chapter 3: *Divine Inspiration*

For years, people believed that the earth was supported by something. The discovery that the earth rests upon nothing was not found until many years after the Book of Job was authored. There was no technology back then that they could have used to figure this out.

It was once commonly believed that blood was harmful to one's health. There was a procedure called bloodletting, which involved removing blood from a sick person's body in the hope that the loss of blood would aid in the patient's recovery. In the 19th century, it was discovered that blood is essential for our health, and removing it has harmful effects. What does the Bible, which was most certainly written before the 19th century, have to say about this?

Chapter 3: *Divine Inspiration*

<u>For the life of the flesh *is* in the blood</u>: and I have given it to you upon the altar to make an atonement for your souls: for it *is* the blood *that* maketh an atonement for the soul. (Leviticus 17:11)

They could have extended many lives if they had just read the Bible, which said all along that blood gives life to the flesh, not death.

In the 1800s, many women died after childbirth due to a condition called puerperal fever. Doctors were puzzled, unaware of the role of germs in spreading infection.

In 1847, a Hungarian physician named Ignaz Semmelweis discovered that doctors who performed autopsies and then delivered babies, without washing their hands, were spreading deadly bacteria. He introduced a practice of washing hands with a chlorinated lime solution between patients. As a result, the maternal death rate dropped dramatically, from as high as 18% to around 2%.

The doctors could have prevented many people from growing up without their mothers if they had just read Leviticus 15:13, which reads:

> And when he that hath an issue is cleansed of his issue; then he shall number to himself seven days for his cleansing, and wash his clothes, and <u>bathe his flesh in running water, and shall be clean</u>. (Leviticus 15:13)

Scripture also says that babies are to get circumcised on the eighth day of their lives: "And in

Chapter 3: *Divine Inspiration*

the eighth day the flesh of the foreskin shall be circumcised." (Leviticus 12:3)

This is because vitamin K levels peak in a baby on the eighth day after birth. The baby, therefore, has a higher chance of bleeding to death if it is circumcised before or after the eighth day.

In Psalm 8, we read: "The fowl of the air, and the fish of the sea, *And whatsoever* passeth through the paths of the seas." (Psalm 8:8)

This reference to "the paths of the seas" inspired Matthew Fontaine Maury (1806–1873) to discover ocean currents. Could ancient Israelites have been aware of ocean currents, given the primitive technology they possessed? Certainly not.

Scripture also speaks of light and radio waves: "Canst thou send lightnings, that they may go, And say unto thee, Here we *are?*" (Job 38:35)

Chapter 3: *Divine Inspiration*

Light and radio waves weren't discovered until the late 1880s by Heinrich Hertz, well after the Bible was written.

Orion is a star constellation mentioned in Job chapter 38: "Canst thou bind the sweet influences of Pleiades, Or loose the bands of Orion?" (Job 38:31)

It was not discovered until thousands of years later that the stars in Orion are not gravitationally bound but are actually drifting apart. God says to Job that He can "loose" Orion, implying Orion's instability well before it was scientifically known.

In that same verse, God mentions the Pleiades and how it is bound together. This was not discovered until the late 19th to the 20th century, over 2,000 years after the Book of Job was written.

The next verse of Job 38 says: "Canst thou guide Arcturus with his sons?" (Job 38:32)

Chapter 3: *Divine Inspiration*

Back in ancient times, Arcturus was only thought to be one star by some. But God said all those years ago that Arcturus has "sons," which refers to the dozens of other stars in the Arcturus Stream. These stars move at 275,000 miles per hour which is why God says they need to be guided. To the naked eye, Arcturus is still.

These ancient descriptions of Orion, the Pleiades, and Arcturus are remarkably consistent with modern discoveries, providing further evidence that the Bible was inspired by a higher power.

The Book of Isaiah mentions that the universe is expanding by saying that God "stretcheth out the heavens as a curtain…" (Isaiah 40:22)

This discovery was made in 1929 by Edwin Hubble, who observed that galaxies were moving away

Chapter 3: *Divine Inspiration*

from one another at an increasing rate. The answer was right there in the Bible all along.

The water cycle explains the movement of water throughout the earth. It consists of evaporation, condensation, precipitation, and collection. This knowledge was not known in ancient times, yet the Bible mentions it:

> For he maketh small the drops of water: They pour down rain according to the vapour thereof: Which the clouds do drop *And* distil upon man abundantly. (Job 36:27–28)

> All the rivers run into the sea; yet the sea *is* not full; unto the place from whence the rivers come, thither they return again. (Ecclesiastes 1:7)

Chapter 3: *Divine Inspiration*

The Bible also mentions quarantining: "All the days wherein the plague *shall be* in him he shall be defiled; he *is* unclean: he shall dwell alone; without the camp *shall* his habitation *be*." (Leviticus 13:46)

Believing that there is an all-powerful creator who inspired ancient writings that contain knowledge people could not have known at the time they were written makes much more sense than believing that ancient people somehow guessed these facts and wrote them in a book for no reason.

Archaeology

Another reason why the Bible is authoritative is the archaeological discoveries that help prove the existence of figures, ethnic groups, and places mentioned in the Scriptures. Many believe the Bible is a fictional book that contains fictional places and fictional people. However, archaeological findings have disproven several of these claims.

Hittites

The Hittites were a group of people from modern-day Turkey. The Bible mentions them numerous times because they had dwelt among the Israelites. Here are some verses that mention the Hittites:

> And Esau was forty years old when he took to wife Judith the daughter of Beeri the Hittite, and Basemath the daughter of Elon the Hittite. (Genesis 26:34).

Chapter 3: *Divine Inspiration*

And it shall be when the LORD shall bring thee into the land of the Canaanites, and the Hittites, and the Amorites, and the Hivites, and the Jebusites, which he sware unto thy fathers to give thee, a land flowing with milk and honey, that thou shalt keep this service in this month. (Exodus 13:5)

Also the valiant men of the armies *were*… Uriah the Hittite… (1 Chronicles 11:26, 41)

Many doubted the existence of these people until the late 19th century, when archaeologists discovered evidence of the Hittites, thereby lending support to the historical credibility of biblical accounts

Chapter 3: *Divine Inspiration*

that mention these ancient people. These findings include city ruins, trade records, and clay tablets.[4]

Egyptian Inscriptions

In 1896, an archaeologist named Flinders Petrie discovered the Merneptah Stele in Thebes, Egypt. The stele's inscription speaks of Pharaoh Merneptah's victories. In line 27, the hieroglyphs have been translated to contain the word "Israel." This supports the idea that the people of Israel are as ancient as the Bible says they are.[5]

Two other Egyptian inscriptions, one from the time of Pharaoh Amenhotep III and the other from the time of Pharaoh Ramses II, contain the phrase "Shasu

---

[4] Trevor Bryce, *Life and Society in the Hittite World* (Oxford: Oxford University Press, 2002), 1–5.
[5] Flinders Petrie, *Six Temples at Thebes, 1896* (London: Egypt Exploration Fund, 1897), 28–30.

Chapter 3: *Divine Inspiration*

of Yahweh." "Shasu" is the word for nomads in Egyptian, and "Yahweh" (YHWH) is the name of the God of the Bible, as revealed in Exodus 3:14. These findings support the idea that the name of Israel's God was known to people in that region in ancient times.[6]

Joseph

Joseph was the eleventh of Jacob's 12 sons and the great-grandson of Abraham, the forefather of Israel. Joseph's brothers envied him because he was their father's favorite, so they sold him to Midianite traders, who in turn sold him to Egypt (Genesis 37). However, their plan backfired when Joseph was made second in command in all of Egypt behind Pharaoh (Genesis 41:41–45).

---

[6] James K. Hoffmeier, *Israel in Egypt: The Evidence for the Authenticity of the Exodus Tradition* (Oxford: Oxford University Press, 1997), 115–117.

Chapter 3: *Divine Inspiration*

Archaeologists have discovered a palace in Egypt that is believed to have belonged to a high-ranking official. The palace contained 12 tombs and 12 pillars. Joseph was one of 12 sons who made up the 12 tribes of Israel.

One of the tombs appeared to be made for royalty, and Joseph was given an incredibly high rank and authority in Egypt. Inside, a statue of a man with yellow skin was displayed, wearing a multicolored coat. The Egyptians would portray northerners with yellow skin and Joseph was given a multicolored coat from his father, as told in Genesis 37:3.

What is even more interesting about this discovery is that no bones were found inside the tomb, supporting the biblical record which tells us that Joseph's bones were taken from Egypt by Moses during the Exodus (Exodus 13:19). This palace could have very well belonged to Joseph.[7]

Tel Dan Inscription

In 1993, an archaeologist named Gila Cook found an ancient inscribed stele in Israel known as the Tel Dan Inscription. The stele mentions biblical kings such as Jehoram and Ahaziah and details a king's (likely King Hazael of Aram-Damascus) victories over these Israelite rulers. It also mentions "the house of David," which provides credible evidence that David was not some fictional character the biblical authors made up but rather that he actually existed.[8]

---

[7] David Rohl, *The Lost Testament: From Eden to Exile – The Five-Thousand-Year History of the People of the Bible* (London: Century, 2002), 224–230.
[8] Avraham Biran and Joseph Naveh, *The Tel Dan Inscription* (Jerusalem: Israel Exploration Society, 1995), 1–12.

Chapter 3: *Divine Inspiration*

David's Palace

In 2 Samuel 5, we're told of the construction of King David's "house" or palace: "And Hiram king of Tyre sent messengers to David, and cedar trees, and carpenters, and masons: and they built David an house." (2 Samuel 5:11)

In 2005, an Israeli archaeologist named Dr. Eilat Mazar discovered a large stone structure in Jerusalem. It was dated to the time of David's reign, approximately 1000 BC. The size of the structure suggests it was built for someone of great power, such as the king of Israel.

It contained Phoenician-style decorations, which makes sense since the biblical record says it was built by Tyrians, who were Phoenicians. The pottery found in the structure was also dated to around the

Chapter 3: *Divine Inspiration*

time of David. All signs point to this discovery being the palace of King David, the second king of Israel.[9]

The Moabite Stone

2 Kings chapter 3 is about King Mesha of Moab rebelling against the Israelites. Mesha rebelled after Ahab, the king of Israel, died and was succeeded by his son Jehoram.

In 1868, a stone was discovered by Frederick Augustus Klein in present-day Jordan. The writings on the stone were written by King Mesha, detailing his victories against the son of Omri. Omri was Ahab's father and Jehoram's grandfather.

The inscription also mentions the Moabite god Chemosh, which is also mentioned in the Bible (1

---

[9] Eilat Mazar, *The Palace of King David: Excavations at the City of David* (Jerusalem: Shoham Academic Research and Publication, 2006), 45–59.

Kings 11:33). This discovery is commonly known as the Moabite Stone or the Mesha Stele. This further helps validate the Bible as a historically accurate source.[10]

Hezekiah's Tunnel

The Scriptures tell us that King Hezekiah built a tunnel in Jerusalem whose purpose was to bring fresh water into the city during a siege:

> And the rest of the acts of Hezekiah, and all his might, and how he made a pool, and a conduit, and brought water into the city, *are* they not written in the book of the chronicles of the kings of Judah? (2 Kings 20:20)

---

[10] F. A. Klein, *Discovery of the Moabite Stone* (London: Palestine Exploration Fund, 1868), 5–12.

Chapter 3: *Divine Inspiration*

This same Hezekiah also stopped the upper watercourse of Gihon, and brought it straight down to the west side of the city of David. And Hezekiah prospered in all his works. (2 Chronicles 32:30)

In 1837, Edward Robinson discovered Hezekiah's Tunnel, also known as the Siloam Tunnel, in eastern Jerusalem. The tunnel extends from the Gihon Spring to the Pool of Siloam, which supports the biblical narrative. The Pool of Siloam was also where Jesus healed the man born blind (John 9:7). Hezekiah's Tunnel helps provide solid evidence that the Israelite kings mentioned in the Bible were real.[11]

---

[11] Edward Robinson, *Biblical Researches in Palestine* (Boston: Crocker & Brewster, 1841), 85–90.

Chapter 3: *Divine Inspiration*

The Sennacherib Prism

In 2 Kings 18 and 19, God brings Sennacherib, king of Assyria, against Judah during the reign of King Hezekiah. He successfully conquers cities in Judah and lays siege to Jerusalem but is not able to capture Hezekiah because God sends an angel, which kills 185,000 of his men, forcing him to withdraw.

In 1830, the Sennacherib Prism, a notable discovery, was found at Nineveh, the ancient Assyrian capital. The prism records Sennacherib boasting about conquering many cities in Judah, but it does not mention him capturing Jerusalem nor Hezekiah, which aligns perfectly with the biblical record.[12]

---

[12] Daniel D. Luckenbill, *The Annals of Sennacherib* (Chicago: University of Chicago Press, 1926), 123–130.

Chapter 3: *Divine Inspiration*

The Cyrus Cylinder

In the Book of Ezra chapter 1, King Cyrus of Persia gives a decree allowing the Jews to return to Jerusalem:

> Now in the first year of Cyrus king of Persia, that the word of the LORD by the mouth of Jeremiah might be fulfilled, the LORD stirred up the spirit of Cyrus king of Persia, that he made a proclamation throughout all his kingdom, and *put it* also in writing, saying, Thus saith Cyrus king of Persia, The LORD God of heaven hath given me all the kingdoms of the earth; and he hath charged me to build him an house at Jerusalem, which *is* in Judah, and build the house of the LORD God of Israel,

Chapter 3: *Divine Inspiration*

(he *is* the God,) which *is* in Jerusalem. And whosoever remaineth in any place where he sojourneth, let the men of his place help him with silver, and with gold, and with goods, and with beasts, beside the freewill offering for the house of God that *is* in Jerusalem. (Ezra 1:1–4)

In 1879, a British archaeologist named Hormuzd Rassam discovered what is now known as the Cyrus Cylinder, a clay cylinder dating back to the 6th century BC. The cylinder praises Cyrus for returning exiles and ordering the rebuilding of temples, aligning with the biblical account.[13]

---

[13] Hormuzd Rassam, *Asshur and the Land of Nimrod* (New York: Harper & Brothers, 1885), 200–210.

Chapter 3: *Divine Inspiration*

Clay Seals

Numerous clay seals have been discovered that mention biblical figures. These include Hezekiah (king of Judah), Ahaz (king of Judah), Jehucal (Zedekiah's royal official), Gedaliah son of Pashur (an official who opposed Jeremiah), Baruch son of Neriah (Jeremiah's scribe), and Isaiah (prophet). These figures are mentioned in the following passages: 2 Kings 18–20, Isaiah 36–39, 2 Kings 15–16, Jeremiah 37:3, Jeremiah 38:1, Jeremiah 36, and the Book of Isaiah. These findings help prove the existence of these biblical figures, further validating the Bible's historical accuracy.[14]

---

[14] Yohanan Aharoni, *The Archaeology of the Land of Israel* (Boulder: Westview Press, 1979), 203–210.
Christopher A. Rollston, "The Seal Impressions of Jehucal and Gedaliah," *Bulletin of the American Schools of Oriental Research*, no. 357 (2010): 41–51.

Chapter 3: *Divine Inspiration*

Pontius Pilate

Pontius Pilate was the fifth Roman governor of Judea, who is notoriously known for ordering Jesus' crucifixion.

> Pilate saith unto them, What shall I do then with Jesus which is called Christ? *They* all say unto him, Let him be crucified. And the governor said, Why, what evil hath he done? But they cried out the more, saying, Let him be crucified. When Pilate saw that he could prevail nothing, but *that* rather a tumult was made, he took water, and washed *his* hands before the multitude, saying, I am innocent of the blood of this just person: see ye *to it*. Then answered all the people, and said, His blood *be*

Chapter 3: *Divine Inspiration*

on us, and on our children. Then released he Barabbas unto them: and when he had scourged Jesus, he delivered *him* to be crucified.

(Matthew 27:22–26)

In 1961, archaeologist Maria Teresa Fortuna Canivet found a block of limestone in Caesarea, Israel. The block contained an inscription that mentioned the name "Pontius Pilate." This helps prove that Pilate did exist, and thus, the events of Jesus' crucifixion are given more credibility.[15]

Dead Sea Scrolls

Perhaps the most significant biblical archaeological discovery is the Dead Sea Scrolls. The

---

[15] Maria Teresa Fortuna Canivet, "The Pontius Pilate Inscription," *Israel Exploration Journal* 13, no. 2 (1963): 79–84.

Chapter 3: *Divine Inspiration*

scrolls were discovered in the Qumran Caves between 1946 and 1956. The manuscripts were allegedly written between the 3rd century BC and the 1st century CE, though it may have been even earlier as people often tend to biasedly date biblical artifacts later to give them less credibility. They are the oldest known copies of biblical writings, containing parts of every Old Testament book, excluding the Book of Esther.

Many skeptics have attempted to argue that the Bible has been altered over time and that its words are not as ancient as they claim to be. However, the Dead Sea Scrolls disprove this claim because our modern Bibles contain the same messages as those found in the Dead Sea Scrolls, indicating that the Scriptures have not been tampered with and that God has kept His holy book preserved.[16]

---

[16] James C. VanderKam and Peter W. Flint, *The Meaning of the Dead Sea Scrolls* (San Francisco: HarperOne, 2002), 45–68.

Chapter 3: *Divine Inspiration*

There are still several more archaeological discoveries that help prove the Bible as a historically accurate source, and I am sure there are plenty more to come.

Fulfilled Prophecies

The most convincing evidence for the Bible's divine inspiration for me is the fulfilled prophecies. The Scriptures have foretold numerous historical events in incredibly accurate detail, which were eventually fulfilled several years after they were written.

Tov, Emanuel (2012) *Textual Criticism of the Hebrew Bible*, Fortress Press, Minneapolis, pp. 102–120.

Chapter 3: *Divine Inspiration*

1948

One of the more prominent of these prophecies concerns the restoration of the nation of Israel. After a series of attacks on the holy land throughout the years, the Jewish homeland was taken, and they were scattered amongst other nations. Not only did God say this would happen, but He also said He would bring them back to their land from which they were scattered.

God gave the prophet Ezekiel a vision, as recorded in Ezekiel chapter 37. In the vision, Ezekiel sees a valley of dry, skeletal remains. The bones eventually fuse together and become covered in flesh and skin. Then, they were given life and became a large army.

Chapter 3: *Divine Inspiration*

Then he said unto me, Son of man, these bones are the whole house of Israel: behold, they say, Our bones are dried, and our hope is lost: we are cut off for our parts. Therefore prophesy and say unto them, Thus saith the Lord GOD; Behold, O my people, I will open your graves, and cause you to come up out of your graves, and bring you into the land of Israel. And ye shall know that I *am* the LORD, when I have opened your graves, O my people, and brought you up out of your graves, and shall put my spirit in you, and ye shall live, and I shall place you in your own land: then shall ye know that I the LORD have spoken *it*, and performed *it*, saith the LORD. (Ezekiel 37:11–14)

Chapter 3: *Divine Inspiration*

What's fascinating is that this was fulfilled in the relatively recent year of 1948 when Israel was reestablished as a nation, and the Jews were brought back to their land.

When have we ever seen an ancient group of people get overthrown, scattered amongst other nations, persecuted at such a level of brutality, and then at last brought back to their land seemingly against all odds? God loves to do things that seem impossible from a human perspective to show us that He controls the odds.

When discussions of Israel's reestablishment were circulating in 1948, the two United States presidential candidates were Harry Truman and Thomas Dewey. Truman was in favor of Israel becoming a nation again, but Dewey was not. It reached a point in the election where they were so

Chapter 3: *Divine Inspiration*

confident Dewey was going to win that a now infamous newspaper headline appeared: "Dewey Defeats Truman." Sure enough, come election night, the Zionist supporter Harry Truman won the election instead, and later that year, Israel was reestablished as a nation.

How ludicrous it would be to believe that ancient people randomly wrote about this improbable prophecy in a book, only for it to be fulfilled thousands of years later unless it was inspired by God.

Egypt's Curse

The nation of Egypt has a vibrant and deep history. The ancient Egyptians were a powerhouse whose technological advancements and culture have left a lasting impact on us today. Despite its former

Chapter 3: *Divine Inspiration*

glory, Egypt has struggled to regain its prosperous past for many years. God tells us why in Ezekiel chapter 29:

> Therefore thus saith the Lord GOD; Behold, I will bring a sword upon thee, and cut off man and beast out of thee. And the land of Egypt shall be desolate and waste; and they shall know that I *am* the LORD: because he hath said, The river *is* mine, and I have made *it*. Behold, therefore I *am* against thee, and against thy rivers, and I will make the land of Egypt utterly waste *and* desolate, from the tower of Syene even unto the border of Ethiopia. No foot of man shall pass through it, nor foot of beast shall pass through it, neither shall it be inhabited forty years. And I will make the land

Chapter 3: *Divine Inspiration*

of Egypt desolate in the midst of the countries *that are* desolate, and her cities among the cities *that are* laid waste shall be desolate forty years: and I will scatter the Egyptians among the nations, and will disperse them through the countries. Yet thus saith the Lord GOD; At the end of forty years will I gather the Egyptians from the people whither they were scattered: and I will bring again the captivity of Egypt, and will cause them to return *into* the land of Pathros, into the land of their habitation; and they shall be there a base kingdom. It shall be the basest of the kingdoms; neither shall it exalt itself any more above the nations: for I will diminish them, that they shall no more rule over the nations. And it shall be no more the confidence of the house of Israel, which bringeth *their* iniquity to remembrance, when they shall look after them: but they shall know that I *am* the Lord GOD. (Ezekiel 29:8–16)

This prophecy of Egypt being made desolate was fulfilled in 605 BC when Egypt was defeated by the Babylonians, led by King Nebuchadnezzar II. Egypt has never been the same since.

An essential piece of this prophecy is how God didn't say He would completely destroy Egypt, but only that they would be severely weakened. This, too, has been fulfilled, as Egypt remains a nation today, although it is no longer as powerful as it once was. It is "the basest of kingdoms" and it's all because God put a curse on them all those years ago.

Chapter 3: *Divine Inspiration*

Tyre

Tyre was a trading power located in modern-day Lebanon that was once allied with Israel. In Ezekiel chapter 26, the fall of Tyre is foretold:

> Therefore thus saith the Lord GOD; Behold, I *am* against thee, O Tyrus, and will cause many nations to come up against thee, as the sea causeth his waves to come up. And they shall destroy the walls of Tyrus, and break down her towers: I will also scrape her dust from her, and make her like the top of a rock. (Ezekiel 26:3–4)

> For thus saith the Lord GOD; Behold, I will bring upon Tyrus Nebuchadrezzar king of

Chapter 3: *Divine Inspiration*

Babylon, a king of kings, from the north, with horses, and with chariots, and with horsemen, and companies, and much people. He shall slay with the sword thy daughters in the field: and he shall make a fort against thee, and cast a mount against thee, and lift up the buckler against thee. (Ezekiel 26:7–8)

And they shall make a spoil of thy riches, and make a prey of thy merchandise: and they shall break down thy walls, and destroy thy pleasant houses: and they shall lay thy stones and thy timber and thy dust in the midst of the water. (Ezekiel 26:12)

And I will make thee like the top of a rock: thou shalt be *a place* to spread nets upon; thou

Chapter 3: *Divine Inspiration*

shalt be built no more: for I the LORD have spoken *it*, saith the Lord GOD. (Ezekiel 26:14)

I will make thee a terror, and thou *shalt be* no *more*: though thou be sought for, yet shalt thou never be found again, saith the Lord GOD. (Ezekiel 26:21).

So God said that He would bring many nations against Tyre, especially the Babylonians led by Nebuchadnezzar, and they would cause such devastation to Tyre that it would never be rebuilt. Nebuchadnezzar II besieged and invaded Tyre from 586 to 573 BC.

Now, this is a controversial prophecy, as Tyre remains a populated city in Lebanon today. However, this prophecy refers to Old Tyre, also known as

Chapter 3: *Divine Inspiration*

Mainland Tyre. New Tyre was an island that the Tyrians moved to after the fall of Old Tyre.

When Alexander the Great was conquering nations, he decided to pursue Tyre. When he arrived, he found that Old Tyre had been abandoned, and the Tyrians had since resided on the island off the coast, which they renamed "Tyre." This fulfills verse 21, which says: "...though thou be sought for, yet shall thou never be found again, saith the Lord GOD." (Ezekiel 26:21)

Alexander, in his ambition, used the stones and wood that once made up Old Tyre and built a mole across the sea, connecting Old Tyre to the island of New Tyre. This fulfilled part of the prophecy which says: "...they shall lay thy stones and thy timber and thy dust in the midst of the water." (Ezekiel 26:12)

Chapter 3: *Divine Inspiration*

As for Old Tyre, it has indeed never been rebuilt, just as the Bible says would happen.

Nebuchadnezzar's Dream

The Book of Daniel is filled with fascinating prophecies. In Daniel chapter 2, King Nebuchadnezzar II of Babylon had a dream that greatly troubled him. He called upon the enchanters and astrologers of Babylon to tell him what his dream meant, but they had no answer for him. Daniel, who was given power from God to interpret dreams, told Nebuchadnezzar what his dream meant.

> Thou, O King, sawest, and behold a great image. This great image, whose brightness *was* excellent, stood before thee; and the form

Chapter 3: *Divine Inspiration*

thereof *was* terrible. The image's head *was* of fine gold, his breast and his arms of silver, his belly and thighs of brass, his legs of iron, his feet part of iron and part of clay. Thou sawest till that a stone was cut out without hands, which smote the image upon his feet *that were* of iron and clay, and brake them into pieces. Then was the iron, the clay, the brass, the silver, and the gold, broken to pieces together, and became like the chaff of the summer threshingfloors; and the wind carried them away, that no place was found for them: and the stone that smote the image became a great mountain, and filled the whole earth. (Daniel 2:31–35)

Chapter 3: *Divine Inspiration*

In verses 36–45, Daniel interprets the meaning of the dream. Each part of the statue represents an empire. The head of gold represents the Babylonian Empire. The chest and arms of silver represent the Medo-Persian Empire, which overthrew the Babylonians. The belly and thighs of brass represent the Greek (Macedonian) Empire, which overthrew the Medo-Persians. The legs of iron represent the Roman Empire, which overthrew the Greeks.

The feet, partly iron and partly clay, is the most unique section of the statue because it doesn't refer to a traditional empire like the others do. Since the iron is continued through it, then it must come from Rome. This is confirmed in Daniel 7, where Daniel is given a vision of four beasts, each representing the first four parts of the statue (Babylon, Medo-Persia, Macedonia, and Rome). Yet the fifth notable thing to arise is not another beast, but it's a little horn that emerges from the fourth beast, which is Rome (Daniel 7:8). The feet of partly iron and partly clay is actually a symbol of the Roman Catholic Church. (We'll go over in the next section why the little horn represents the Catholic Church.)

The Western Roman Empire was broken up into ten main barbarian kingdoms: Vandals, Suevians, Visigoths, Alemanni, Franks, Burgundians, Anglo-Saxons, Ostrogoths, Lombards, and the Heruli. These ten kingdoms are representative of the ten toes on the statue's feet. These European kingdoms, or just more broadly Europe, are the clay part of the feet and the Catholic Church is the iron (Roman) part of the feet. Roman power continued through the Catholic Church, which has had a massive influence on Europe since its rise to power.

Chapter 3: *Divine Inspiration*

For those who believe that there were actually more than ten kingdoms that Western Rome was divided into, it's important to note that ten is also used in the Bible as a symbol of a multitude or completeness (Exodus 7–12, Exodus 20:1–17).

We are currently living in the feet of partly iron and partly clay. The stone striking the image represents the Messiah putting an end to the nations of the world. The rise and fall of these mighty empires and deceptive religion were foretold in the Holy Scriptures all along.

Four Beasts

Daniel chapter 7 is sort of a continuation of the chapter 2 prophecy, but this time, it's Daniel who's given a dream, and his dream gives us more details concerning these empires:

Chapter 3: *Divine Inspiration*

In the first year of Belshazzar king of Babylon Daniel had a dream and visions of his head upon his bed: then he wrote the dream, *and* told the sum of the matters. Daniel spake and said, I saw in my vision by night, and, behold, the four winds of the heaven strove upon the great sea. And four great beasts came up from the sea, diverse one from another. The first *was* like a lion, and had eagle's wings: I beheld till the wings thereof were plucked, and it was lifted up from the earth, and made stand upon the feet as a man, and a man's heart was given to it. (Daniel 7:1–4)

This beast is representative of Babylon (head of gold) as lions and eagles have been used in Scripture

Chapter 3: *Divine Inspiration*

as symbols of Babylon (Jeremiah 49:19, Lamentations 4:19).

The wings of the beast getting torn off so that it has to stand as a man, as well as it being given the mind of a man, represents King Nebuchadnezzar getting humbled as his kingdom was stripped from him. He was given the mind of an animal before his sanity was eventually restored (Daniel 4).

> And behold another beast, a second, like to a bear, and it raised up itself on one side, and *it had* three ribs in the mouth of it between the teeth of it: and they said thus unto it, Arise, devour much flesh. (Daniel 7:5)

This beast represents the Medo-Persian Empire (chest and arms of silver). The beast being "raised up

Chapter 3: *Divine Inspiration*

on one side" refers to the Persians' greater dominance in the alliance compared to the inferior Medes. The three ribs in the mouth of the beast are a reference to the Medo-Persian conquests of Lydia (546 BC), Babylon (539 BC), and Egypt (525 BC).

> After this I beheld, and lo another, like a leopard, which had upon the back of it four wings of a fowl; the beast had also four heads; and dominion was given to it. (Daniel 7:6)

This third beast is representative of the Macedonian Empire (belly and thighs of brass), which was spearheaded by Alexander the Great. The beast being depicted as a leopard with wings symbolizes the swiftness of Alexander's conquests.

Chapter 3: *Divine Inspiration*

The four heads represent Alexander's four generals: Ptolemy, Seleucus, Cassander, and Lysimachus. After Alexander's death, his empire was divided among these four generals.

> After this I saw in the night visions, and behold a fourth beast, dreadful and terrible, and strong exceedingly; and it had great iron teeth: it devoured and brake in pieces, and stamped the residue with the feet of it: and it *was* diverse from all the beasts that *were* before it; and it had ten horns. I considered the horns, and, behold, there came up among them another little horn, before whom there were three of the first horns plucked up by the roots: and, behold, in this horn *were* eyes like the eyes of man, and a mouth speaking great things. (Daniel 7:7–8)

Chapter 3: *Divine Inspiration*

This most terrifying beast represents the Roman Empire, which the legs of iron in Daniel chapter 2 symbolize, hence the iron teeth.

The ten horns represent the ten European barbarian kingdoms (feet of partly iron and partly clay) that Rome was broken up into, which we've previously discussed (Vandals, Suevians, Visigoths, Alemanni, Franks, Burgundians, Anglo-Saxons, Ostrogoths, Lombards, and the Heruli).

The little horn represents the Roman Church, which ultimately became the papacy. The three uprooted horns represent the Vandals, Ostrogoths, and Heruli, whose fall, whether directly or indirectly, was brought about by the Roman Church.

When Rome was divided, the western part of the Roman Empire fell (5th century AD), while the

Chapter 3: *Divine Inspiration*

eastern part survived and became what we know today as the Byzantine Empire.

The first Byzantine emperor was Constantine I (r. AD 306–337), who legalized Christianity and unified the Church with the state. Constantine exploited his alliance with Christianity to lend legitimacy to his rule, making it appear divinely supported. This, however, was not true Christianity, as they taught false doctrines, which we'll explore later on in this book.

The Byzantine Empire utilized Christianity to consolidate its power and control the population. The Vandals were overthrown by the Byzantine Empire in the Vandalic War (AD 533–534). Emperor Justinian I (r. AD 527–565) commanded his general, Belisarius, to lead the Eastern Romans against the Vandals to reclaim the land they had taken from Western Rome.

Chapter 3: *Divine Inspiration*

The war ended at the Battle of Tricamarum, where the Byzantine Empire quelled the Vandal Kingdom, uprooting the first of the three horns.

The Roman Church further supported Justinian's ambitions to take back Rome's land from the Ostrogoths, who were Arians, and the Church, who were Catholics, saw them as heretics. The Church endeavored to build alliances for the Byzantines against the Ostrogoths. They were able to win over the Franks, as well as the Italian nobility, who strongly disliked the Ostrogoths.

The Byzantine Empire subdued the Ostrogothic Kingdom in AD 553 at the Battle of Mons Lactarius, uprooting the second of the three horns.

The Heruli were not conquered by the Byzantine Empire but were instead absorbed into it. After their defeat at the hands of the Lombards (c. AD

Chapter 3: *Divine Inspiration*

508), the Heruli migrated to the lands of the Byzantine Empire. Many of them became mercenaries for the Byzantines, even helping to defeat the Ostrogoths in the Gothic War (AD 535–554). The Heruli ultimately adopted Byzantine customs and intermarried with them, resulting in their once-independent kingdom becoming integrated into the Byzantine Empire.

This was the last of the three horns which were uprooted by the little horn. The Roman Church supported all of these conquests and gained more power as a result.

The Little Horn

After Daniel was told that the four beasts represent four kingdoms, he wanted to know more about the fourth beast (Rome).

Chapter 3: *Divine Inspiration*

Daniel says in verse 21 about the little horn that emerged from the fourth beast: "I beheld, and the same horn made war with the saints, and prevailed against them." (Daniel 7:21)

This refers to the period when the Christian Empire of Rome, under Constantine, persecuted other Christian groups after the Trinity was established at the Council of Nicaea in AD 325. The Christian groups who did not accept the Nicene Christian teachings were exiled, their properties confiscated, their writings terminated, and legal action was taken against them, which included fines and imprisonment. This persecution continued past the reign of Constantine.

The angel then further explained the fourth beast to Daniel:

Chapter 3: *Divine Inspiration*

Thus he said, The fourth beast shall be the fourth kingdom upon earth, which shall be diverse from all kingdoms, and shall devour the whole earth, and shall tread it down, and break it in pieces. And the ten horns out of this kingdom *are* ten kings *that* shall arise: and another shall rise after them; and he shall be diverse from the first, and he shall subdue three kings. And he shall speak *great* words against the most High, and shall wear out the saints of the most High, and think to change times and laws: and they shall be given into his hand until a time and times and the dividing of time. (Daniel 7:23–25)

Let's take a look at this phrase: "until a time and times and the dividing of time." What does this

Chapter 3: *Divine Inspiration*

mean? There is a teaching known as the day-year principle, which holds that in specific biblical prophecies, a day is equivalent to a year. This is based on Numbers 14:34 and Ezekiel 4:6, where a day is used to represent a year.

This principle is also applied to the phrase "until a time and times and the dividing of time." The ancient Hebrew year was about 360 days. When it says "a time," it is speaking of a period of 360 years. When it says "times," it refers to a time (360 years) multiplied by two, which equals 720 years. When it says "the dividing of time," it is speaking of a time (360 years) divided in half, which equals 180 years.

Now, if it says "until a time and times and the dividing of time" together, it means to add 360 plus 720 plus 180, which equals 1,260 years. What Scripture is telling us here is that the little horn

Chapter 3: *Divine Inspiration*

(Roman Church/papacy) will persecute Christians for 1,260 years. When does this 1,260-year period begin?

In AD 533, Emperor Justinian I decreed that the Pope (Bishop of Rome) be made the "head of all the holy churches."[17] Following this decree, the Catholic Church began to experience a significant increase in power. They burned non-Catholic writings, including Bibles, so only their church leaders could read them and thus dictate what they allegedly said.

Some historical events of the Catholic Church's persecution include the Albigensian Crusade (1209–1229), St. Bartholomew's Day Massacre (1572), the Piedmontese Easter (1655), The Hussite Wars (1419–1434), the Thirty Years' War

---

[17] Philip Schaff, *History of the Christian Church*, vol. 3, *Nicene and Post-Nicene Christianity* (New York: Charles Scribner's Sons, 1884), 327.

Chapter 3: *Divine Inspiration*

(1618–1648), and the reign of Mary I "Bloody Mary" (1553–1558).

The Catholic Church taught and still teaches many doctrines that do not align with what the Bible says, persecuted and oppressed those who wouldn't accept their teachings, and invented their own laws, which they forced upon others.

This all lines up perfectly with verse 25 of Daniel chapter 7. But does the timeframe line up?

As we've discussed, this persecution is supposed to have lasted for 1,260 years if we follow the day-year principle. So, from the time of Justinian's decree in AD 533 plus 1,260 years, we get to the year 1793.

1793 was the exact year that the Reign of Terror (1793–1794) began during the French

Chapter 3: *Divine Inspiration*

Revolution (1789–1799). Now, what does the French Revolution have to do with this?

During the French Revolution, the Catholic Church suffered a significant setback. All church properties were taken away from them in 1789 by the National Assembly. The Civil Constitution of the Clergy (1790) brought the Church under the control of the state, which greatly harmed the power of the papacy.

Secularization was on the rise, and Catholicism was on the decline with the introduction of the Cult of Reason and the Cult of the Supreme Being becoming popularized by the state. The Reign of Terror turned the tables on the Catholic Church as they were now the ones who started to get persecuted and killed.

The Concordat (1801) reestablished Catholicism as the main religion in France, but their

Chapter 3: *Divine Inspiration*

power remained subordinate to the state. The fact that the Bible essentially foretells the exact year the Reign of Terror in the French Revolution would begin is genuinely remarkable.

These years could also be applied to the decree of Phocas (606 AD), which also declared the Pope as "head of all churches."[18] 606 AD plus 1,260 years equals the year 1866, which was around the time when Garibaldi put an end to the Papal States in Italy, thereby weakening the power and influence of the Catholic Church.

The Ram and the Goat

In the next chapter, Daniel has another vision:

---

[18] Philip Schaff, *History of the Christian Church*, vol. 4, *Medieval Christianity* (New York: Charles Scribner's Sons, 1884), 222.

Chapter 3: *Divine Inspiration*

Then I lifted up mine eyes, and saw, and, behold, there stood before the river a ram which had *two* horns: and the *two* horns *were* high; but one *was* higher than the other, and the higher came up last. I saw the ram pushing westward, and northward, and southward; so that no beasts might stand before him, neither *was there any* that could deliver out of his hand; but he did accordingly to his will, and became great. And as I was considering, behold, an he goat came from the west on the face of the whole earth, and touched not the ground: and the goat *had* a notable horn between his eyes. And he came to the ram that had *two* horns, which I had seen standing before the river, and ran unto him in the fury of his power. And I saw him come close unto the

Chapter 3: *Divine Inspiration*

ram, and he was moved with choler against him, and smote the ram, and brake his two horns: and there was no power in the ram to stand before him, but he cast him down to the ground, and stamped upon him: and there was none that could deliver the ram out of his hand. Therefore the he goat waxed very great: and when he was strong, the great horn was broken; and for it came up four notable ones toward the four winds of heaven. (Daniel 8:3–8)

The ram with two horns represents the Medo-Persian Empire. The horn, which was higher than the other and came up last, represents the Persians, who were more powerful than the Medes (the smaller horn). This detail is also given in the four

Chapter 3: *Divine Inspiration*

beasts prophecy in chapter 7: "...it raised up itself on one side..." (Daniel 7:5)

The goat that came from the west represents the Macedonian Empire, which overthrew the Medo-Persians, and the horn between the goat's eyes represents Alexander the Great. Macedonia destroyed Medo-Persia during Alexander's conquests, just like how the goat destroys the ram. When it says: "...the he goat waxed very great..." (Daniel 8:8), this is a subtle nod to Alexander <u>the Great</u>.

Verse 8 goes on to say: "...and when he was strong, the great horn was broken; and for it came up four notable ones toward the four winds of heaven." (Daniel 8:8)

This is a prophecy concerning the dividing of Alexander's empire. Alexander unexpectedly died from illness in 323 BC while he was still in his prime.

Chapter 3: *Divine Inspiration*

This is why it says: "...and when he was strong, the great horn was broken..."

The four horns toward the four winds of heaven that come up represent the four divisions of the Macedonian Empire following Alexander's death, which was given to each of his four generals: Ptolemy, Seleucus, Cassander, and Lysimachus.

These interpretations are confirmed later in the chapter when the angel Gabriel tells Daniel the meaning of the vision:

> The ram which thou sawest having *two* horns *are* the kings of Media and Persia. And the rough goat *is* the king of Grecia: and the great horn that *is* between his eyes is the first king. Now that being broken, whereas four stood up

Chapter 3: *Divine Inspiration*

for it, four kingdoms shall stand up out of the nation, but not in his power. (Daniel 8:20–22)

Going back to Daniel's vision, we're told of another horn emerging:

> And out of one of them came forth a little horn, which waxed exceeding great, toward the south, and toward the east, and toward the pleasant *land*. And it waxed great, *even* to the host of heaven; and it cast down *some* of the host and of the stars to the ground, and stamped upon them. Yea, he magnified *himself* even to the prince of the host, and by him the daily *sacrifice* was taken away, and the place of his sanctuary was cast down. And an host was given *him* against the daily *sacrifice* by reason

Chapter 3: *Divine Inspiration*

of transgression, and it cast down the truth to the ground; and it practised, and prospered. (Daniel 8:9–12)

Let's see what the angel had to say about who this little horn was, and then we'll figure out which historical figure the description matches up with:

And in the latter time of their kingdom, when the transgressors are come to the full, a king of fierce countenance, and understanding dark sentences, shall stand up. And his power shall be mighty, but not by his own power: and he shall destroy wonderfully, and shall prosper, and practise, and shall destroy the mighty and the holy people. And through his policy also he shall cause craft to prosper in his hand; and he

Chapter 3: *Divine Inspiration*

shall magnify *himself* in his heart, and by peace shall destroy many: he shall also stand up against the Prince of princes; but he shall be broken without hand. And the vision of the evening and the morning which was told *is* true: wherefore shut thou up the vision; for it *shall be* for many days. (Daniel 8:23–26)

Most scholars believe this prophecy concerns Antiochus IV Epiphanes, who was king of the Seleucid Empire from 175 to 164 BC. Let's examine this theory.

Daniel tells us that this "little horn" is someone who will come out of the latter period of the four kingdoms of Alexander's generals. We're also told that this person would succeed in their attempts to deceive and destroy the holy people. Lastly, they will rise up

Chapter 3: *Divine Inspiration*

against God ("Prince of princes") and be defeated by Him.

Now, does Antiochus IV fit this description? Yes, he does.

He was a king of the latter period of the Seleucid Empire, which was founded by Alexander the Great's general Seleucus.

He persecuted the Jewish people ("the mighty and the holy people") through boldness and deception. In 167 BC, Antiochus built an altar dedicated to Zeus in the Jewish Temple and sacrificed pigs on it. Pigs are seen as unclean in Judaism (Deuteronomy 14:8), so this was considered a great abomination.

He got rid of Jewish customs such as keeping the Sabbath, circumcision, and reading the Torah. He forced many Jews to convert to worshiping the Greek

Chapter 3: *Divine Inspiration*

gods. Any Jews who refused to accept his blasphemous decrees were tortured and killed.

He had Jerusalem seized, looted, and fortified to severely limit the religious freedom of the Jewish people. He even went so far as to mint coins of himself with the inscription: "God manifest" (Greek: "theos epiphanes").

God put an end to Antiochus IV's brutal treatment of His people after the successful Maccabean Revolt (167–160 BC), which led to the recapture of the Temple and the liberation of the Jews from the oppression they had suffered.

> Then I heard one saint speaking, and another saint said unto that certain *saint* which spake, How long *shall be* the vision *concerning* the daily *sacrifice*, and the transgression of

Chapter 3: *Divine Inspiration*

desolation, to give both the sanctuary and the host to be trodden under foot? And he said unto me, Unto two thousand and three hundred days; then shall the sanctuary be cleansed. (Daniel 8:13–14)

This passage tells us that the abomination of desolation set up by Antiochus IV (the altar to Zeus in the Temple) will be removed after "two thousand and three hundred days." These days don't refer to years, as they would in the day-year principle, but rather to daily sacrifices, which is the context of the passage, as we can see in verses 11–12.

Since there were two sacrifices a day, 2,300 sacrifices equals 1,150 days, which is a little over three years. The abominable altar was constructed in 167 BC and was taken down three years later in 164 BC by the Maccabees, just as the prophecy says.

I think we can confidently say that Antiochus IV Epiphanes is, in fact, the little horn prophesied about in Daniel chapter 8.

Hellenistic Conflicts

We'll delve into the Daniel chapter 9 prophecy in a later section of this book. But for now, let's look at the prophecies in Daniel 11 and analyze their immense accuracy.

> Also I in the first year of Darius the Mede, *even* I, stood to confirm and to strengthen him. And now will I shew thee the truth. Behold, there shall stand up yet three kings in Persia; and the

Chapter 3: *Divine Inspiration*

> fourth shall be far richer than *they* all: and by his strength through his riches he shall stir up all against the realm of Grecia. (Daniel 11:1–2)

The three Persian kings who would arise were Cambyses II, Bardiya (also called Smerdis), and Darius I. The fourth Persian king, Xerxes, would be richer than the others. And, as verse 2 states, Xerxes attempted to conquer Greece (480–479 BC).

> And a mighty king shall stand up, that shall rule with great dominion, and do according to his will. (Daniel 11:3)

This is yet another prophecy about the coming of Alexander the Great. Alexander was one of the most

Chapter 3: *Divine Inspiration*

successful conquerors of all time, hence his alias "the Great."

> And when he shall stand up, his kingdom shall be broken, and shall be divided toward the four winds of heaven; and not to his posterity, nor according to his dominion which he ruled: for his kingdom shall be plucked up, even for others beside those. (Daniel 11:4)

This, too, is very accurate. Alexander died in his prime, and instead of his kingdom being ruled by his son ("his posterity") Alexander IV, it was divided into four separate kingdoms ("four winds of heaven") and given to his four generals.

Chapter 3: *Divine Inspiration*

And the king of the south shall be strong, and *one* of his princes; and he shall be strong above him, and have dominion; his dominion *shall be* a great dominion. (Daniel 11:5)

The "king of the south" refers to Ptolemy, whose kingdom included Egypt and parts of modern-day Sudan. Ptolemy's land was located farther south than the other kingdoms that emerged after Alexander's empire was divided.

One of Ptolemy's "princes" whose kingdom would be more potent than his refers to Seleucus. The Seleucid Kingdom was larger than the Ptolemaic Kingdom and, at its height, encompassed territories in the modern-day nations of Syria, Lebanon, Iraq, Iran, Jordan, Israel, Palestine, Armenia, southeastern Turkey, and parts of Kuwait. Initially, it also controlled

Chapter 3: *Divine Inspiration*

vast eastern regions, including parts of present-day Afghanistan, Pakistan, Turkmenistan, Uzbekistan, and Tajikistan; however, many of these eastern areas later broke away to form independent Hellenistic kingdoms, such as the Greco-Bactrian Kingdom.

> And in the end of years they shall join themselves together; for the king's daughter of the south shall come to the king of the north to make an agreement... (Daniel 11:6)

Interpretation: This indicates that after a specific period, these two kingdoms would form an alliance through the marriage of a Ptolemaic king's daughter to a Seleucid king.

Historical Fulfillment: This is precisely what happened in 252 BC when Berenice, the daughter of

Chapter 3: *Divine Inspiration*

Ptolemy II Philadelphus, married the Seleucid king Antiochus II Theos to forge an alliance between the two kingdoms.

Verse 6 goes on to say:

>...But she shall not retain the power of the arm; neither shall he stand, nor his arm: but she shall be given up, and they that brought her, and he that begat her, and he that strengthened her in *these* times. (Daniel 11:6)

Interpretation: This marriage would not end well for Berenice ("she shall not retain the power of the arm") nor Antiochus Theos ("neither shall he stand").

Historical Fulfillment: After Ptolemy Philadelphus died, Antiochus Theos divorced Berenice

Chapter 3: *Divine Inspiration*

and remarried his first wife, Laodice, whom he had previously divorced to marry Berenice. To solidify her son's claim to the Seleucid throne, Laodice had her husband Antiochus Theos, Berenice, and Berenice's son killed.

> But out of a branch of her roots shall *one* stand up in his estate, which shall come with an army, and shall enter into the fortress of the king of the north, and shall deal against them, and shall prevail: and shall also carry captives into Egypt their gods, with their princes, *and* with their precious vessels of silver and of gold; and he shall continue *more* years than the king of the north. So the king of the south shall come into *his* kingdom, and shall return into his own land. (Daniel 11:7–9)

Chapter 3: *Divine Inspiration*

Interpretation: Despite the tragic ending to Berenice's life, the Scriptures tell us that she would be avenged. Verses 7 and 8 of Daniel chapter 11 say that someone from Berenice's family ("a branch from her roots") will successfully attack the king of the Seleucid Empire ("king of the north"), looting their prized possessions and taking them to Egypt.

Historical Fulfillment: Berenice's brother, Ptolemy III Euergetes, was king of the Ptolemaic dynasty in Egypt from 246 to 222 BC. In response to the death of his sister and nephew, Ptolemy III invaded Syria, which was a part of the Seleucid Empire. This is known today as the Third Syrian War or the Laodicean War (246–241 BC). The king of the Seleucid Empire at the time was Seleucus II Callinicus (the son of Laodice). He is the "king of the north" here.

Chapter 3: *Divine Inspiration*

Ptolemy III's invasion was a success, and just like verse 8 says, they brought the spoils of war back to Egypt. Verse 9 states that Seleucus II would attempt to attack the Ptolemaic Kingdom in response, but to no avail. Historical records suggest that this was, in fact, the case.[19]

> But his sons shall be stirred up, and shall assemble a multitude of great forces: and *one* shall certainly come, and overflow, and pass through: then shall he return, and be stirred up, *even* to his fortress. (Daniel 11:10)

---

[19] Polybius, *The Histories*, trans. Evelyn S. Shuckburgh (London: Macmillan, 1899), book 5, chap. 40.
Appian (1899) *Syrian Wars*, Trans. Horace White. Macmillan, London, Section 65.
Justinus (1853) *Epitome of the Philippic History of Pompeius Trogus*, Trans. Rev. John Selby Watson, Henry G. Bohn, London, Book 27, Chapter 1.
Diodorus Siculus (1933) *Library of History*, Trans. C.H. Oldfather, Harvard University Press, Cambridge, Book 33 (Fragments), Fragment 23.

Chapter 3: *Divine Inspiration*

Interpretation: Seleucus II's sons will gather large armies and attack the Ptolemaic Kingdom, but only one of his sons will succeed in doing so.

Historical Fulfillment: The sons of Seleucus II, Seleucus III Ceraunus (r. 225 to 223 BC), and Antiochus III the Great (r. 223 to 187 BC) both attacked the Ptolemaic Kingdom during their reigns. Seleucus III's efforts did not come to fruition, however, as he was assassinated three years into his reign. His brother, Antiochus III, on the other hand, achieved greater success in his ambitions to regain lost territories for the Seleucid Empire. He initiated the Fourth (219–217 BC) and Fifth (202–195 BC) Syrian Wars, which ultimately led to the Seleucids recapturing Coele-Syria in 200 BC.

Chapter 3: *Divine Inspiration*

And the king of the south shall be moved with choler, and shall come forth and fight with him, *even* with the king of the north: and he shall set forth a great multitude, but the multitude shall be given into his hand. *And* when he hath taken away the multitude, his heart shall be lifted up; and he shall cast down *many* ten thousands: but he shall not be strengthened *by it*. (Daniel 11:11–12)

Interpretation: A Ptolemaic king will attack and defeat a Seleucid king. Verse 12 says: "...but he shall not be strengthened *by it*." This means the victory would not last.

Historical Fulfillment: These verses foretell when King Ptolemy IV, Philopator of Egypt (r. 221 to

Chapter 3: *Divine Inspiration*

204 BC), defeated Antiochus III ("king of the north") at the Battle of Raphia in 217 BC.

> For the king of the north shall return, and shall set forth a multitude greater than the former, and shall certainly come after certain years with a great army and with much riches. And in those times there shall many stand up against the king of the south: also the robbers of thy people shall exalt themselves to establish the vision; but they shall fall. So the king of the north shall come, and cast up a mount, and take the most fenced cities: and the arms of the south shall not withstand, neither his chosen people, neither *shall there be any* strength to withstand. (Daniel 11:13–15)

Chapter 3: *Divine Inspiration*

Interpretation: These verses indicate that a Seleucid king will raise a larger army and engage in battle against a Ptolemaic king. Many will join him against this Ptolemaic king, including some Jews who will think that they are fulfilling a prophecy ("exalt themselves to establish the vision"), but their efforts would fail. Then, the Seleucid king will successfully capture a fortified city, which will be too much for the Ptolemaic forces to handle.

Historical Fulfillment: This provides us with more details regarding the Fifth Syrian War. The "king of the north" is still Antiochus III the Great, but the "king of the south" is now Ptolemy V Epiphanes (r. 204 to 180 BC).

Several Jews joined the fight against the Ptolemaic Kingdom for various political and religious

Chapter 3: *Divine Inspiration*

reasons. However, they did not get the outcomes they wanted as Hellenism continued to flourish.

The fortified city captured by Antiochus III refers back to the taking of Coele-Syria at the Battle of Panium (200 BC), which, as we've been over, is also prophesied about in verse 10 of Daniel chapter 11. This was a significant victory for the Seleucids, as it severely weakened the Ptolemies.

> But he that cometh against him shall do according to his own will, and none shall stand in the glorious land, which by his hand shall be consumed. He shall also set his face to enter with the strength of his whole kingdom, and upright ones with him; thus shall he do: and he shall give him the daughter of women,

corrupting her: but she shall not stand *on his side*, neither be for him. (Daniel 11:16–17)

Interpretation: These verses indicate that Antiochus III would become extremely powerful and would occupy the land of Israel ("the glorious land"). Verse 17 tells us that Antiochus will give his daughter in marriage to the king of the south (Ptolemy V) in an unsuccessful attempt at overthrowing the Ptolemaic Empire.

Historical Fulfillment: After the Battle of Panium in 200 BC, Israel became a part of the Seleucid Empire. Antiochus III married his daughter Cleopatra I Syra to Ptolemy V in 194 BC. He wanted to use his daughter to spread his influence over Egypt, but this backfired as she chose to stay loyal to her Ptolemaic husband instead of conspiring against him.

Chapter 3: *Divine Inspiration*

After this shall he turn his face unto the isles, and shall take many: but a prince for his own behalf shall cause the reproach offered by him to cease; without his own reproach he shall cause *it* to turn upon him. Then he shall turn his face toward the fort of his own land: but he shall stumble and fall, and not be found. (Daniel 11:18–19)

Interpretation: These verses tell us that Antiochus III will invade many coastlands ("isles") before being stopped by a "prince" who will turn the tables against him. Antiochus will then retreat to his own land, where he will be defeated.

Historical Fulfillment: Antiochus III invaded coastal areas of Asia Minor and Greece. The "prince" who put a halt to his ambitions was the Roman general

Chapter 3: *Divine Inspiration*

Lucius Scipio Asiaticus, who defeated Antiochus III at the Battle of Magnesia in 190 BC. After the battle, Antiochus fled back to his own land, and due to financial struggles, he resorted to looting temples within his kingdom. In 187 BC, Antiochus was killed ("stumble and fall") while trying to plunder a temple in Elymais.

> Then shall stand up in his estate a raiser of taxes *in* the glory of the kingdom: but within few days he shall be destroyed, neither in anger, nor in battle. (Daniel 11:20)

Interpretation: This suggests that Antiochus III's successor will send out a tax collector and will ultimately be killed, but not in battle.

Chapter 3: *Divine Inspiration*

Historical Fulfillment: Antiochus III's successor was his son Seleucus IV Philopator (r. 187 to 175 BC). Seleucus IV sent his finance minister Heliodorus to collect taxes from the Temple in Jerusalem. Seleucus ended up getting assassinated (probably at the orchestration of Heliodorus) instead of dying in battle.

> And in his estate shall stand up a vile person, to whom they shall not give the honour of the kingdom: but he shall come in peaceably, and obtain the kingdom by flatteries. (Daniel 11:21)

Interpretation: This verse says that Seleucus IV's successor would be a detestable person who would not be the rightful heir but would seize the throne through cunning.

Chapter 3: *Divine Inspiration*

Historical Fulfillment: Seleucus IV's successor was his brother Antiochus IV Epiphanes, who killed his nephew (Seleucus' son Antiochus) and claimed the throne for himself.

> And with the arms of a flood shall they be overflown from before him, and shall be broken; yea, also the prince of the covenant. And after the league *made* with him he shall work deceitfully: for he shall come up, and shall become strong with a small people." (Daniel 11:22–23)

Interpretation: A large army will be defeated by Antiochus IV and someone whom Scripture calls "the prince of the covenant" will be killed. Antiochus

Chapter 3: *Divine Inspiration*

will then make an alliance but will use deception to gain more power despite having limited support.

Historical Fulfillment: The overwhelming army defeated by Antiochus IV refers to the Ptolemaic forces that were defeated by Antiochus' forces multiple times.

The "prince of the covenant" is Onias III, the Jewish High Priest who was killed in approximately 171 BC after being deposed from his position by Antiochus IV, sometime between 175 and 171 BC.

Antiochus had made an alliance with Jewish Hellenizers. Still, he then turned his back on them once the coalition wasn't beneficial for him anymore and started to persecute the Jews and had the Temple desecrated.

Antiochus used cunning and deception to rise from being a hostage in Rome to becoming king of the

Chapter 3: *Divine Inspiration*

Seleucid Empire despite having a small number of supporters. These supporters included Eumenes II of Pergamum, Attalus II of Pergamum, Heliodorus, Ptolemy VI Philopator, as well as a faction within the Seleucid nobility and military commanders.

> He shall enter peaceably even upon the fattest places of the province; and he shall do *that* which his fathers have not done, nor his fathers' fathers; he shall scatter among them the prey, and spoil, and riches: *yea*, and he shall forecast his devices against the strong holds, even for a time. (Daniel 11:24)

Interpretation: Antiochus IV will invade and plunder rich provinces and try to overthrow strongholds for some time.

Chapter 3: *Divine Inspiration*

Historical Fulfillment: The rich province that Antiochus invaded refers to Egypt, which he invaded twice during the Sixth Syrian War (170–168 BC).

The strongholds that Antiochus sought to capture were Pelusium (successfully captured in 170 BC), Memphis (reached by Antiochus in 168 BC, but was unable to keep his power there for long), and Alexandria (besieged by Antiochus in 168 BC, but his attempts at invasion were unsuccessful).

> And he shall stir up his power and his courage against the king of the south with a great army; and the king of the south shall be stirred up to battle with a very great and mighty army; but he shall not stand: for they shall forecast devices against him. Yea, they that feed of the portion of his meat shall destroy him, and his

Chapter 3: *Divine Inspiration*

army shall overflow: and many shall fall down slain. And both these kings' hearts *shall be* to do mischief, and they shall speak lies at one table; but it shall not prosper: for yet the end *shall be* at the time appointed. (Daniel 11:25–27)

Interpretation: Antiochus IV Epiphanes will go to war against a Ptolemaic king. The Ptolemaic king will attempt to fight back but will be defeated due to being betrayed by his own men. The two kings will be in each other's presence but will lie and try to deceive each other; however, neither of them will succeed because God's appointed time will have not yet come.

Historical Fulfillment: This also refers to Antiochus IV's invasions of Egypt during the Sixth Syrian War. Egypt was a large part of the Ptolemaic

Chapter 3: *Divine Inspiration*

Kingdom, which was ruled by Ptolemy VI at the time. The Ptolemies tried to invade Palestine but were ultimately defeated by the Seleucids in the Sinai Peninsula.

Ptolemy VI was betrayed by his officials ("they that feed of the portion of his meat") during the war. Two of his generals, Comanus and Cineas, usurped control over Egypt from him.

Ptolemy VI and Antiochus IV met with each other and made a truce, and Ptolemy began to live in Antiochus' custody. Antiochus placed Ptolemy back on the throne to rule as his puppet king. However, both of them were trying to deceive the other to gain the upper hand.

> Then shall he return into his land with great riches; and his heart *shall be* against the holy

Chapter 3: *Divine Inspiration*

> covenant; and he shall do *exploits*, and return to his own land. (Daniel 11:28)

Interpretation: This verse tells us that Antiochus IV will oppose the "holy covenant." The "holy covenant" refers to the Jewish people's worship of God (Exodus 19:5).

Historical Fulfillment: Antiochus IV opposed the Jewish people's worship of God when he plundered the Temple in Jerusalem in 169 BC, persecuted the Jews, and tried to put an end to their religious freedom.

> At the time appointed he shall return, and come toward the south, but it shall not be as the former, or as the latter. For the ships of Chittim shall come against him: therefore he shall be grieved, and return, and have indignation

Chapter 3: *Divine Inspiration*

against the holy covenant: so shall he do; he shall even return, and have intelligence with them that forsake the holy covenant. And arms shall stand on his part, and they shall pollute the sanctuary of strength, and shall take away the daily *sacrifice*, and they shall place the abomination that maketh desolate. And such as do wickedly against the covenant shall he corrupt by flatteries: but the people that do know their God shall be strong, and do *exploits*. (Daniel 11:29–32)

Interpretation: Antiochus IV will attack the Ptolemaic Kingdom again but will not prevail, as ships from Kittim (in Cyprus) will attack him. This will cause him to retreat and direct his anger at the holy covenant. Antiochus and his followers will desecrate

Chapter 3: *Divine Inspiration*

the Jewish Temple, stop the daily offerings, and set up an abomination that will cause desolation.

Historical Fulfillment: While Antiochus was waging war against Egypt, the Romans sought to curb his ambitions. The "ships of Chittim" represent Rome and the Roman power over the Mediterranean. Popillius Laenas (fl. 172–158 BC), a Roman general, met with Antiochus and forced him to retreat.

Due to his humiliation, Antiochus took his anger out on the Jewish people and targeted their religious practices ("holy covenant"). As we've already been over, he plundered the Jewish Temple and set up laws that opposed Judaism, which included outlawing Jewish sacrifices. The "abomination that maketh desolate" refers to the altar dedicated to Zeus that Antiochus had constructed in the Temple. This caused indignation among the Jewish people, which

Chapter 3: *Divine Inspiration*

led to the Maccabean Revolt (167–160 BC), a revolt that caused widespread desolation.

> And they that understand among the people shall instruct many: yet they shall fall by the sword, and by flame, by captivity, and by spoil, *many* days. Now when they shall fall, they shall be holpen with a little help: but many shall cleave to them with flatteries. And *some* of them of understanding shall fall, to try them, and to purge, and to make *them* white, *even* to the time of the end: because *it is* yet for a time appointed. (Daniel 11:33–35)

Interpretation: Wise Jewish teachers will be killed, imprisoned, and persecuted. They will receive some help for their troubles, though it will not

Chapter 3: *Divine Inspiration*

completely end their struggles. Some of these teachers will die, but for their own benefit so that they die as righteous martyrs who will be rewarded at the time appointed by God.

Historical Fulfillment: Many of the Jewish leaders were killed during the persecution led by Antiochus IV. The help which the Jews would receive refers to the early success of the Maccabean Revolt.

A Jewish priest named Mattathias refused to worship the pagan gods and killed the Seleucid official who had ordered him to do so. He then fled to the Gophna Hills, assembled a guerilla force, and started the rebellion. After Mattathias' death, his son Judas Maccabeus took charge of the revolt. He led the Maccabees to several decisive victories, including the Battle of Beth Horon (166 BC), the Battle of Emmaus (165 BC), and the Battle of Beth-Zur (164 BC). These

Chapter 3: *Divine Inspiration*

victories led to the recapture of Jerusalem and the Temple (164 BC).

Some righteous Jews died, but it was for their temporary life to end in uprightness so they could later be rewarded with eternal life from God when the time comes.

The King Who Does According to His Will

> And the king shall do according to his will; and he shall exalt himself, and magnify himself above every god, and shall speak marvellous things against the God of gods, and shall prosper till the indignation be accomplished: for that that is determined shall be done.
>
> (Daniel 11:36)

Chapter 3: *Divine Inspiration*

Interpretation: Here, we're told of a ruler who will selfishly rise to power, exalt himself, and blaspheme against God. He will succeed until a specific time.

Historical Fulfillment: This verse transfers us from the Greek period to the Roman period. The "king" being spoken of here is actually the pope or, more broadly, the Catholic Church.

The Catholic Church has always tried to exalt itself above God while aiming to become as rich and as powerful as possible. Several Catholic authorities through the years have made incredibly blasphemous claims on how the pope possesses the authority of God on earth. Here are some examples:

Chapter 3: *Divine Inspiration*

"The Lord our God no longer reigns. He has resigned all power to the Pope."[20]

"We hold upon this earth the place of God Almighty."[21]

"The Pope is not a mere man, but as it were God, and the vicar of God."[22]

"The Pope is the guardian of dogma and morals; he is the supreme judge of the faithful … he is the way, the truth, and the life."[23]

---

[20] J. A. Wylie, *The History of Protestantism*, vol. 1 (London: Cassell & Company, 1878), 48.
[21] Pope Leo XIII, *Praeclara Gratulationis Publicae* (New York: Benziger Brothers, 1894), 2.
[22] Martin Luther, *Against the Roman Papacy: An Institution of the Devil*, in *Luther's Works*, vol. 41 (Philadelphia: Fortress Press, 1966), 263. Originally published 1545.
[23] Pope Pius IX (attributed), in Karl Joseph von Hefele, *History of the Councils*, vol. 7 (Edinburgh: T. & T. Clark, 1870), 26.

Chapter 3: *Divine Inspiration*

This is absolute blasphemy! Where does it ever say in the Bible that we are to have a hierarchy within the church, let alone a "pope"? The only people who say that the pope has this authority are the Catholic Church themselves. Why, therefore, should anyone believe and follow them?

So far, the papacy aligns perfectly with verse 36 of Daniel 11. Let's see if the following verses do as well.

> Neither shall he regard the God of his fathers, nor the desire of women, nor regard any god: for he shall magnify himself above all. But in his estate shall he honour the God of forces: and a god whom his fathers knew not shall he honour with gold, and silver, and with precious stones, and pleasant things. (Daniel 11:37–38)

Chapter 3: *Divine Inspiration*

Interpretation: The papacy will not teach the same faith as their ancestors. They will abstain from marriage, practice celibacy, and worship themselves. They will believe in the so-called "God of forces." They will use materialistic riches in their worship of a god whom their ancestors did not worship.

Historical Fulfillment: The Catholic Church began in Rome. The ancient Romans were pagans for thousands of years, believing in gods and goddesses such as Minerva, Ceres, Juno, Vesta, Diana, Venus, Mars, Mercury, Jupiter, Neptune, Vulcan, and Apollo. This is what verse 37 refers to when it says: "Neither shall he regard the God of his fathers…"

Instead of Paganism, the Catholic Church claims to worship the God of the Bible, but they instead worship and "magnify" themselves.

Chapter 3: *Divine Inspiration*

Many members within the Catholic Church's hierarchy are required to be celibate:

> All the ordained ministers of the latin church are normally chosen from among men of faith who live a celibate life and who intend to remain celibate for the sake of the kingdom of heaven. Celibacy is a sign of this new life to the service of which the Church's minister is consecrated; accepted with a joyous heart celibacy radiantly proclaims the Reign of God.[24]

In 1 Timothy chapter 4, the Apostle Paul writes about how there will be a falling astray of true Christianity:

---

[24] Catholic Church, *Catechism of the Catholic Church* (Vatican City: Libreria Editrice Vaticana, 1994), 395.

Chapter 3: *Divine Inspiration*

Now the Spirit speaketh expressly, that in the latter times some shall depart from the faith, giving heed to seducing spirits, and doctrines of devils; speaking lies in hypocrisy; having their conscience seared with a hot iron; <u>forbidding to marry</u>, *and commanding* to abstain from meats, which God hath created to be received with thanksgiving of them which believe and know the truth. (1 Timothy 4:1–3)

So once again, we see this prophecy of false teachers that would come and practice abstinence from marriage (and thus sex), which fits the Catholic Church's teachings. Despite this doctrine, there have been several cases of the sexual abuse of children by the clergy, which further goes to show the corruption of this system.

Chapter 3: *Divine Inspiration*

The phrase "God of forces" (Daniel 11:38) figuratively represents human protection. The Hebrew word translated as "of forces" is *maoz* (מָעוֹז), which means "a place of safety." This word is used to describe human protection in Isaiah 30:2–3, Psalm 60:7, and Psalm 108:8.

The Catholic Church has long believed that the dead saints protect them. John Chrysostom, a Roman Church leader, wrote:

> The bodies of these saints fortify the city more effectually for us than impregnable walls of adamant, and like towering rocks placed around on every side, repel not only the assaults of enemies that are visible, but the insidious stratagems also of invisible demons, and counteract and defeat every artifice of the devil

Chapter 3: *Divine Inspiration*

as easily as a strong man overturns the toys of children.[25]

It's quite ironic that a Roman said this, considering the Roman Empire was overthrown years later. Where were the dead saints then? They were dead. This is what Scripture refers to when it says: "...shall he honour the God of forces..." (Daniel 11:38)

The Catholic Church pursues extravagant wealth and likes to display it, making it seem religious. They have grand cathedrals that display impressive architecture, and inside, they contain artwork that is very pleasing to the eye. They build statues of those whom they deem important religious figures, despite the Bible condemning idolatry (Exodus 20:4). The

---

[25] John Chrysostom, *Homilies on the Martyrs*, in *Patrologia Graeca*, ed. J.-P. Migne, vol. 50 (Paris: Migne, c. 347–407 AD), 693.

Chapter 3: *Divine Inspiration*

leaders, especially the pope, are often dressed in fine, expensive clothing and jewelry. The wealth of the Catholic Church is estimated to be in the billions.

The descriptions given in Daniel 11:37–38 accurately match the Catholic Church.

> Thus shall he do in the most strong holds with a strange god, whom he shall acknowledge *and* increase with glory: and he shall cause them to rule over many, and shall divide the land for gain. (Daniel 11:39)

Interpretation: The papacy will use its power to subdue fortified cities and will be rewarded with land and power.

Chapter 3: *Divine Inspiration*

Historical Fulfillment: This verse refers to the Holy Roman Empire, an imperial alliance between the Roman Empire and the Catholic Church.

Charlemagne, king of the Franks and Lombards (r. AD 768–814), was crowned Roman Emperor by Pope Leo III in AD 800. The empire lasted for about 1,000 years before being abdicated in 1806 during the Napoleonic Wars.

However, during those 1,000 years, the large Holy Roman Empire consisted of the modern-day countries of Germany, Austria, Switzerland, the Netherlands, Belgium, Luxembourg, the Czech Republic, and parts of Italy, France, and Poland. Notable victories of the Holy Roman Empire include the Battle of Lechfeld (AD 955), the Battle of Mühldorf (1322), the Battle of the White Mountain (1620), the Battle of Nördlingen (1634), and the Siege

Chapter 3: *Divine Inspiration*

of Vienna (1683). The more the empire expanded, so did the power of the papacy.

The final verses of Daniel 11, verses 40–45, provide details about an end-time prophecy that hasn't yet occurred but is likely on the verge of happening. We will explore this prophecy in a future chapter of this book.

Six-Day War

The Six-Day War of 1967 was a war fought between Israel and certain surrounding nations about 20 years after Israel's reestablishment. The odds were heavily stacked against Israel, but they reigned victorious after six days and regained control over the Sinai Peninsula, the Gaza Strip, the West Bank, the Golan Heights, and East Jerusalem.

Chapter 3: *Divine Inspiration*

Winning a war in six days is unheard of, especially for a nation as small and outnumbered as Israel was. Once again, God proved that the odds don't matter to Him because He controls the odds.

Jesus, after foretelling the fall of Jerusalem, which was later fulfilled in AD 70 at the hands of the Romans, said this: "And they shall fall by the edge of the sword, and shall be led away captive into all nations: and Jerusalem shall be trodden down of the Gentiles, until the times of the Gentiles be fulfilled." (Luke 21:24)

Jesus speaks of how after the Romans took Jerusalem, the Jews would be killed, scattered, and "trodden down" by the Gentiles (non-Jews), signifying that this Gentile occupation of Israel would last for a long time and the Jews would get oppressed during it. This would continue until "the times of the Gentiles be

Chapter 3: *Divine Inspiration*

fulfilled," meaning the Gentile occupation of Jerusalem would come to an eventual end. This was fulfilled after the Six-Day War, about 1,900 years after the events of AD 70.

Revelation

The Book of Revelation is an incredibly metaphorical book written by the Apostle John detailing the prophetic visions he received. Many of these prophecies are sort of continuations of specific prophecies foretold in the Book of Daniel, which we've already been over (French Revolution, rise and fall of the Catholic Church) or end-time prophecies that we'll discuss in a future chapter of this book. So we'll now examine the prophecies from Revelation that have already been fulfilled but which we haven't covered yet, specifically those in chapters 6, 8, 9, and 16.

Seven Seals

> And I saw when the Lamb opened one of the seals, and I heard, as it were the noise of thunder, one of the four beasts saying, Come and see. And I saw, and behold a white horse: and he that sat on him had a bow; and a crown was given unto him: and he went forth conquering, and to conquer. (Revelation 6:1–2)

Interpretation: White is a symbol of victory and peace (Ecclesiastes 9:8, Isaiah 1:18, Daniel 7:9, Revelation 3:4). The bow, crown, and conquering mentality of the horseback rider indicate this vision concerns a prosperous nation focused on expansion.

Historical Fulfillment: The first four of these seven seals unleash different horses with different riders, symbolizing different periods of the Roman Empire. This first seal refers to the period from AD 96 to 180, during the reigns of Rome's "Five Good Emperors": Nerva, Trajan, Hadrian, Antoninus Pius, and Marcus Aurelius. This was a time of prosperity for Rome, known as the "Pax Romana."

> And when he had opened the second seal, I heard the second beast say, Come and see. And there went out another horse *that was* red: and *power* was given to him that sat thereon to take peace from the earth, and that they should kill

Chapter 3: *Divine Inspiration*

one another: and there was given unto him a great sword. (Revelation 6:3–4)

Interpretation: Red is a symbol of blood, war, and sin (Isaiah 1:18, Isaiah 63:2–3, Nahum 2:3). This seal indicates that following the Roman period of peace, a period of conflict and bloodshed will ensue.

Historical Fulfillment: This represents the Roman period, which lasted from AD 193 to 250, starting with the assassination of Commodus. On December 31, AD 192, Emperor Commodus was assassinated, marking the beginning of a period of chaos. This consisted of the Year of the Five Emperors (AD 193), the tumultuous Severan Dynasty (AD 193–235), and the Crisis of the Third Century (AD 235–284), a period of rapid succession and constant civil wars.

Chapter 3: *Divine Inspiration*

And when he had opened the third seal, I heard the third beast say, Come and see. And I beheld, and lo a black horse; and he that sat on him had a pair of balances in his hand. And I heard a voice in the midst of the four beasts say, A measure of wheat for a penny, and three measures of barley for a penny; and *see* thou hurt not the oil and the wine. (Revelation 6:5–6)

Interpretation: This third horse is black, which is a symbol of mourning, suffering, grief, and judgment (Job 30:30, Jeremiah 14:2, Lamentations 4:8, Joel 2:6, Nahum 2:10). The rider is holding scales, which further shows the theme of judgment as well as symbolizing taxation and famine rationing.

Chapter 3: *Divine Inspiration*

The voice that emerges from amidst the four beasts speaks of a time of economic struggle ("A measure of wheat for a penny, and three measures of barley for a penny") and imbalance where the wealthy aren't as affected ("thou hurt not the oil and the wine").

Historical Fulfillment: This refers to the period from AD 250 to 284, when heavy taxation, economic instability, and food shortages were prevalent in the Roman Empire. This was primarily due to the plague of Cyprian (AD 250–270), which coincided with the worsening of the Crisis of the Third Century.

This period ended with the ascension of Diocletian in AD 284, whose reforms helped bring economic stability back to Rome.

Chapter 3: *Divine Inspiration*

And when he had opened the fourth seal, I heard the voice of the fourth beast say, Come and see. And I looked, and behold a pale horse: and his name that sat on him was Death, and Hell followed with him. And power was given unto them over the fourth part of the earth, to kill with sword, and with hunger, and with death, and with the beasts of the earth. (Revelation 6:7–8)

Interpretation: The pale horse, followed by death, makes it quite evident that this refers to a time of death in Rome.

Historical Fulfillment: This fourth seal refers to the period of AD 284 to 312, which began with the brutal reign of Diocletian (AD 284–305) in which

Chapter 3: *Divine Inspiration*

many Christians were killed which led to the Great Persecution of Christians (AD 303–311).

This period also consisted of civil wars (AD 306–312). These included Constantine versus Maxentius (AD 306–312) and Galerius' eastern struggles (AD 306–311).

The period ended in AD 312 after Constantine's victory at the Battle of the Milvian Bridge.

> And when he had opened the fifth seal, I saw under the altar the souls of them that were slain for the word of God, and for the testimony which they held: and they cried with a loud voice, saying, How long, O Lord, holy and true, dost thou not avenge our blood on them that dwell on the earth? And white robes were given

Chapter 3: *Divine Inspiration*

unto every one of them; and it was said unto them, that they should rest yet for a little season, until their fellowservants also and their brethren, that should be killed as they *were*, should be fulfilled. (Revelation 6:9–11)

Interpretation: This fifth seal is about dead Christian martyrs ("them that were slain for the word of God") calling out for justice against those who killed them so their blood may be avenged ("dost thou not avenge our blood on them that dwell on the earth?").

Historical Fulfillment: Pagan Rome were the ones responsible for the death of these Christian martyrs. This period of redemption for the deceased Christians began in AD 312, when Constantine won the Battle of the Milvian Bridge, solidifying his power.

Chapter 3: *Divine Inspiration*

In AD 313, Christianity became legalized by the Edict of Milan. In AD 391, Theodosius I declared Christianity the official religion of the Roman Empire, ending Rome's long, oppressive history of Paganism.

This period ended in AD 395 when Rome became permanently divided into the East and West.

> And I beheld when he had opened the sixth seal, and, lo, there was a great earthquake; and the sun became black as sackcloth of hair, and the moon became as blood; and the stars of heaven fell unto the earth, even as a fig tree casteth her untimely figs, when she is shaken of a mighty wind. And the heaven departed as a scroll when it is rolled together; and every mountain and island were moved out of their places. And the kings of the earth, and the great

Chapter 3: *Divine Inspiration*

men, and the rich men, and the chief captains, and the mighty men, and every bondman, and every free man, hid themselves in the dens and in the rocks of the mountains; and said to the mountains and rocks, Fall on us, and hide us from the face of him that sitteth on the throne, and from the wrath of the Lamb: For the great day of his wrath is come; and who shall be able to stand. (Revelation 6:12–17)

Interpretation: Romans will turn fearful as divine wrath comes down upon Rome for its many sins.

Historical Fulfillment: This period began with the death of Theodosius I and the dividing of the Roman Empire in AD 395. God sent judgments upon Rome, such as the sack at the hands of the Visigoths

(AD 410), the Vandals (AD 455), and the ultimate fall of Western Rome in AD 476, primarily due to Rome's history of Christian persecution. This marked the end of the pagan Roman Empire.

First Six Trumpets

> And when he had opened the seventh seal, there was silence in heaven about the space of half an hour. And I saw the seven angels which stood before God; and to them were given seven trumpets. And another angel came and stood at the altar, having a golden censer; and there was given unto him much incense, that he should offer *it* with the prayers of all the saints upon the golden altar which was before the throne. And the smoke of the incense, *which*

Chapter 3: *Divine Inspiration*

came with the prayers of the saints, ascended up before God out of the angel's hand. And the angel took the censer, and filled it with fire of the altar, and cast *it* into the earth: and there were voices, and thunderings, and lightnings, and an earthquake. (Revelation 8:1–5)

Interpretation: There being "silence in heaven about the space of half an hour" means there would be a temporary period of calmness followed by a series of judgments.

The seven trumpets, given to seven angels, represent seven judgments from God to be unleashed on Rome, which is compared to "voices, and thunderings, and lightnings, and an earthquake." (v. 5)

Historical Fulfillment: When verse one mentions silence in heaven for half an hour, this refers

Chapter 3: *Divine Inspiration*

to the period during Constantine's reign when Christianity was spreading, and thus, the persecution of Christians was halted.

The seventh trumpet has yet to be fulfilled, and it details a future time; therefore, we'll now review the first six trumpets, as these are already historically fulfilled prophecies.

> And the seven angels which had the seven trumpets prepared themselves to sound. The first angel sounded, and there followed hail and fire mingled with blood, and they were cast upon the earth: and the third part of trees was burnt up, and all green grass was burnt up. (Revelation 8:6–7)

Chapter 3: *Divine Inspiration*

Interpretation: The first four trumpets represent judgments on Western Rome, culminating in its eventual fall in AD 476. Hail and fire mixed with blood clearly symbolize violent war and destruction. In these Revelation prophecies, the earth is often used as a symbol for the Roman Empire. So, this bloody war would be "cast upon" Rome. The trees and grass burning up means this would cause widespread devastation.

Historical Fulfillment: This first trumpet represents the Visigoth invasion led by King Alaric, which led to the sack of Rome in AD 410. This was a bloody invasion that sent shockwaves throughout the world since it was the first time in about 800 years that Rome fell to a foreign invasion. Roman cities and the Roman countryside were destroyed, thereby fulfilling

Chapter 3: *Divine Inspiration*

the part of the prophecy that involved the burning of trees and grass.

> And the second angel sounded, and as it were a great mountain burning with fire was cast into the sea: and the third part of the creatures which were in the sea, and had life, died; and the third part of the ships were destroyed. (Revelation 8:8–9)

Interpretation: The great mountain burning on fire being cast into the sea represents something powerful related to the nations, which are represented by the sea (Daniel 7:2–3, Isaiah 17:12–13, Psalm 65:7), being overthrown.

Though the sea can be used metaphorically to describe the nations of the world, this judgment seems

Chapter 3: *Divine Inspiration*

to suggest a literal involvement of the sea ("the ships were destroyed"). A bloody naval battle is heavily implied in these verses.

Historical Fulfillment: This judgment refers to the naval attacks against Rome led by the Vandal king Genseric from AD 429 to 468. King Genseric began the Vandalic invasion of North Africa, Rome's naval base, in AD 429, eventually capturing Carthage in AD 439. This allowed the Vandals to build a powerful navy, which established their dominance over the Western Mediterranean.

Following the assassination of Emperor Petronius Maximus, the Vandals sailed to Rome and sacked it in AD 455.

In AD 468, Rome attempted to reclaim Carthage from the Vandals and assembled a fleet of over 1,000 ships. King Genseric, however, surprisingly attacked them and destroyed the Roman fleet at the Battle of Cape Bon, thus bringing a bloody naval judgment upon Rome, just as the prophecy says would happen.

> And the third angel sounded, and there fell a great star from heaven, burning as it were a lamp, and it fell upon the third part of the rivers, and upon the fountains of waters; and the name of the star is called Wormwood: and the third part of the waters became wormwood; and many men died of the waters, because they were made bitter. (Revelation 8:10–11)

Interpretation: Stars can be used in Scripture to symbolically refer to world leaders (Isaiah 14:12, Daniel 8:10, Matthew 24:29). This third trumpet tells

Chapter 3: *Divine Inspiration*

us that a powerful ruler ("great star") will rapidly come down and bring destruction ("burning as it were a lamp") on populated regions ("third part of the rivers, and upon the fountains of waters"). Water represents life in Scripture (Isaiah 55:1, Jeremiah 2:13, Isaiah 41:17–18, Psalm 1:3).

This mighty ruler is called "Wormwood," which is the name of a bitter herb. This ruler will, therefore, bring about bitterness and sorrow.

Historical Fulfillment: This prophecy refers to the Hunnic attacks on Rome, led by Attila the Hun. Attila is this "Wormwood."

The first of these major attacks against Rome led by Attila happened at around AD 441 when the Huns successfully invaded the Eastern Roman Empire (Byzantine Empire).

Chapter 3: *Divine Inspiration*

In AD 451, Attila invaded Gaul, which led to the Battle of the Catalaunian Plains. The Huns were ultimately put down in this battle, but not before causing great devastation by weakening the Roman army, looting, and pillaging.

Attila invaded Italy in 452 AD, causing widespread destruction.

This period of the third trumpet ended in AD 453 when Attila died from a hemorrhage.

> And the fourth angel sounded, and the third part of the sun was smitten, and the third part of the moon, and the third part of the stars; so as the third part of them was darkened, and the day shone not for a third part of it, and the night likewise. (Revelation 8:12)

Chapter 3: *Divine Inspiration*

Interpretation: The sun, moon, and stars represent worldly powers and authorities in Scripture (Genesis 37:9–10, Isaiah 13:10, Ezekiel 32:7–8, Joel 2:10). This suggests that the ruling authorities in Rome will be destroyed, as they are likened to the "darkened" sun, moon, and stars.

Historical Fulfillment: This fourth trumpet represents the final judgment upon Western Rome, specifically its official collapse in AD 476 at the hands of several barbarian kingdoms. These include the Visigoths, Ostrogoths, Vandals, Suevi, Alemanni, Burgundians, Franks, Anglo-Saxons, Heruli, and the Lombards. While Western Rome fell, the Eastern Roman Empire remained intact.

> And the fifth angel sounded, and I saw a star fall from heaven unto the earth: and to him was

Chapter 3: *Divine Inspiration*

given the key of the bottomless pit. And he opened the bottomless pit; and there arose smoke out of the great pit, as the smoke of a great furnace; and the sun and the air were darkened by reason of the smoke of the pit. (Revelation 9:1–2)

Interpretation: A leader ("star") will arise with great power ("to him was given the key") and will unleash chaos and desolation ("he opened the bottomless pit"), which will spread like smoke. This will cause confusion and turmoil ("the sun and the air were darkened").

Historical Fulfillment: The two following trumpets detail judgments against the Byzantine Empire.

Chapter 3: *Divine Inspiration*

The authoritative "star" is Muhammad (or rather, the idea of Muhammad and the rise of Islam if he didn't exist). The alleged date of the start of Muhammad's ministry (or the beginning of the spread of Islam) is c. AD 612.

The "bottomless pit" symbolizes the Arabian Desert. From this "bottomless pit" came Islam, which spread like smoke throughout regions, including the Byzantine Empire. The Islamic teachings "darkened" the Christian teachings of the Byzantines.

> And there came out of the smoke locusts upon the earth: and unto them was given power, as the scorpions of the earth have power. And it was commanded them that they should not hurt the grass of the earth, neither any green thing, neither any tree; but only those men which

Chapter 3: *Divine Inspiration*

have not the seal of God in their foreheads. And to them it was given that they should not kill them, but that they should be tormented five months: and their torment *was* as the torment of a scorpion, when he striketh a man. And in those days shall men seek death, and shall not find it; and shall desire to die, and death shall flee from them. (Revelation 9:3–6)

Interpretation: A harmful force will emerge from Islam. They will quickly sweep across regions, much-resembling locust swarms. However, they will demonstrate some restraint ("they should not hurt the grass of the earth, neither any green thing, neither any tree"). But they will harm those who are not true believers ("but only those men which have not the seal of God in their foreheads"). The locust-like force will

Chapter 3: *Divine Inspiration*

not completely destroy these false believers, but they will terrorize them for five months ("they should not kill them, but that they should be tormented five months").

This reference to "five months" is another application of the day-year principle. Five months is about 150 days, and when we apply the day-year principle to this, we change it to 150 years. So, the torture of these false believers would last for approximately 150 years. This oppression will be so severe that the victims will wish for death ("in those days shall men seek death").

Historical Fulfillment: The locusts that emerge from the smoke (Islam) are the Saracens, a group of early Islamic warriors centered in the Arabian Desert. The Saracens attacked many regions, rapidly

Chapter 3: *Divine Inspiration*

spreading Islam, including large parts of the Byzantine Empire.

Despite the widespread destruction they brought, the Arab invaders did not harm any plants because it is against Islamic law to do so. So the part of the prophecy that says the locusts would not harm any green thing is actually literal. However, it's also symbolic, with the plants symbolizing those within the Byzantine Empire who were not associated with Byzantine corruption.

The Saracens did practice restraint on specific populations who submitted to them, only bringing judgments upon those whom God wanted to be judged. These are those who "...have not the seal of God on their foreheads." (v. 4)

Chapter 3: *Divine Inspiration*

Despite these damaging Islamic attacks on the Byzantine Empire, they didn't bring complete destruction to it.

Now, let's see if these harmful attacks actually lasted for 150 years. If this period began in AD 612, the apparent start of Muhammad's ministry, then it would end in AD 762. This is precisely what happened!

In AD 762, the city of Baghdad (the capital of Iraq) was founded by Caliph Al-Mansur of the Abbasid Caliphate. This made Islam more centralized and less expansive. The rapid locust-like conquests ended, and so did the fifth trumpet.

> And the sixth angel sounded, and I heard a voice from the four horns of the golden altar which is before God, saying to the sixth angel

which had the trumpet, Loose the four angels which are bound in the great river Euphrates. And the four angels were loosed, which were prepared for an hour, and a day, and a month, and a year, for to slay the third part of men. And the number of the army of the horsemen *were* two hundred thousand: and I heard the number of them. (Revelation 9:13–16)

Interpretation: Four powers will arise ("Loose the four angels") out of a region symbolized by the Euphrates River ("which are bound in the great river Euphrates"). These powers will bring destruction upon a group of people which make up one-third of something ("to slay the third part of men") for "an hour, and a day, and a month, and a year."

Chapter 3: *Divine Inspiration*

This is yet another example of the day-year principle. An hour is 1/24 of a day, and 1/24 of a year is about 15 days. One day would be equivalent to one year, one month would be equivalent to 30 years, and one year would be equivalent to 360 years.

Applying the day-year principle to these periods, considering that the Jewish year was approximately 360 days and the Jewish month was approximately 30 days, we can calculate that this period spans 391 years and 15 days.

So, these four powers would wage war for 391 years and 15 days. These powers would consist of a vast army ("the number of the army of the horsemen *were* two hundred thousand").

Historical Fulfillment: This prophecy refers to the Turkish powers' attacks on the Byzantine Empire. These powers include the Seljuks, the Mongols, the

Chapter 3: *Divine Inspiration*

Tatars, and the Ottomans. (Mongols aren't actually Turkic but are often associated with Turkic groups due to living in a similar region and sharing cultural similarities.) These four groups all crossed the Euphrates River to launch their attacks against the Byzantine Empire.

The Seljuks were the first of these groups to attack the Byzantines. Examples of their successes include the capture of Ani (1064), the Battle of Manzikert (1071), and the Battle of Myriokephalon (1176).

The Mongols were the next of the "four angels" to attack. Examples of these attacks include their raids on Thrace (1263–1265) and the Battle of Köse Dağ (1243).

Next were the Tatars, who also participated in the raids on Thrace alongside the Mongols. They also

Chapter 3: *Divine Inspiration*

conducted minor naval and border raids on the Byzantine Empire from the late 1200s through the 1300s.

The last of these four powers to attack the Byzantines were the Ottomans. Examples of these aggressions include the capture of Bursa (1326), the capture of Nicaea (1331), and the capture of Constantinople which marks the termination of the Byzantine Empire (1453).

The destruction brought by them upon a third part of the people is a reference to the Byzantine Empire, which is a third part of Rome, the other two-thirds being Western Rome and the Holy Roman Empire.

So, according to the prophecy, this period of attacks against the Byzantine Empire should have lasted for 391 years and 15 days, which is what we calculated when we used the day-year principle. This period ended on May 29, 1453 when Constantinople fell at the hands of the Ottomans. When we subtract 391 years and 15 days from May 29, 1453, we get to May 14, 1062. This was right during the time when the Seljuks, the first of the "four angels" to be released, began hostilities against the Byzantine Empire. This proves that these attacks against "the third part of men" lasted for about 391 years and 15 days, just as Scripture says would happen.

First Five Vials

We will now be analyzing Revelation chapter 16. This chapter details the seven vials of God's judgments. But once again, since we're only going

Chapter 3: *Divine Inspiration*

over the prophecies that have already been fulfilled, we're just going to go over the first five vials.

> And I heard a great voice out of the temple saying to the seven angels, Go your ways, and pour out the vials of the wrath of God upon the earth. And the first went, and poured out his vial upon the earth; and there fell a noisome and grievous sore upon the men which had the mark of the beast, and *upon* them which worshipped his image. (Revelation 16:1–2)

> **Interpretation:** Judgment will come against a corrupt group ("a noisome and grievous sore") who have the "mark of the beast" and worship its image. In Revelation 13, "the beast" is used to represent the Catholic Church and their persecution of true

believers, giving us more symbolic detail of the "little horn" as spoken of in Daniel chapter 7. The "mark of the beast" refers to those who follow these teachings. According to the first vial of Revelation 16, the corruption within the Catholic Church will lead to a judgment against it.

Historical Fulfillment: This, much like Daniel 7:25, refers to the French Revolution (1789–1799), when the tables were turned on the Catholic Church, and it finally became the victim instead of the oppressor.

> And the second angel poured out his vial upon the sea; and it became as the blood of a dead *man*: and every living soul died in the sea. (Revelation 16:3)

Chapter 3: *Divine Inspiration*

Interpretation: There will be a bloody, destructive judgment ("the blood of a dead man") centered around maritime power ("the sea").

Historical Fulfillment: The following vials represent judgments rendered during the Napoleonic Wars, specifically detailing the years 1793–1809.

Napoleon rose to power due to the French Revolution (the first vial) because the overthrow of the monarchy meant people like himself could rise up the ranks without coming from a particularly powerful family.

In 1793, Britain declared war on France, starting a massive naval conflict between the two nations. This led to the Battle of the Nile (1798), in which the French fleet was destroyed in Egypt by the British, and the Battle of Trafalgar (1805), in which Britain defeated the French and Spanish fleets, thereby

Chapter 3: *Divine Inspiration*

establishing naval dominance for over a century. This was God's hand directing Napoleon's army to only invade the nations He wanted them to.

> And the third angel poured out his vial upon the rivers and fountains of waters; and they became blood. And I heard the angel of the waters say, Thou art righteous, O Lord, which art, and wast, and shalt be, because thou hast judged thus. For they have shed the blood of saints and prophets, and thou hast given them blood to drink; for they are worthy. And I heard another out of the altar say, Even so, Lord God Almighty, true and righteous *are* thy judgments. (Revelation 16:4–7)

Chapter 3: *Divine Inspiration*

Interpretation: Violence, death, and destruction ("they became blood") will come upon nations that are potent sources of influence and vitality ("the rivers and fountains of waters"). This is a judgment from God ("Thou art righteous, O LORD… because thou hast judged thus") on nations who persecuted faithful believers ("For they have shed the blood of saints and prophets").

Based on the context, we can infer that this refers to nations that were at the heart of the Catholic Church's influence.

Historical Fulfillment: This third vial is about Napoleon's conquests against countries such as Italy, Germany, and Austria, which were heavily influenced by the papacy.

The Catholic Church was founded in Rome, Italy. The Papal States existed in Italy for over a

Chapter 3: *Divine Inspiration*

thousand years (AD 756–1870) and were governed by the pope. Germany was the heart of the Holy Roman Empire, which was founded as a Catholic realm, an alliance between the Church and secular authority. Austria was the home of the royal Habsburg family who were fierce loyalists of the Catholic Church.

The Catholic influence on these nations was severely weakened by the Napoleonic Wars. Specific battles include the Battle of Arcole (1796), the Battle of Marengo (1800), the Battle of Ulm (1805), and the Battle of Wagram (1809).

These were righteous judgments from God on the Catholic Church for their persecution of the faithful throughout the years.

And the fourth angel poured out his vial upon the sun; and power was given unto him to

Chapter 3: *Divine Inspiration*

scorch men with fire. And men were scorched with great heat, and blasphemed the name of God, which hath power over these plagues: and they repented not to give him glory.
(Revelation 16:8–9)

Interpretation: A powerful figure ("the sun") will be given power by God ("power was given unto him") to bring destruction ("scorch men with fire") upon those who blaspheme against God ("men were scorched with great heat, and blasphemed the name of God").

Despite God bringing these judgments upon them ("God, which hath power over these plagues"), they would not change their blasphemous ways ("they repented not to give him glory").

Chapter 3: *Divine Inspiration*

Historical Fulfillment: The influential figure symbolized by the sun is Napoleon. The blasphemers whom God brings judgment upon through Napoleon are once again the Catholic Church, this time referring to the end of the Holy Roman Empire at the hands of Napoleon in 1806. Despite this major blow, the Catholic Church persisted rather than repenting.

> And the fifth angel poured out his vial upon the seat of the beast; and his kingdom was full of darkness; and they gnawed their tongues for pain, and blasphemed the God of heaven because of their pains and their sores, and repented not of their deeds. (Revelation 16:10–11)

Chapter 3: *Divine Inspiration*

Interpretation: Judgment will come against the papacy ("seat of the beast"). The Catholic Church's influence will be weakened ("his kingdom was full of darkness") and turmoil within the Church will brew ("they gnawed their tongues for pain").

Despite this judgment, they will still not repent nor give up their blasphemous ways ("blasphemed the God of heaven … and repented not of their deeds").

Historical Fulfillment: This vial was fulfilled in 1809 when Pope Pius VII was imprisoned following the annexation of the Papal States by French troops led by Napoleon. From the time of his imprisonment (July 6, 1809) to his release (March 1814), the Catholic Church faced uncertainty and a decline in its power. But even after the Pope's release, the Catholic Church still carried on with its sinful, self-glorifying ways.

Chapter 3: *Divine Inspiration*

When examining these prophecies, which we've exhaustively analyzed, the immense detail and accuracy of them (especially those in Daniel, as the Revelation prophecies employ more figurative language) have led many critics to claim that they must have been written after the events took place. Well, what's their proof? And if that was the case, how and why would anyone believe the Scriptures?

Let's say I were to write a book about the 2024 United States presidential election, in which I describe how Donald Trump would be elected as the new president over Kamala Harris. Then, I tell everyone that the book was written 1,000 years before the election. Why should anyone believe me?

Why, then, did the Jewish people believe and follow the Book of Daniel if it was allegedly written after the prophesied events had taken place? And why

Chapter 3: *Divine Inspiration*

did the Christians believe and follow the Book of Revelation if it was also written after the prophesied events took place?

Also, how would the biblical authors have been able to foretell the French Revolution, the Napoleonic Wars, Israel's reestablishment, and other world events, so accurately since they came along several years after the critics claim these books must've been written anyway?

Do they mean to claim that the Book of Ezekiel was written after 1948 or that the Book of Revelation was written after the 1800s? Surely, they cannot be in that much denial. All of these eye-opening fulfilled prophecies should convince us that the Bible is divinely inspired and thus give us no reason not to fully believe and follow it.

Chapter 4: Authority

Now that we've gone over how the Bible is divinely inspired, let's examine other religious texts to determine if they also hold the same authority.

The three major religions are Christianity, Judaism, and Islam. Christians follow the Bible, which includes the Old Testament and the New Testament. Jews follow the Tanakh (also known as the Old Testament) but reject the New Testament. Muslims follow the Quran, which they believe contains teachings from God, divinely revealed to the Prophet Muhammad. Let's first examine Islam.

Chapter 4: *Authority*

Islam

The five core pillars of Islam are Shahadah (faith), Salah (prayer), Sawm (fasting), Zakah (almsgiving), and Hajj (pilgrimage). Let's go through each of these five pillars.

Shahadah: God, whom they call "Allah," created everything. Muslims believe the last Prophet was named Muhammad, who was visited by the angel Gabriel in a cave called Hira, where God revealed Himself to him through divine revelations. Muhammad began to preach these teachings and had them written in a book called the Quran, which led to the creation of Islam.

Salah: Muslims pray five times a day, facing the direction of the Kaaba, the most sacred Islamic mosque in Mecca, Saudi Arabia. They pray before sunrise, early in the afternoon, late in the afternoon, after sunset, and at night.

Sawm: Muslims abstain from eating and drinking in daylight hours during their holy month of Ramadan.

Zakah: Giving money to help those in need.

Hajj: A religious journey to Mecca, Saudi Arabia, at least once in a Muslim's lifetime.

Although it is its own religion, Islamic beliefs are heavily influenced and inspired by the Bible. Some people from the Bible who are also mentioned in the Quran include Adam, Noah, Abraham, Ishmael, Isaac, Jacob, Joseph, Moses, David, Job, Jonah, Mary, John the Baptist, Jesus, and so on. They believe that Jesus was a prophet but not that he is the Son of God, which is what the Bible claims.

Chapter 4: *Authority*

So, the question now arises: Is the Quran reliable? The answer is no, it's not. We have absolutely zero reasons to believe that the Quran is divinely inspired and should be followed.

The Quran was written at the earliest, 600 years after the Bible was written. Since Muslims believe in certain people, stories, and teachings from the Bible, it means they believe the Bible is, at least in many ways, the inspired word of God.

So, why do they follow the Quran instead of the Bible? Well, if you ask a Muslim this question, they'll say it's because the Bible has been tampered with and altered over time. However, in the Quran, it says that God's word cannot be changed:

(Unless otherwise noted, all Quran quotations are taken from the Saheeh International translation.)

Chapter 4: *Authority*

And the word of your Lord has been fulfilled in truth and in justice. <u>None can alter His words</u>, and He is the Hearing, the Knowing. (Qur'an 6:115)

And recite, [O Muhammad], what has been revealed to you of the Book of your Lord. <u>There is no changer of His words</u>, and never will you find in other than Him a refuge. (Qur'an 18:27)

For them are good tidings in the worldly life and in the Hereafter. <u>No change is there in the words of Allah</u>. That is what is the great attainment. (Qur'an 10:64)

Chapter 4: *Authority*

These passages in the Quran completely contradict the Islamic reasoning for why the Quran should be followed instead of the Bible.

Let's now examine how the teachings in the Quran differ from those in the Bible. Muslims believe that Muhammad was the last Prophet: "Muhammad is not the father of [any] one of your men, but [he is] the Messenger of Allah and last of the prophets. And ever is Allah, of all things, Knowing." (Qur'an 33:40)

What does the Bible have to say about this? Jesus says: "I am the Alpha and the Omega, the beginning and the end, the first and the last." (Revelation 22:13)

The Bible tells us that Jesus is the beginning and the end, not Muhammad. In fact, Muhammad isn't mentioned in the Bible at all! Is Jesus mentioned in the Quran? Yes, he is (Qur'an 2:87, Qur'an 3:45, Qur'an

Chapter 4: *Authority*

4:157–159, Qur'an 5:17, Qur'an 6:85, Qur'an 19:16–36, etc.).

Muslims pray five times a day while facing Mecca, which they believe to be the holiest city since it is the alleged birthplace of Muhammad:

> And establish prayer at the two ends of the day and at the approach of the night… (Qur'an 11:114)

> Establish prayer at the decline of the sun [from its meridian] until the darkness of the night and [also] the Qur'an [i.e., recitation] of dawn. Indeed, the recitation of dawn is ever witnessed. (Qur'an 17:78)

Chapter 4: *Authority*

We have certainly seen the turning of your face, [O Muhammad], toward the heaven, and We will surely turn you to a qiblah with which you will be pleased. <u>So turn your face toward al-Masjid al-Haram. And wherever you [believers] are, turn your faces toward it [in prayer]</u>. Indeed, those who have been given the Scripture well know that it is the truth from their Lord. And Allah is not unaware of what they do. (Qur'an 2:144)

And [mention] when We made the House a place of return for the people and [a place of] security. And take, [O believers], from the standing place of Abraham a place of prayer. And We charged Abraham and Ishmael, [saying], "Purify My House for those who perform ṭawāf and those who are staying [there] for worship and those who bow and prostrate [in prayer]." (Qur'an 2:125)

Now what does the Bible say about this?

Rejoice evermore. <u>Pray without ceasing</u>. In every thing give thanks: for this is the will of God in Christ Jesus concerning you. (1 Thessalonians 5:16–18)

And take the helmet of salvation, and the sword of the Spirit, which is the word of God: <u>Praying always with all prayer and supplication in the Spirit</u>, and watching thereunto with all perseverance and supplication for all saints. (Ephesians 6:17–18)

Chapter 4: *Authority*

For the LORD hath chosen Zion; he hath desired it for his habitation. This is my rest for ever: here will I dwell; for I have desired it. (Psalm 132:13–14)

And he carried me away in the spirit to a great and high mountain, and shewed me <u>that great city, the holy Jerusalem</u>, descending out of heaven from God. (Revelation 21:10)

Thus saith the LORD; I am returned unto Zion, and will dwell in the midst of Jerusalem: and Jerusalem shall be called a city of truth; and the mountain of the LORD of hosts the holy mountain. (Zechariah 8:3)

Chapter 4: *Authority*

The Bible teaches that there is no limit on how often we should pray and that Jerusalem is God's holy city, not Mecca.

Now, let's examine the Prophet Muhammad a little bit more. The Bible teaches that the promised Prophet would be an Israelite, not an Arab.

Moses said to the Israelites: "The LORD thy God will raise up unto thee a Prophet from the midst of thee, of thy brethren, like unto me; unto him ye shall hearken." (Deuteronomy 18:15)

God said to David, the second king of Israel: "And when thy days be fulfilled, and thou shalt sleep with thy fathers, I will set up thy seed after thee, which shall proceed out of thy bowels, and I will establish his kingdom." (2 Samuel 7:12)

There are also little to no credible historical sources that prove Muhammad even existed. The

Chapter 4: *Authority*

sources detailing Muhammad's life were written after his supposed death, and there are no reliable contemporary sources written during his alleged lifetime.

What I believe could have happened is when the Arabs invaded Jerusalem in AD 638, they saw how the Jews had Moses and the Christians had Jesus, so they made up Muhammad and wrote the Quran to spread Arab influence and increase their power.

If Muhammad did exist, I think it's safe to say that he was a false prophet who never had any divine encounter but sought to be seen as the most important human to have ever lived and bring glory to the city of Mecca, leading many astray in the process. I believe one of the only verses in the Bible where you could say speaks of Muhammad would be in Matthew 24 when

Chapter 4: *Authority*

Jesus says: "And many false prophets shall rise, and shall deceive many." (Matthew 24:11)

Is Jesus the Messiah?

Jews and Christians both accept and follow the Tanakh, also known as the Old Testament. However, Christians also accept and follow the New Testament because they believe that Jesus Christ is the promised Messiah. Messiah, which means "anointed one," is a figure prophesied about in the Old Testament who would come from the line of King David, establish God's Kingdom, restore Israel, and bring in worldwide peace.

Followers of Judaism, however, do not believe that Jesus is the Messiah, thus rejecting the New

Chapter 4: *Authority*

Testament. Instead, they think that Jesus was a fraud because he didn't completely fulfill all of the Messianic prophecies written in the Old Testament.

Let's now examine the Messianic prophecies in the Old Testament and draw a conclusion on whether or not Jesus is the Messiah. Here are some of the Messianic prophecies that Jesus fulfilled (if the New Testament is to be believed):

1. **He (the seed of the woman) would defeat sin (the seed of the serpent).**

And I will put enmity between thee and the woman, between thy seed and her seed; it shall bruise thy head, and thou shalt bruise his heel. (Genesis 3:15)

Chapter 4: *Authority*

Fulfillment: When Jesus died without ever sinning, he defeated sin. Because the wages of sin is death (Romans 6:23) and Jesus died without sin, he was raised from the dead, made immortal, and thus gave his followers the same hope (Acts 2:24, Romans 6:4).

2. He would be a descendant of Abraham and David from the tribe of Judah.

And in thy [Abraham's] seed shall all the nations of the earth be blessed; because thou hast obeyed my voice. (Genesis 22:18)

The sceptre shall not depart from Judah, Nor a lawgiver from between his feet, Until Shiloh

Chapter 4: *Authority*

come; And unto him *shall* the gathering of the people *be*. (Genesis 49:10)

Behold, the days come, saith the LORD, that I will raise unto David a righteous Branch, and a King shall reign and prosper, and shall execute judgment and justice in the earth. (Jeremiah 23:5)

Fulfillment: We're given two genealogies of Jesus in Scripture: his legal genealogy through Joseph (since he had no human father) in the Book of Matthew and his biological genealogy through his mother, Mary, in the Book of Luke (Matthew 1:1–16, Luke 3:23–38). The genealogies tell us that Jesus is both a legal and physical descendant of David, Judah, and Abraham.

3. He would be from Bethlehem.

But thou, Beth-lehem Ephratah, *though* thou be little among the thousands of Judah, *yet* out of thee shall he come forth unto me *that* is to be ruler in Israel; whose goings forth *have been* from of old, from everlasting." (Micah 5:2)

Fulfillment: Although Jesus was raised in Nazareth, he was born in Bethlehem (Matthew 2:1).

4. He would be the Son of God.

I will be his father, and he shall be my son. (2 Samuel 7:14)

Chapter 4: *Authority*

Fulfillment: Jesus' mother, Mary, became pregnant with him through the Holy Spirit when she was a virgin, so Jesus has no human father and is, therefore, the Son of God (Matthew 1:18–25, Matthew 3:17).

Now let's take a look at the prophecies that Jesus didn't fulfill, which Jews use for their reasoning as to why he cannot be the Messiah:

1. **The Messiah will raise the faithful believers from the dead, and they will be given immortality.**

Thy dead *men* shall live, *together with* my dead body shall they arise. Awake and sing, ye that dwell in dust: for thy dew *is as* the dew of herbs, and the earth shall cast out the dead. (Isaiah 26:19)

And many of them that sleep in the dust of the earth shall awake, some to everlasting life, and some to shame and everlasting contempt. (Daniel 12:2)

> **2. The Messiah will bring all the Jews to Israel. Although the Jewish people are back in their land, there are still many who remain scattered amongst the nations, especially those from the lost ten tribes of Israel.**

And he shall set up an ensign for the nations, and shall assemble the outcasts of Israel, and

Chapter 4: *Authority*

gather together the dispersed of Judah from the four corners of the earth. (Isaiah 11:12)

For, lo, the days come, saith the LORD, that I will bring again the captivity of my people Israel and Judah, saith the LORD: and I will cause them to return to the land I gave to their fathers, and they shall possess it. (Jeremiah 30:3)

3. **The Messiah will establish God's Kingdom on earth, ushering in a new world of peace and righteousness.**

And he shall judge among the nations, and shall rebuke many people: and they shall beat their swords into plowshares, and their spears into

Chapter 4: *Authority*

pruninghooks: nation shall not lift up sword against nation, neither shall they learn war any more. (Isaiah 2:4)

And in the days of these kings shall the God of heaven set up a kingdom, which shall never be destroyed: and the kingdom shall not be left to other people, *but* it shall break in pieces and consume all these kingdoms, and it shall stand for ever. (Daniel 2:44)

The Christian response to these seemingly unfulfilled prophecies is that Jesus is currently in heaven and will fulfill them when he returns to earth at his second coming (Matthew 24:30, Acts 1:11, Hebrews 9:28, etc.). For Jesus to be proven as the Messiah, there would need to be verses in the Old

Chapter 4: *Authority*

Testament, which both Jews and Christians follow, that indicate how the Messiah would suffer during his first time on earth and not immediately fulfill all of the Messianic prophecies. Well, there are:

> He is despised and rejected of men; a man of sorrows, and acquainted with grief: and we hid as it were *our* faces from him; he was despised, and we esteemed him not. Surely he hath borne our griefs, and carried our sorrows: yet we did esteem him stricken, smitten of God, and afflicted. But he *was* wounded for our transgressions, *he was* bruised for our iniquities: the chastisement of our peace *was* upon him; and with his stripes we are healed. (Isaiah 53:3–5)

Chapter 4: *Authority*

This doesn't sound like someone who instantly becomes the king of the world. This is someone who would live a life of suffering and hardship. Is this not what Jesus went through as he was hated and despised by many (John 15:18) and flogged and crucified (John 19:1–16)?

> For dogs have compassed me: The assembly of the wicked have inclosed me: They pierced my hands and my feet. I may tell all my bones: They look *and* stare upon me. They part my garments among them, And cast lots upon my vesture. (Psalm 22:16–18)

Is this once again not identical to what happened to Jesus? In Mark chapter 15, concerning Jesus' crucifixion, we're told: "And when they had

Chapter 4: *Authority*

crucified him, they parted his garments, casting lots upon them, what every man should take." (Mark 15:24)

Zechariah chapter 12 is a prophecy concerning the future Battle of Armageddon, where many nations will be gathered against the land of Israel. In this chapter, God says how He will protect Israel that day and destroy the nations that attack it. We're also told that the Messiah will reveal himself to the Jewish people following the battle after they had just been delivered from the hands of the opposing nations:

> And I will pour upon the house of David, and upon the inhabitants of Jerusalem, the spirit of grace and of the supplications: and they shall look upon me whom they have pierced, and they shall mourn for him, as one mourneth for

Chapter 4: *Authority*

> *his* only *son*, and shall be in bitterness for him, as one that is in bitterness for *his* firstborn. (Zechariah 12:10)

The Jews reject Jesus as the Messiah, but when he comes to save them and they see how he was pierced (probably by noticing the holes in his hands), they will weep bitterly and mourn over their guilt of rejecting him. The Jewish people rejecting Jesus as the Messiah is literally prophesied about in the Tanakh.

In Daniel 9:24–27, the angel Gabriel visits Daniel and gives him what is commonly known as the "Seventy Weeks Prophecy":

> Seventy weeks are determined upon thy people and upon thy holy city, to finish the transgression, and to make reconciliation for

Chapter 4: *Authority*

iniquity, and to bring in everlasting righteousness, and to seal up the vision and prophecy, and to anoint the most Holy. (Daniel 9:24)

The seventy weeks here is another example of the day-year principle, where each week represents seven years instead of seven days. This would mean that these seventy weeks refer to 490 years. This verse is saying that there will be a period of 490 years when sin will be defeated ("finish the transgression"), when sins can become forgiven ("make reconciliation for iniquity"), when eternal righteousness will be made to eventually come into the world ("bring in everlasting righteousness"), when the prophecy would be fulfilled ("seal up the vision and prophecy"), and when the Messiah would be anointed ("anoint the most Holy").

Chapter 4: *Authority*

So when does this period begin, and was it fulfilled?

> Know therefore and understand, *that* from the going forth of the commandment to restore and to build Jerusalem unto the Messiah the Prince *shall be* seven weeks, and threescore and two weeks: the street shall be built again, and the wall, even in troublous times. (Daniel 9:25)

"Seven weeks, and threescore and two weeks" = 69 weeks. Since each day represents a year and every week represents seven years in the day-year principle, this equals approximately 483 years. This verse tells us that the Messiah would come 483 years after the command to rebuild Jerusalem was given.

Chapter 4: *Authority*

Well, when did this commandment take place? King Artaxerxes of Persia gave the decree to rebuild Jerusalem (Ezra 7:12–26) in the year 457 BC. Since there is no year 0, one year gets added when going from BC to AD. So 457 BC + 483 + 1 = AD 27.

What happened in AD 27? It just so happens to be the commonly believed year when Jesus was baptized and thus began his ministry (Luke 3:23). The Jewish belief of Jesus not being the Messiah is becoming increasingly more difficult to prove.

Now, we have covered 483 years of the 490-year prophecy, which leaves seven more years to go. The last two verses of Daniel 9 tell us what will happen within these seven years:

> And after threescore and two weeks shall Messiah be cut off, but not for himself: and the

Chapter 4: *Authority*

people of the prince that shall come shall destroy the city and the sanctuary; and the end thereof *shall be* with a flood, and unto the end of the war desolations are determined. (Daniel 9:26)

This verse tells us that the Messiah would be "cut off, but not for himself." This means that the Messiah would die for the sake of others. That doesn't sound like the Jewish view of the Messiah, who is expected to immediately usher in a new world of peace and righteousness and reign as king. This says that the Messiah would be killed! Does this match with what happened to Jesus? Yes, it absolutely does. Jesus was crucified to bring about the hope of salvation to mankind (John 3:16).

Chapter 4: *Authority*

The second part of the verse which says: "the people of the prince that shall come shall destroy the city and the sanctuary; and the end thereof *shall be* with a flood, and unto the end of the war desolations are determined," refers to the destruction of the Temple and of Jerusalem at the hands of the Romans in AD 70. This led to the continuation of the Jewish Diaspora, which began with the Babylonian conquest in 587 BC.

> And he shall confirm the covenant with many for one week: and in the midst of the week he shall cause the sacrifice and the oblation to cease, and for the overspreading of abominations he shall make *it* desolate, even until the consummation, and that determined shall be poured upon the desolate. (Daniel 9:27)

Chapter 4: *Authority*

This verse tells us that the Messiah will fulfill God's new covenant of faith and grace (Jeremiah 31:31–34, Matthew 26:28), which will replace the old covenant centered on the Law of Moses (Hebrews 9:26–28). The verse goes on to say that within one week (the last seven years of the prophecy), the Old Testament sacrificial system would be abolished.

The last part of the verse, which says, "for the overspreading of abominations he shall make *it* desolate," also refers to the Roman destruction of the Temple and Jerusalem (AD 70), which left Jerusalem "desolate" (Luke 21:20–24).

The first part of this final seven-year section of the 490-year prophecy relates to Jesus' ministry, which led to his crucifixion. The other part relates to the spreading of the gospel after Jesus' death. The 490-year period ended at around AD 34 when Stephen

Chapter 4: *Authority*

was stoned (Acts 7:54–60). This marked Israel's formal rejection of the gospel and the turning of the message to the Gentiles.

The New Testament teachings of Jesus as the Messiah do not contradict the Old Testament Messianic prophecies; instead, they reinforce them. Now that we've established this, the question arises of whether Jesus even existed at all or whether all that the New Testament says about him is fabricated. To answer this, we need to find reliable, unbiased historical sources that prove Jesus was, in fact, a real person. It just so happens that there are several. In fact, almost every historian today, whether they're a Christian or not, would agree that there was a man from Nazareth named Jesus who gained a large following and was killed on the orders of Pontius Pilate. Let's take a look at the evidence.

Chapter 4: *Authority*

The early Christians were severely persecuted following Jesus' death. The Roman Emperor Nero (r. AD 54–68) initiated this oppression. In AD 64, Nero blamed The Great Fire of Rome on Christians to build up anger and hostility towards them when, in actuality, the fire was probably started by Nero himself.

Christians were then imprisoned and killed in brutal ways such as crucifixion, getting burned alive, and getting eaten alive by dogs and lions. These facts are proven by the Roman historian Tacitus in his *Annals* (c. AD 116):

> Therefore, to scotch the rumor, Nero substituted as culprits, and punished with the utmost refinements of cruelty, a class of men, loathed for their vices, whom the crowd styled Christians. Christus, from whom the name had

Chapter 4: *Authority*

its origin, suffered the extreme penalty during the reign of Tiberius at the hands of one of our procurators, Pontius Pilatus, and a most mischievous superstition, thus checked for the moment, again broke out not only in Judea, the first source of the evil, but even in Rome, where all things hideous and shameful from every part of the world find their center and become popular. Accordingly, an arrest was first made of all who pleaded guilty; then, upon their information, an immense multitude was convicted, not so much of the crime of firing the city, as of hatred against mankind. Mockery of every sort was added to their deaths. Covered with the skins of beasts, they were torn by dogs and perished, or were nailed to crosses, or were doomed to the flames and

Chapter 4: *Authority*

burnt, to serve as a nightly illumination, when daylight had expired.[26]

This quote from Tacitus supports the biblical account that Jesus Christ ("Christus") existed, gained a large following known as Christians (Acts 11:26), and was killed on the orders of Pontius Pilate (Luke 23:23–25).

Now ask yourself why those early Christians, who knew the punishments they would've had to endure, willingly died those horrific deaths when all they had to do was stop being Christians or at least claim that they weren't unless they were 100 percent certain that Jesus was, in fact, the Son of God? If Jesus was just some fraud, why would these people rather

---

[26] Tacitus. *The Annals of Imperial Rome*. Translated by Alfred John Church and William Jackson Brodribb. London: Macmillan, 1876, 365–66.

Chapter 4: *Authority*

die in these brutal ways than renounce their faith unless they saw him do things (healing the sick, raising the dead, walking on water, etc.) that wouldn't be possible unless he was given power from God to do so?

Also, crucifixion was used as a public display of humiliation. People back then certainly wanted nothing to do with someone who was crucified. Yet, for whatever reason, Jesus' followers were proud to follow a crucified man and more than willing to suffer the temporary yet brutal consequences for it.

And if they somehow stole Jesus' body and made up the idea that he was raised in order to maintain their pride, why would they do that and write about it knowing the consequences that would follow in which they would be publicly humiliated and

Chapter 4: *Authority*

ridiculed as fanatics seemingly until the end of time? That completely goes against their pride.

The only logical explanation is that Jesus is indeed the Son of God, and everything the Bible says about him is true. Knowing that Jesus is the Messiah led these faithful men and women to follow in his footsteps by willingly dying as martyrs.

Flavius Josephus (AD 37–c. 100) was a Roman-Jewish historian who mentions Jesus in one of his writings:

> About this time, there lived Jesus, a wise man, if indeed one ought to call him a man. For he was one who wrought surprising feats and was a teacher of such people as accept the truth gladly. He won over many Jews and many of the Greeks. He was the Messiah. When Pilate,

Chapter 4: *Authority*

upon hearing him accused by men of the highest standing amongst us, had condemned him to be crucified, those who had in the first place come to love him did not give up their affection for him. On the third day he appeared to them restored to life, for the prophets of God had prophesied these and countless other marvelous things about him. And the tribe of the Christians, so called after him, has still to this day not disappeared.[27]

Now, this quote about Jesus was quite possibly tampered with later on to make more people believe in Jesus as the Messiah. Josephus' original quote probably doesn't contain phrases such as: "if indeed

---

[27] Josephus. *The Works of Josephus: Complete and Unabridged.* Translated by William Whiston. Peabody, MA: Hendrickson Publishers, 1998, 480.

Chapter 4: *Authority*

one ought to call him a man" and "He was the Messiah." However, it is generally agreed upon by scholars that Josephus did indeed write something about Jesus since he was born a few years after Jesus' death. Although we cannot fully accept that Josephus wrote all of those words (although he may have), we can accept that he did write about Jesus, which further supports his existence.

Pliny the Younger (AD 61/62–c. 113) was a lawyer, author, and magistrate of Rome. Around AD 112, Pliny wrote a letter to Emperor Trajan in which he mentioned Jesus and the early Christians:

> I asked them whether they were Christians. If they admitted it, I repeated the question a second and a third time, threatening them with punishment; if they persisted, I ordered them to

Chapter 4: *Authority*

be led away for execution. For whatever the nature of their admission, I had no doubt that stubbornness and unyielding obstinacy deserved to be punished.[28]

They also declared that the sum of their guilt or error amounted only to this, that on an appointed day they had been accustomed to meet before daybreak and to sing responsively a hymn to Christ as to a god...[29]

This letter proves the presence of Christianity in those days and the influence Jesus had on that part of the world.

---

[28] Pliny the Younger. *The Letters of the Younger Pliny*. Translated by Betty Radice. London: Penguin Books, 1969, 294.
[29] Pliny the Younger. *The Letters of the Younger Pliny*. Translated by Betty Radice. London: Penguin Books, 1969, 294.

Chapter 4: *Authority*

Suetonius (c. AD 69–after 122) was a Roman historian who wrote *The Twelve Caesars*. In this set of bibliographies, Suetonius also writes about the Christian persecution under Emperor Nero, and many believe that he mentions Jesus as well:

> Punishment was inflicted on the Christians, a class of men given to a new and mischievous superstition.[30]

> He expelled the Jews from Rome, who were constantly making disturbances at the instigation of Chrestus.[31]

---

[30] Suetonius. *The Twelve Caesars*. Translated by Robert Graves. London: Penguin Books, 2007, 127.
[31] Suetonius. *The Twelve Caesars*. Translated by Robert Graves. London: Penguin Books, 2007, 91.

Chapter 4: *Authority*

This mention of a man called "Chrestus" who started Jewish "disturbances" is commonly believed to be a reference to Jesus Christ. According to James D.G. Dunn, most scholars believe that:

> Most infer that Suetonius misheard the name (the pronunciation of *Christus* and *Chrestus* would have been very similar) and misunderstood the report as a reference to someone (Chrestus) active in the Jewish community at the time.[32]

Christianity spreading throughout pagan Rome was seen by the Romans as a cult that caused disruptions for them.

---

[32] Dunn, James D. G. *The Partings of the Ways: Between Christianity and Judaism and Their Significance for the Character of Christianity.* London: SCM Press, 2003, 68.

Chapter 4: *Authority*

After everything we've analyzed, I see no logical reasons to deny that Jesus existed and that everything the Bible says about him is true.

> Now when the centurion, and they that were with him, watching Jesus, saw the earthquake, and those things that were done, they feared greatly, saying, Truly this was the Son of God. (Matthew 27:54)

Chapter 5: The Apostasy

Now that we've gone over why the Bible (both the Old and New Testament) is divinely inspired and should be believed and followed, the question arises of why are there so many Christian denominations? Shouldn't there only be one? Does the Bible teach multiple different faiths that contradict each other?

No. God is not trying to trick us. He revealed the truth in His holy book for all to read and understand. The reason why there are so many denominations has nothing to do with how the Bible was written but has everything to do with us and our flawed nature.

Chapter 5: *The Apostasy*

Scripture actually issues several warnings about apostasy (the abandonment of a religious belief) and the rise of many false teachers who would deceive many. It also emphasizes the importance of holding on to the truth and not being influenced by the false doctrines they teach. Such verses include:

> Now the Spirit speaketh expressly, that in the latter times some shall depart from the faith, giving heed to seducing spirits, and doctrines of devils. (1 Timothy 4:1)

> Beloved, believe not every spirit, but try the spirits whether they are of God: because many false prophets are gone out into the world. (1 John 4:1)

Chapter 5: *The Apostasy*

For the time will come when they will not endure sound doctrine; but after their own lusts shall they heap to themselves teachers, having itching ears; and they shall turn away *their* ears from the truth, and shall be turned unto fables. (2 Timothy 4:3–4)

But there were false prophets also among the people, even as there shall be false teachers among you, who privily shall bring in damnable heresies, even denying the Lord that bought them, and bring upon themselves swift destruction. (2 Peter 2:1)

Beware of false prophets, which come to you in sheep's clothing, but inwardly they are ravenous wolves. (Matthew 7:15)

Chapter 5: *The Apostasy*

And many false prophets shall rise, and shall deceive many. (Matthew 24:11)

Beware lest any man spoil you through philosophy and vain deceit, after the tradition of men, after the rudiments of the world, and not after Christ. (Colossians 2:8)

And have no fellowship with the unfruitful works of darkness, but rather reprove *them*. (Ephesians 5:11)

These are only a few of the many verses that warn us about the coming of these false teachings. Therefore, the fact that there are numerous denominations actually validates the Bible, as that's what Scripture predicts would happen.

Chapter 5: *The Apostasy*

Now, which denomination is the right one? Which doctrines were started by false teachers? Fortunately for us, all we have to do is read the Bible and find out.

Sola Scriptura

First, it's essential to establish the importance of "Sola Scriptura," which is the belief that the Bible is the only source of authority that Christians should follow. We've already established why the Bible is God's inspired word, which should make it 100 percent authoritative since it is from the higher power who created the universe.

However, there are those, such as Catholics, who claim that the pope has the same authority or even greater authority than God Himself, claiming they were divinely appointed. Now, why would anyone in their right mind believe this blasphemy? Why would anyone believe these sinful, mortal men share or have more authority than the creator and sustainer of the universe? Because they said so? If their Church leaders were appointed by God to their positions, then why does what they teach contradict what the Bible says?

In Acts chapter 5, the apostles were gaining a large following, which angered the Jewish authorities. When confronted and ordered to stop preaching, they responded by saying:

> Then Peter and the *other* apostles answered and said, <u>We ought to obey God rather than man</u>. (Acts 5:29)

Chapter 5: *The Apostasy*

We must also obey God rather than men. The Bible, therefore, is the sole authority of divine revelation and the only reliable source from which we should base our beliefs.

The Trinity Fallacy

One of the most widely accepted doctrines in mainstream Christianity is the doctrine of the Trinity. The Trinity is the belief that God exists as three separate beings within one: the Father, the Son, and the Holy Spirit. Three in one. Trinitarians believe that God is Yahweh, that He is also another entity called the Holy Spirit, and that He turned Himself into a man (Jesus) to be His own Son and sacrificed Himself on the cross to save His followers.

Chapter 5: *The Apostasy*

Is this one of the "damnable heresies" (2 Peter 2:1) that God warns us about? Most certainly.

The doctrine of the Trinity began to be formally defined in Christianity at the First Council of Nicaea in AD 325, approximately 300 years after Jesus' time on earth. The Council affirmed the divinity of the Son, a concept earlier explored by theologians such as Tertullian (c. AD 160–220).

Tertullian was born approximately 160 years after the birth of Christ. The Council made what is known as the Nicene Creed, which was later expanded at the First Council of Constantinople in AD 381, which reads:

> We believe in one God, the Father, the Almighty, maker of heaven and earth, of all that is, seen and unseen. We believe in one

Chapter 5: *The Apostasy*

Lord, Jesus Christ, the only Son of God, eternally begotten of the Father, God from God, Light from Light, true God from true God, begotten, not made, of one Being with the Father. Through him all things were made. For us and for our salvation he came down from heaven: by the power of the Holy Spirit he became incarnate from the Virgin Mary, and was made man. For our sake he was crucified under Pontius Pilate; he suffered death and was buried. On the third day he rose again in accordance with the Scriptures; he ascended into heaven and is seated at the right hand of the Father. He will come again in glory to judge the living and the dead, and his kingdom will have no end. We believe in the Holy Spirit, the Lord, the giver of life, who proceeds from the

Chapter 5: *The Apostasy*

Father and the Son. With the Father and the Son he is worshiped and glorified. He has spoken through the Prophets. We believe in one holy catholic and apostolic Church. We acknowledge one baptism for the forgiveness of sins. We look for the resurrection of the dead, and the life of the world to come. Amen.[33]

The fact that the Bible warns us about false teachings that would arise, then this central doctrine was established about 300 years after Jesus' time on earth, leads me to believe it is no coincidence. Let's examine what Scripture has to say concerning this doctrine.

---

[33] The Episcopal Church (1979) *The Book of Common Prayer*, Church Publishing, New York, 358.

Chapter 5: *The Apostasy*

The Father and the Son

Trinitarians claim that God is "three in one," although the phrase "three in one" does not appear in Scripture. The Bible tells us that God is one. Not three, not three in one, just one. Some verses include:

> Hear, O Israel: The LORD our God *is* one LORD. (Deuteronomy 6:4)

> Thou believest that there is one God; thou doest well: the devils also believe, and tremble. (James 2:19)

> Remember the former things of old: for I *am* God, and *there is* none else; *I am* God, and *there is* none like me. (Isaiah 46:9)

Chapter 5: *The Apostasy*

Trinitarians believe that Jesus is God, often referring to him as "God the Son." They believe that God turned himself into a man, overcame sin, and died for us. This contradicts several basic biblical teachings.

The phrase "God the Son" appears zero times in Scripture. The Bible clearly teaches that Jesus is the Son of God, with the title appearing numerous times.

> And Jesus, when he was baptized, went up straightway out of the water: and, lo, the heavens were opened unto him, and he saw the Spirit of God descending like a dove, and lighting upon him: and lo a voice from heaven saying, This is my beloved Son, in whom I am well pleased. (Matthew 3:16–17)

Chapter 5: *The Apostasy*

According to Trinitarians, this is God calling out to Himself and declaring Himself to be His own Son, stating that He loves and is pleased with Himself. Now, ask yourself if that makes any sense.

> For God so loved the world, that he gave his only begotten Son, that whosoever believeth in him should not perish, but have everlasting life. (John 3:16)

According to Trinitarians, this verse states that God is His own Son, whom He begat into the world.

In John chapter 10, the Jewish authorities accuse Jesus of claiming to be God. Look at his response:

Chapter 5: *The Apostasy*

Then the Jews took up stones again to stone him. Jesus answered them, Many good works I shewed you from my Father; for which of those works do ye stone me? The Jews answered him, saying, For a good work we stone thee not; but for blasphemy; and because that thou, being, makest thyself God. Jesus answered them, Is it not written in your law, I said, Ye are gods? If he called them gods, unto whom the word of God came, and the scripture cannot be broken; say ye of him, whom the Father hath sanctified, and sent into the world, Thou blasphemest; <u>because I said, I am the Son of God</u>? (John 10:31–36)

So here, Jesus is asking the Jewish leaders why they are saying he blasphemously claimed to be God

Chapter 5: *The Apostasy*

when all he said was that he was God's Son. He is literally saying no, I'm not claiming to be God but rather the Son of God.

Jesus also prayed to God. Would God pray to Himself? The night before Jesus was crucified, he prayed to God and said: "O my Father, if it be possible, let this cup pass from me: nevertheless not as I will, but as thou *wilt*." (Matthew 26:39)

Jesus had seen people get crucified, so he was terrified to endure the same slow and excruciating death. So he prayed to God and asked Him if it was possible for him to not have to endure that horrible death. As we know, Jesus was indeed crucified. According to the Trinity, this was God praying to Himself and then not fulfilling His own prayer.

Jesus was always separating himself from God and exalting God over himself. When the young rich ruler came to Jesus, he asked him: "Good Master, what shall I do that I may inherit eternal life? And Jesus said unto him, Why callest thou me good? *there is* none good but one, *that is*, God." (Mark 10:17–18)

Jesus is saying that he is not good, but only God is good, which means they cannot be equal. Although Jesus is good since he died without sinning, he still hadn't defeated sin at that time, so he wasn't officially "good" yet.

Another key example comes in John chapter 14:

> Ye have heard how I said unto you, I go away, and come *again* unto you. If ye loved me, ye would rejoice, because I said, I go unto the Father: <u>for my Father is greater than I</u>. (John 14:28)

Chapter 5: *The Apostasy*

This is Jesus clearly teaching his subordination to God.

Scripture also reveals major differences to us between God and Jesus. James tells us that God cannot be tempted: "Let no man say when he is tempted, I am tempted of God: <u>for God cannot be tempted by evil</u>, neither tempteth he any man." (James 1:13)

Yet we're also told that Jesus was tempted:

Then was Jesus led up of the Spirit into the wilderness to be tempted of the devil. (Matthew 4:1)

For we have not an high priest which cannot be touched with the feeling of our infirmities; <u>but was in all points tempted like as *we are*</u>, *yet* without sin. (Hebrews 4:15)

Chapter 5: *The Apostasy*

In the Book of Luke, we're told that as Jesus grew up, he increased in wisdom: "And Jesus increased in wisdom and stature, and in favour with God and man." (Luke 2:52)

This creates yet another complication for the Trinity as God cannot increase in wisdom because He is all-knowing (1 John 3:20).

When speaking of the time when he will establish the Kingdom of God at his second coming, Jesus said: "But of that day and hour knoweth no *man*, no, not the angels of heaven, but my Father only." (Matthew 24:36)

How could Jesus not know when his second coming would be, but God does if he is God?

Moses writes in Numbers chapter 23: "God *is* not a man, that he should lie; Neither the son of man, that he should repent." (Numbers 23:19)

Chapter 5: *The Apostasy*

God is not a man. Jesus is a man (Acts 2:22, 1 Timothy 2:5). It even adds on how God is not the "son of man." The "Son of man" was one of Jesus' titles (Mark 10:45, Mark 14:62, Luke 19:10, John 3:13, etc.).

God does not change: "For I *am* the LORD, I change not…" (Malachi 3:6)

Why, then, would He change into a man? Was He lying? Obviously not, because we're told that He cannot lie (Numbers 23:19, Hebrews 6:18, Titus 1:2).

God cannot die (1 Timothy 6:16). Jesus died (Mark 15:37). If God turned Himself into a man to defeat sin and sacrifice Himself for our sake, not only does that contradict all of those verses, but also his death would mean nothing since that's not man overcoming sin, but God, who can't even sin anyway.

Chapter 5: *The Apostasy*

Now, several verses are completely misinterpreted by Trinitarians. They claim certain verses prove that Jesus preexisted his birth and that he is God. Let's take a look at them:

> <u>And God said, Let us make man in our image, after our likeness</u>: and let them have dominion over the fish of the sea, and over the fowl of the air, and over the cattle, and over all the earth, and over every creeping thing that creepeth upon the earth. (Genesis 1:26)

Trinitarians have misinterpreted the "us" in this verse to refer to the plurality of God's nature (Father, Son, Holy Spirit) and as proof that Jesus preexisted.

This doesn't make any sense. You cannot preexist yourself. Jesus is a man (Acts 2:22, 1 Timothy

Chapter 5: *The Apostasy*

2:5). How then could he exist before Adam, the first man (Genesis 2:7, 1 Corinthians 15:45)?

The "us" in Genesis 1:26 refers to the angels. The angels played a significant role in creation. The first verse of the Bible states: "In the beginning God created the heaven and the earth." (Genesis 1:1)

The Hebrew word translated as "God" in this verse is the word *Elohim* (אֱלֹהִים), which can refer to God, but it can also be used to describe angels. A good example of this comes in Psalm 8: "For thou hast made him a little lower than the angels [*Elohim*], And hast crowned him with glory and honour." (Psalm 8:5)

Several verses support the idea that God used the angels in the creation process:

Chapter 5: *The Apostasy*

By the word of the LORD were the heavens made; And all the host of them by the breath of his mouth. (Psalm 33:6)

Through faith we understand that <u>the worlds were framed by the word of God</u>, so that things which are seen were not made of things which do appear. (Hebrews 11:3)

For this they willingly are ignorant of, that <u>by the word of God</u> the heavens were of old, and the earth standing out of the water and in the water. (2 Peter 3:5)

These verses imply that God created the world through commands given to the angels (who get their power from Him).

Chapter 5: *The Apostasy*

Throughout Scripture, it is proven that God uses His angels to carry out His will: "Bless the LORD, ye his angels, that excel in strength, that do his commandments, hearkening unto the voice of his word." (Psalm 103:20)

Oftentimes, angels are referred to as God because they were given power and authority from God to carry out His righteous judgments. A great example of this comes in Genesis chapter 18 when three angels visited Abraham: "And he lift up his eyes and looked, and, lo, three men [angels] stood by him…" (Genesis 18:2)

(Scripture calls the angels men because they were initially mistaken as men but later proven to be angels.)

Later in the chapter, God says that He will bring judgment upon the corrupt people of Sodom and

Chapter 5: *The Apostasy*

Gomorrah for their sins. Read the following verses carefully:

> And the LORD said, Because the city of Sodom and Gomorrah is great, and because their sin is very grievous; I will go down now, and see whether they have done altogether according to the cry of it, which is to come unto me; and if not, I will know. And the men turned their faces from thence, and went toward Sodom: but Abraham stood yet before the LORD. (Genesis 18:20–22)

Notice how God says He would go down to Sodom and Gomorrah and examine the people there, but then it says the angels ("men") went down to Sodom. It says: "Abraham stood yet before the LORD"

Chapter 5: *The Apostasy*

(v. 22) because one of the three angels (Genesis 18:2) had stayed with Abraham. At the same time, the other two went to Sodom and Gomorrah, as confirmed in Genesis 19:1.

So Abraham remained in the presence of one of the angels, who had taken on the name of the LORD. The angels going down to Sodom and Gomorrah is equated to God going down to Sodom and Gomorrah, further proving that the angels can take on the name of God.

In Exodus 23, God is speaking to Moses and the Israelites, and He says:

> Behold, I send an Angel before thee, to keep thee in the way, and to bring thee into the place which I have prepared. Beware of him, and obey his voice, provoke him not; for he will not

Chapter 5: *The Apostasy*

pardon your transgressions: <u>for my name *is* in him</u>. (Exodus 23:20–21)

Here, God says that His name is in the angel He was sending. This proves without a doubt that angels can take on the name of God.

This also helps to confirm that the angels are made in God's image (moral and intellectual capability). And since we know that humans are created in God's image (Genesis 1:26), it validates the idea that the "us" in the creation account refers to the angels, not to Jesus.

In the Book of Zechariah, when speaking of the future time when Jesus will reveal himself to his fellow Jews, it says:

Chapter 5: *The Apostasy*

And I will pour upon the house of David, and upon the inhabitants of Jerusalem, the spirit of grace and of supplications: and they shall look upon me whom they have pierced, and they shall mourn for him, as one mourneth for *his* only *son*, and shall be in bitterness for him, as one that is in bitterness for *his* firstborn. (Zechariah 12:10)

This verse is confusing since God is the one speaking. He says: "they [the Jews] shall look upon me whom they have pierced," which would imply that He is talking about Himself having been crucified. However, as we read further into the verse, the language shifts and God begins speaking in the third person, as seen in phrases such as "they shall mourn for him" and "shall be in bitterness for him." It

Chapter 5: *The Apostasy*

wouldn't make sense why He would switch to the third person if He was only talking about Himself.

When God says "him," He is referring to Jesus. The reason why He starts this verse by speaking in the first person by saying "me" is to highlight how Jesus was the perfect manifestation of God and how God was figuratively in Christ on the cross (2 Corinthians 5:19). Since Jesus represented God so thoroughly, it could be said that God was "pierced" because an act against God's perfect representative is, therefore, an act against God Himself.

But as God cannot die (1 Timothy 6:16), then it is "him" (Jesus) who was ultimately pierced and who will be mourned over. This explanation is reinforced for us in John chapter 19, which says: "And again another scripture saith, They shall look on him whom they have pierced." (John 19:37) This verse, which is

Chapter 5: *The Apostasy*

about Jesus being pierced on the cross, uses the third person ("him"), not the first person ("me").

> But unto the Son *he saith*, Thy throne, O God, *is* for ever and ever: A sceptre of righteousness *is* the sceptre of thy kingdom. (Hebrews 1:8)

In this verse, it seems as if God is calling Jesus ("the Son") God. This presents some challenges, however. If God is speaking to Himself here, why does He say: "<u>Thy</u> throne" and "<u>thy</u> kingdom"? Shouldn't He say "my throne" and "my kingdom"?

The next verse reads: "Thou hast loved righteousness, and hated iniquity; Therefore God, *even* thy God, hath anointed thee With the oil of gladness above thy fellows." (Hebrews 1:9)

Chapter 5: *The Apostasy*

Why would God refer to Himself in the third person here? Shouldn't He say: "I, thy God, hath anointed thee"? And also, why would God refer to Himself as His own God?

These two verses are actually quoting Psalm 45:

> Thy throne, O God *is* for ever and ever: The sceptre of thy kingdom *is* a right sceptre. Thou lovest righteousness, and hatest wickedness: Therefore God, thy God, hath anointed thee with the oil of gladness above thy fellows. (Psalm 45:6–7)

This passage was written by the sons of Korah to a king in a royal wedding song. So, did they call this king God? No, of course not.

Chapter 5: *The Apostasy*

The Hebrew word translated as "God" is once again the word *Elohim*, which is used in the following verses to describe human judges: Exodus 21:6; Exodus 22:8–9; Psalm 82:1, 6. The word is essentially used for someone who is mighty. Jesus is not called God in Hebrews 1 but instead is called a mighty one, which he certainly is.

> Let this mind be in you, which was also in Christ Jesus: who, being in the form of God, thought it not robbery to be equal with God: but made himself of no reputation, and took upon him the form of a servant, and was made in the likeness of men: and being found in fashion as a man, he humbled himself, and became obedient unto death, even the death of the cross. (Philippians 2:5–8)

Chapter 5: *The Apostasy*

This has been interpreted by Trinitarians as meaning that Jesus was equal to God and became a man to defeat sin on the cross, thereby proving his divinity and preexistence.

This is another misinterpretation. These verses clearly separate Jesus and God. Why would Jesus consider equality with God something to not grasp if he was already God?

When it says Jesus is "in the form of God" (v. 6), that is referring to Jesus being a man who is made in God's image (Genesis 1:26) as well as him being the perfect representative of God (Hebrews 1:3).

Jesus "made himself of no reputation," was "found in fashion as a man," and "humbled himself" by submitting to God's will instead of trying to exalt himself which many men have strived to do throughout

Chapter 5: *The Apostasy*

the ages. A great example would be the Tower of Babel (Genesis 11:4).

Verse 9 of Philippians chapter 2 tells us: "Wherefore God also hath highly exalted him, and given him a name which is above every name." (Philippians 2:9)

See how it says that God exalted him, not that Jesus exalted himself, because God is greater than Jesus, and they are not the same.

> Jesus said unto them, Verily, verily, I say unto you, Before Abraham was, I am. (John 8:58)

Trinitarians believe this verse is Jesus proving his preexistence by saying that he existed before Abraham. They also think that Jesus is calling himself

Chapter 5: *The Apostasy*

God here when he says: "I am" because God had told Moses: "I AM THAT I AM." (Exodus 3:14)

Both of these interpretations are wrong. Jesus did not say: "Before Abraham was, I was." The very first verse of the New Testament says: "The book of the generation of Jesus Christ, the son of David, the son of Abraham." (Matthew 1:1)

How is Jesus the son of David and the son of Abraham if he somehow lived before them? We're even given two genealogies of Jesus; his legal genealogy through Joseph (Matthew 1:1–16) and his biological genealogy through Mary (Luke 3:23–38), neither of which mention that he existed before his ancestors.

Just because Jesus said "I am," certainly does not mean that he's God. In the very next chapter, the

Chapter 5: *The Apostasy*

man born blind is asked if he's the man born blind, and he says: "I am *he*." (John 9:9)

Does this mean the man born blind is God, too? Of course not.

Jesus was not saying that he physically existed before Abraham, but that he was God's purpose for the world before Abraham lived, and thus has more authority than Abraham, being the Messiah. If we take a look a couple of verses back, Jesus says how Abraham knew that one day the Messiah would come, reinforcing this idea: "Your father Abraham rejoiced to see my day: and he saw *it*, and was glad." (John 8:56)

In John 10, Jesus says: "I and *my* Father are one." (John 10:30)

Trinitarians often reference this verse to support the Trinity because Jesus seemingly says that he and God are the same.

Chapter 5: *The Apostasy*

Jesus is not saying that he and the Father are one being but instead that they are of one mind and purpose. This is proven later on in the Book of John. In John chapter 17, Jesus is praying to God for his followers (I don't know why he'd be praying to himself), and he says:

> Neither pray I for these alone, but for them also which shall believe on me through their word; <u>that they all may be one; as thou, Father, *art* in me, and I in thee, that they also may be one in us</u>: that the world may believe that thou hast sent me. (John 17:20–21)

Now, do you really think Jesus is asking God to make his followers all the same person? Of course not. He's asking God to make them of one mind and

Chapter 5: *The Apostasy*

purpose, as he and God are. This is similar to how the bond between David and Jonathan is described in 1 Samuel 18:1.

In Colossians 2, we're told concerning Jesus: "For in him dwelleth all the fulness of the Godhead bodily." (Colossians 2:9)

Trinitarians believe this means that God lives in Jesus' body, so therefore, Jesus is God. This, however, cannot be the case since according to the Trinity, God is three persons: the Father, the Son, and the Holy Spirit. So, Jesus being the "fulness of the Godhead" would contradict the Trinity because it would disregard the Father and the Holy Spirit.

This verse refers to how Jesus is the perfect manifestation of God, not that he is God himself. Jesus never sinned (Hebrews 4:15) and always perfectly followed God's will. Being the Son of God and the

Chapter 5: *The Apostasy*

Messiah, he was given great power and authority from God (John 3:34, John 5:26–27). Since Jesus was the perfect manifestation of God, "in him dwelleth all the fulness of the Godhead bodily."

> Go ye therefore, and teach all nations, baptizing them in the name of the Father, of the Son, and of the Holy Ghost. (Matthew 28:19)

Trinitarians believe that since the Father, the Son, and the Holy Spirit ("Holy Ghost") are all mentioned here, it means they're equal.

Just because the Father, the Son, and the Holy Spirit are mentioned in this verse does not mean that they are all God. The Father is God, who is the creator and sustainer of the universe. The Son is Jesus, who is the Son of God and Messiah, who died on the cross so

Chapter 5: *The Apostasy*

that those who believe and are baptized may be saved. The Holy Spirit is God's divine power, which we'll explore further later in this chapter. These are all listed as part of a singular name to signify the unity of purpose between them.

Understanding the importance of these powerful names is crucial for baptism and, ultimately, salvation. Nowhere in this verse does it say that the Father, the Son, and the Holy Spirit are all the same.

In John chapter 20, Thomas calls Jesus "God": "And Thomas answered and said unto him, My Lord and my God." (John 20:28)

From a Trinitarian perspective, Thomas is calling Jesus God, thereby affirming Jesus' divinity.

In the Old Testament, representatives of God were sometimes referred to as "God." Angels are referred to as God at times (Genesis 16:7, Genesis

Chapter 5: *The Apostasy*

22:8, Exodus 23:20–21, etc.) It, therefore, makes perfect sense for Jesus also to be able to take on the name of God since Jesus was made greater than the angels: "Being made so much better than the angels, as he hath by inheritance obtained a more excellent name than they." (Hebrews 1:4)

Moses is referred to as a "god to Pharaoh" (Exodus 7:1). And as we've previously discussed, human judges can be called *Elohim*, which can be translated as "God" (Exodus 21:6, Exodus 22:8–9, Psalm 82:1, John 10:34–35).

Also, earlier in John 20, Jesus tells Mary: "I ascend unto my Father, and your Father; and *to* my God, and your God." (John 20:17) Since Jesus was to ascend to his God, it is clear that he is not God himself.

Chapter 5: *The Apostasy*

In the beginning was the Word, and the Word was with God, and the Word was God. The same was in the beginning with God. All things were made by him; and without him was not any thing made that was made. In him was life; and the life was the light of men. And the light shineth in darkness; and the darkness comprehended it not. There was a man sent from God, whose name *was* John. The same came for a witness, to bear witness of the Light, that all *men* through him might believe. He was not that Light, but *was sent* to bear witness of that Light. *That* was the true Light, which lighteth every man that cometh into the world. He was in the world, and the world was made by him, and the world knew him not. He came unto his own, and his own received him not.

Chapter 5: *The Apostasy*

> But as many as received him, to them gave he power to become the sons of God, *even* to them that believe on his name: which were born, not of blood, nor of the will of the flesh, nor of the will of man, but of God. And the Word was made flesh, and dwelt among us, (and we beheld his glory, the glory as of the only begotten of the Father) full of grace and truth. (John 1:1–14)

Trinitarians interpret this passage as meaning that Jesus ("the Word") was always God from the beginning who created everything. He became flesh by turning himself into a man and lived amongst humans on earth.

The first mistake Trinitarians make when reading this passage is overlooking the meaning of the

Chapter 5: *The Apostasy*

word "Word" and assuming it is merely a name for Jesus. The Greek word translated as "Word" is *logos* (λόγος), which refers to God's purpose and His words. This means that "all things were made by" God's purposeful decrees. This is reinforced by the following verse: "For this they willingly are ignorant of, that by the word [*logos*] of God the heavens were of old, and the earth standing out of the water and in the water." (2 Peter 3:5)

In verses 3 and 4 of John chapter 1, "the Word" is referred to as "him," leading many to further believe that this is a reference to Jesus.

However, this is another misunderstanding. In the Greek language, nouns are given a gender. Since the Greek word *logos* is masculine, the pronouns he, him, and his are attributed to it. The "him" in verses 3

Chapter 5: *The Apostasy*

and 4 is a reference to Greek nouns, not to the man Jesus Christ.

Now let's see what verses 4 and 5 are actually telling us:

> In him was life; and the life was the light of men. And the light shineth in darkness; and the darkness comprehended it not. (John 1:4–5)

The "light" here is actually a reference to the Lord Jesus, even though "the Word" isn't. Jesus gave life to God's purposeful commands by teaching and reinforcing them. This is proven in the following verses, which state that John the Baptist bore witness to "the Light" (John 1:6–8). We know that John's purpose was to: "Prepare ye the way of the Lord." (Mark 1:3)

Chapter 5: *The Apostasy*

Verse 10 reads: "The world was made by him." (John 1:10) The Greek word translated as "by" here is the word *dia* (διά), which means "because of" or "on account of." This does not mean that Jesus created the world, but rather that God created everything because of Jesus since Jesus was God's plan and purpose for the world from the beginning of creation.

Verse 14 reads: "The Word was made flesh." (John 1:14) This has been misinterpreted to mean that Jesus wasn't always in the flesh but became flesh by putting himself into the world as a man. This cannot be the case since we've already discussed why "the Word" isn't a name for Jesus but rather refers to God's divine purpose and His words.

God's purpose "became flesh" when Jesus was born since Jesus, being the one and only begotten Son

Chapter 5: *The Apostasy*

of God and the promised Messiah, was God's purpose all along, and he taught the words of God perfectly.

A verse commonly used to prove Jesus' preexistence is found in John 17 which reads: "And now, O Father, glorify thou me with thine own self with the glory which I had with thee before the world was." (John 17:5)

The Trinitarian interpretation is that Jesus said he had glory with God before the world began which proves his preexistence.

This does not mean that Jesus actually experienced glory with God before the world began, but rather that he had foreordained glory from God, which he was destined to receive. This is proven in the following verses:

Chapter 5: *The Apostasy*

<u>Who [Jesus] verily was foreordained before the foundation of the world</u>, but was manifest in these last times for you. (1 Peter 1:20)

<u>Him [Jesus], being delivered by the determinate counsel and foreknowledge of God</u>, ye have taken, and by wicked hands have crucified and slain. (Acts 2:23)

Some verses say that the believers are chosen in Christ before the foundation of the world (Matthew 25:34, Ephesians 1:4–5), further disproving the preexistence interpretation.

In the last chapter of the Bible, Revelation 22, Jesus says: "I am the Alpha and Omega, the beginning and the end, the first and the last." (Revelation 22:13)

Trinitarians claim this is proof that Jesus is God, as God also calls Himself the first and the last

Chapter 5: *The Apostasy*

(Isaiah 44:6). And since Jesus claims to be the beginning, they interpret it as meaning that He was alive from the beginning of creation.

If Jesus was truly claiming to be equal with God here, it would contradict several verses in which he clearly teaches his subordination to God, such as John 14:28 and 1 Corinthians 15:28. So, what does this mean?

Jesus has been given immense authority by God and is called the "Alpha and Omega" because he is the ultimate fulfillment of God's plan. Being the Son of God, Jesus is the "heir of all things" (Hebrews 1:2) and thus shares the title of being the "Alpha and Omega" with his Father, though he certainly isn't his Father himself and didn't preexist his own birth.

Chapter 5: *The Apostasy*

The Holy Spirit

Trinitarians believe that the third person who makes up God is the Holy Spirit. They often use the following passage as proof for this teaching:

> And I will pray the Father, and he shall give you another Comforter, that he may abide with you for ever; *even* the Spirit of truth; whom the world cannot receive, because it seeth him not, neither knoweth him: but ye know him; for he dwelleth with you, and shall be in you. (John 14:16–17)

Trinitarian Interpretation: Since Jesus calls the Holy Spirit ("Spirit of Truth") "another Comforter"

Chapter 5: *The Apostasy*

that was to come, it means that the Holy Spirit is a distinct person within the Godhead.

Explanation: The Holy Spirit is God's divine power, not some separate deity. This is proven in the following verses:

> And the angel answered and said unto her, <u>The Holy Ghost shall come upon thee, and the power of the Highest shall overshadow thee</u>: therefore also that holy thing which shall be born of thee shall be called the Son of God. (Luke 1:35)

See how the angel tells Mary that the Holy Spirit ("Holy Ghost") will come upon her and that the power of God ("the Highest") will therefore come upon her also, equating them.

Chapter 5: *The Apostasy*

> But truly I am full of power <u>by the spirit of the LORD</u>, and of judgment, and of might, to declare unto Jacob his transgression, and to Israel his sin. (Micah 3:8)

Notice how Micah doesn't just say "the spirit" but instead says "the spirit of the LORD" and how God's Spirit gives him power.

Isaiah 32:15 reads: "Until the spirit be poured upon us from on high…" (Isaiah 32:15) "From on high" means from God. So Isaiah is saying that "the spirit" comes from God, meaning it is God's power.

> And the earth was without form, and void; and darkness was upon the face of the deep. And <u>the Spirit of God</u> moved upon the face of the waters. (Genesis 1:2)

Chapter 5: *The Apostasy*

In the second verse of the entire Bible, the Holy Spirit is referred to as "the Spirit of God." It is Yahweh's Spirit.

> Thou sendest forth thy spirit, they are created: And thou renewest the face of the earth. (Psalm 104:30)

Here, the psalmist says how God creates through His Spirit, proving that God's Spirit is His power.

> He therefore that despiseth, despiseth not man, but God, who hath also given unto us <u>his holy Spirit</u>. (1 Thessalonians 4:8)

Chapter 5: *The Apostasy*

Instead of simply saying "God's Spirit" or the "Spirit of God," this verse literally refers to the Holy Spirit as God's "holy Spirit."

Suppose anyone were to try to refute these claims by saying that the Holy Spirit being from God doesn't contradict the Trinity since God is made up of the Father, the Son, and the Holy Spirit. In that case, another verse officially puts that argument down: "For it is not ye that speak, but <u>the Spirit of your Father</u> which speaketh in you." (Matthew 10:20)

In this verse, Jesus attributes the Spirit to the Father. If the Father is only a third of God, rather than the entirety of God, this would contradict the Trinity because it would mean that the Holy Spirit belongs to the Father rather than being its own entity within the Godhead as well. God is the Father, and the Holy Spirit is the power of the Father: the power of God.

Chapter 5: *The Apostasy*

Looking back at John 14:16–17, Jesus is saying that he will pray to God, and God will give His power (the Holy Spirit) to his disciples for them to spread the truth effectively. Nowhere in those verses nor anywhere in Scripture is the Trinitarian view of the Holy Spirit supported.

God's power being given to the disciples was fulfilled in the Book of Acts:

> And when the day of Pentecost was fully come, they were all with one accord in one place. And suddenly there came a sound from heaven as of a rushing mighty wind, and it filled all the house where they were sitting. And there appeared unto them cloven tongues like as of fire, and it sat upon each of them. And they were all filled with the Holy Ghost, and began

Chapter 5: *The Apostasy*

to speak with other tongues, as the Spirit gave them utterance. And there were dwelling at Jerusalem Jews, devout men, out of every nation under heaven. Now when this was noised abroad, the multitude came together, and were confounded, because that every man heard them speak in his own language. And they were all amazed and marvelled, saying one to another, Behold, are not all these which speak Galilaeans? And how hear we every man in our own tongue, wherein we were born? Parthians, and Medes, and Elamites, and the dwellers in Mesopotamia, and in Judaea, and Cappadocia, in Pontus, and Asia, Phrygia, and Pamphylia, in Egypt, and in the parts of Libya about Cyrene, and strangers of Rome, Jews and proselytes, Cretes and Arabians, we do hear

Chapter 5: *The Apostasy*

them speak in our tongues the wonderful works of God. And they were all amazed, and were in doubt, saying one to another, What meaneth this? (Acts 2:1–12)

The Holy Spirit gave the disciples the power to speak in different languages and to also perform miracles (Acts 5:12, 15, 16; Acts 6:8; Acts 14:3).

Some believe that the Holy Spirit is still given to people today to perform miracles and preach. This is not true. The Holy Spirit was given to specific individuals at a particular time for a specific purpose. The purpose was to spread Christianity and establish the early church. Once the true first-century Christian church was established, there was no more need for the Holy Spirit's gifts.

Chapter 5: *The Apostasy*

Charity never faileth: but whether *there be* prophecies, they shall fail; whether *there be* tongues, they shall cease; whether *there be* knowledge, it shall vanish away. For we know in part, and we prophesy in part. But when that which is perfect is come, then that which is in part shall be done away. (1 Corinthians 13:8–10)

"When that which is perfect is come" refers to the completion of the Scriptures. The Greek word translated as "perfect" is *teleios* (τέλειος), which can also mean "complete." Paul is saying that once the Scriptures are completed, there will be no more of the Holy Spirit's gifts ("prophecies," "tongues," "knowledge").

Chapter 5: *The Apostasy*

Once the Bible was completed, filled with God's word and purpose, the gifts of the Holy Spirit ceased to exist on the earth. It will stay this way until the return of the Lord Jesus Christ.

The Trinity is confusing for a reason. One plus one plus one does not equal one for a reason. It is a lie. It's a manmade doctrine invented several years after true first-century Christianity, and it has deceived many.

Is the Soul Immortal?

Another standard teaching found within mainstream Christianity is the doctrine of the immortal soul. This is the belief that when we die, although our physical bodies decay, our "soul" lives on. This, too, is

Chapter 5: *The Apostasy*

incredibly unscriptural. First of all, the belief in the immortal soul isn't found in the Bible but rather stems from Hinduism, Ancient Egypt, Greek philosophy, and other sources.

The soul is not some immortal thing that is separate from the body, but rather, it refers to a living person: "And the LORD God formed man *of* the dust of the ground, and breathed into his nostrils the breath of life; <u>and man became a living soul</u>." (Genesis 2:7)

When Adam was brought to life, he became a "living soul." The Hebrew word translated as "soul" is *nephesh* (נֶפֶשׁ), which refers to a living being. *Nephesh* is even used for animals as well: "And God said, Let the waters bring forth abundantly the moving creature [*nephesh*] that hath life, and fowl *that* may fly above the earth in the open firmament of heaven." (Genesis 1:20)

Chapter 5: *The Apostasy*

Here, the word *nephesh* is translated as "creature," referring to animals. Those who believe that the immortal soul is taught in the Bible would say that it applies only to humans, not to animals. This verse contradicts that claim and proves that the word "soul" just refers to life.

Let's now look at how "soul" is used in the New Testament: "For what is a man profited, if he shall gain the whole world, and lose his own soul? or what shall a man give in exchange for his soul?" (Matthew 16:26)

The Greek word translated as "soul" is *psuché* (ψυχή), which means "life." And if you replace the word "soul" in this verse with "life," it fits perfectly.

Chapter 5: *The Apostasy*

Hell

The false doctrine of the immortal soul also teaches that if you have lived a sinful life, you will go to this place called hell, which is commonly believed to be a fiery underworld realm where sinners are eternally burned. Let's take a look at some of the verses which have been misinterpreted to mean this:

> For fire is kindled in mine anger, And shall burn unto the lowest hell, And shall consume the earth with her increase, And set on fire the foundations of the mountains. (Deuteronomy 32:22)

Chapter 5: *The Apostasy*

In this verse, Moses compares his fiery anger with hell, which might make it seem as if he's saying hell is a fiery place. This is not true.

The Hebrew word used for "hell" is *sheol* (שְׁאוֹל), which refers to the grave or death. It is used again in 1 Samuel chapter 2: "The LORD killeth, and maketh alive: He bringeth down to the grave [*sheol*], and bringeth up." (1 Samuel 2:6)

Sheol is used to refer to "the grave" (death). In Deuteronomy 32:22, Moses is speaking figuratively about how his fiery anger will extend even to the grave.

In Genesis chapter 37, after Jacob is led to believe that his beloved son Joseph has died, it says:

> And all his sons and all his daughters rose up to comfort him; but he refused to be comforted;

Chapter 5: *The Apostasy*

and he said, <u>For I will go down into the grave</u> [*sheol*] <u>unto my son mourning</u>. Thus his father wept for him. (Genesis 37:35)

Jacob said that he would go down to the grave mourning for his son because he knew that when we die, we all go to the grave, not to any spiritual realm. Jacob was an overall righteous man, so he wouldn't even go to hell anyway if the common interpretation of hell is to be believed.

Let's now look at how hell is spoken of in the New Testament:

And fear not them which kill the body, but are not able to kill the soul: but rather fear him which is able to destroy both soul and body in hell. (Matthew 10:28)

Chapter 5: *The Apostasy*

This verse references the hope of eternal life through God's grace. Jesus is saying not to fear humans who can kill you, thus ending your temporary life, but to instead fear God, who can end your temporary life and also your hope of eternal life.

The Greek word used for "hell" here is *geenna* (γέεννα). This refers to the Valley of Gehenna, located outside Jerusalem. Gehenna was a place where children were sacrificed to pagan gods (Jeremiah 7:31) and later became a place where trash was burned.

Gehenna's association with fire and hell has led people to believe that hell is a place where your "soul" is tormented by eternal burning. However, the children and the refuse that were burned in Gehenna did not burn forever. They withered away until they were gone. Gehenna is a symbol of ultimate destruction and

Chapter 5: *The Apostasy*

death, not eternal burning in some underworld dimension.

In Luke 12, Jesus says:

> Consider the lilies how they grow: they toil not, they spin not; and yet I say unto you, that Solomon in all his glory was not arrayed like one of these. If then God so clothe the grass, which is to day in the field, and to morrow is cast into the oven; how much more *will he clothe* you, O ye of little faith? (Luke 12:27–28)

Jesus parallels plants withering with being thrown into "the oven" (or fire), which proves that fire is used symbolically for death and destruction and is not to be taken literally.

Chapter 5: *The Apostasy*

In Matthew 25, when Jesus was telling the parable of the sheep and the goats, he said: "And these shall go away into everlasting punishment: but the righteous into life eternal." (Matthew 25:46)

This verse seems to support the idea that sinners will endure everlasting torture. Well, this cannot be the case since Paul writes in Romans: "For the wages of sin *is* death; but the gift of God *is* eternal life through Jesus Christ our Lord." (Romans 6:23)

The punishment for sin is death, not eternal burning. And everlasting death would certainly qualify as "everlasting punishment." It's a punishment which is everlasting.

John writes in Revelation 14: "And the smoke of their torment ascendeth up for ever and ever: and they have no rest day nor night, who worship the beast

Chapter 5: *The Apostasy*

and his image, and whosoever receiveth the mark of his name." (Revelation 14:11)

Revelation is a very metaphorical book. For example, there was not an actual beast with seven heads and ten horns (Revelation 13:1), but rather, John saw it in a prophetic vision.

The smoke continually rising is used metaphorically to describe the punishment of everlasting death inflicted upon sinners. This is reinforced in 2 Thessalonians, which reads: "Who shall be punished with everlasting destruction from the presence of the Lord, and from the glory of his power." (2 Thessalonians 1:9)

Here, Paul calls the punishment of the ungodly "everlasting destruction." Destruction means dying or ceasing to exist, not eternal torture.

Chapter 5: *The Apostasy*

The parable of the rich man and Lazarus is commonly used as proof that hell is a place of eternal torment for the unrighteous. Let's take a look at it:

> There was a certain rich man, which was clothed in purple and fine linen, and fared sumptuously every day: and there was a certain beggar named Lazarus, which was laid at his gate, full of sores, and desiring to be fed with the crumbs which fell from the rich man's table: moreover the dogs came and licked his sores. And it came to pass, that the beggar died, and was carried by the angels into Abraham's bosom: the rich man also died, and was buried; and in hell he lift up his eyes, being in torments, and seeth Abraham afar off, and Lazarus in his bosom. And he cried and said,

Chapter 5: *The Apostasy*

Father Abraham, have mercy on me, and send Lazarus, that he may dip the tip of his finger in water, and cool my tongue; for I am tormented in this flame. But Abraham said, Son remember that thou in thy lifetime received thy good things, and likewise Lazarus evil things: but now he is comforted, and thou art tormented. And beside all this, between us and you there is a great gulf fixed: so that they which would pass from hence to you cannot; neither can they pass to us, that *would come* from thence. Then he said, I pray thee therefore, father, that thou wouldest send him to my father's house: for I have five brethren; that he may testify unto them, lest they also come into this place of torment. Abraham saith unto him, They have Moses and the prophets; let them hear them.

Chapter 5: *The Apostasy*

And he said, Nay, father Abraham: but if one went unto them from the dead, they will repent. And he said unto him, If they hear not Moses and the prophets, neither will they be persuaded, though one rose from the dead. (Luke 16:19–31)

It's essential to keep in mind that this is a parable (Matthew 13:13). Parables are stories intended to teach a lesson. They are not to be taken literally, as seen in Judges 9:7–15, which tells the story of trees asking an olive tree, a fig tree, and a vine to be their king. They all decline, allowing them to continue producing their fruits. The trees then ask a bramble, who agrees but says that if they are not sincere in wanting him to be their king, they will burn and not be allowed to be within the shade of the bramble.

Chapter 5: *The Apostasy*

Obviously, this is not to be taken literally, but it teaches a lesson on the importance of choosing a worthy leader. Now that we understand parables are not to be taken literally let's further examine the story of the rich man and Lazarus.

We're told that when the beggar named Lazarus died, he was taken by angels to "Abraham's bosom." After the rich man died, he was being tormented in hell. The Greek word used for "hell" here is *hadés* (ᾅδης), which refers to the realm in which all of the dead reside (the grave, death). But this rich man was conscious in Hades, and he sees Abraham with the beggar and calls out to him, asking the father of the Jews to save him from the unbearable torment he was enduring.

Abraham refused because the rich man was not worthy, and there was a "great gulf" fixed between

Chapter 5: *The Apostasy*

Hades and where Abraham and Lazarus were, so they wouldn't be able to cross anyway. The rich man then asks Abraham to send the beggar to his family so they may be warned and not also enter the place of torment.

Abraham says that they have Moses and the prophets to listen to. The rich man says that if someone from the dead warns them, they will repent. Abraham finishes the conversation by saying that Moses and the prophets should be convincing enough.

This parable contradicts several fundamental biblical teachings. Scripture teaches us that when we die, we are just dead (Genesis 3:19, Psalm 146:4, Ecclesiastes 9:5, Romans 6:23, etc.). Once we die, we are unconscious and cease to exist.

Yet in this passage, the rich man goes to a place of torment after death, and the beggar goes to a place of comfort, where Abraham also resides. This has been

Chapter 5: *The Apostasy*

used to prove that when we die, the immortal souls of the righteous go to heaven, and the immortal souls of the sinful go to hell. However, we're told that the judgment does not happen at death but after the resurrection of the dead: "And many of them that sleep in the dust of the earth shall awake, some to everlasting life, and some to shame *and* everlasting contempt." (Daniel 12:2)

The story of the rich man and Lazarus is actually an example of a Jewish fable. Scripture warns us about believing in such fables: "This witness is true. Wherefore rebuke them sharply, that they may be sound in the faith; <u>not giving heed to Jewish fables, and commandments of men, that turn from the truth</u>." (Titus 1:13–14)

The Book of Enoch is a religious text, likely written by multiple authors over the years, attributed to

Chapter 5: *The Apostasy*

the prophet Enoch who we read about in Genesis 5:21–24. The book is not considered canonical, and assuming that God was in control of deciding which books were to be included in the Bible, it makes perfect sense why the Book of Enoch is not part of it. It contains ideas that the Bible completely rejects, such as fallen angels and giant human-angel hybrids. However, the book does provide some context regarding the Jewish myths that were believed in during those times:

> These hollow places have been created for this very purpose, that the spirits of the souls of the dead should assemble therein... And this has been made for the spirits of the righteous, who will be separated from this great punishment...

Chapter 5: *The Apostasy*

a spring of water shall be given to the righteous and they shall dwell in blessing and light.[34]

We can see certain similarities between this passage and the parable of the rich man and Lazarus. They both teach that the souls of the righteous will be separated from the souls of the wicked, the souls of the wicked will experience torment ("great punishment"), and the souls of the righteous will dwell in a realm of peace and comfort.

The Babylonian Talmud is a text rich in ancient Jewish commentary, serving as the primary source of Jewish law and theology today. It also contains fabled teachings that are echoed in this parable given by Jesus:

---

[34] R. H. Charles, *The Book of Enoch* (London: SPCK, 1912), 71–72.

Chapter 5: *The Apostasy*

The righteous sit with their crowns upon their heads and enjoy the radiance of the Shechinah, as it is said, "And they shall be gathered one by one, O children of Israel." (Isaiah 27:12) This is the meaning of the words of our father Abraham, as it is said, "They shall come and rest in the bosom of Abraham."[35]

Here, we can see that Abraham was believed to be a figure who would provide comfort for the righteous in the afterlife, where they would be brought to the "bosom of Abraham," as mentioned in Luke 16:22.

Luke 16:23–24 tells us that those in Hades have eyes, fingers, and tongues instead of being immortal souls separate from the body, which goes against the

---

[35] I. Epstein, ed., *The Babylonian Talmud: Tractate Bava Batra* (London: Soncino Press, 1935), 10b.

Chapter 5: *The Apostasy*

popular teaching of hell within mainstream Christianity. Taking this parable literally contradicts both biblical teachings and the modern view of hell.

The parable of the rich man and Lazarus is one of those fables that Paul warns us not to believe (Titus 1:13–14). Jesus utilized common beliefs of the time to teach a lesson, even though some of them may have been unscriptural.

So, what is the lesson of this parable? It teaches that the righteous will be rewarded after the resurrection (Isaiah 26:19) and that the unrighteous will be overwhelmed with regret on the Day of Judgment (Matthew 8:11–12, Luke 13:28–29) by using "Abraham's bosom" as a symbol for acceptance and peace and using hell as a symbol of death and loss.

Chapter 5: *The Apostasy*

Hell is a word used for death. When we die, we are unconscious and return to the dust from which we were made (Genesis 3:19).

Lucifer

You cannot discuss hell without mentioning the devil. Most Christians today would tell you that hell is ruled by a fallen angel called the devil or Satan, who tempts us to sin. This also is not true. Why would God punish an angel for sinning by giving it more power than it had before?

The idea of a fallen angel makes no sense anyway because angels cannot sin. We're told that the punishment of sin is death (Romans 6:23), and we're also told that angels cannot die (Luke 20:36). So if

Chapter 5: *The Apostasy*

angels cannot die, then they cannot sin because sin results in death. Also, if angels could sin, how are they any different from us, and why would God trust them to be His messengers who can bear His name?

A verse that many use to prove that angels can sin comes in 2 Peter: "For if God spared not the angels that sinned, but cast *them* down to hell, and delivered *them* into chains of darkness, to be reserved unto judgment." (2 Peter 2:4)

This verse appears to suggest that there have been angels who sinned, were cast down to hell, and were judged. This cannot be the case since, as we've just gone over, angels cannot die, so they, therefore, cannot go to hell (the grave). So, what does this verse mean?

The Greek word used for "angels" is *aggelos* (ἄγγελος) which means "messenger." While this term

Chapter 5: *The Apostasy*

is commonly used to refer to angels, it can also be applied to human messengers. For example, the word is used to describe John the Baptist in Matthew 11: "For this is *he*, of whom it is written, Behold, I send my <u>messenger</u> [*aggelos*] before thy face, Which shall prepare thy way before thee." (Matthew 11:10)

So what 2 Peter 2:4 must be saying is that human messengers (righteous servants of God) that sinned, died, and now await the resurrection and judgment.

The passage that convinces people that the devil is a fallen angel who was cast out of heaven comes in Isaiah chapter 14:

> How art thou fallen from heaven, O Lucifer, son of the morning! *how* art thou cut down to the ground, which didst weaken the nations!

Chapter 5: *The Apostasy*

> For thou hast said in thine heart, I will ascend into heaven, I will exalt my throne above the stars of God: I will sit also upon the mount of the congregation, in the sides of the north: I will ascend above the heights of the clouds; I will be like the most High. Yet thou shalt be brought down to hell, to the sides of the pit. (Isaiah 14:12–15)

This passage has been heavily misinterpreted to mean that an angel named Lucifer was cast out of heaven by God because he sinned. This is taken entirely out of context. If this passage is read in context as it should be, then everyone should come to the conclusion that it refers to King Nebuchadnezzar II of Babylon. The previous chapter is a prophecy against the Babylonian Empire:

Chapter 5: *The Apostasy*

The burden of Babylon which Isaiah the son of Amoz did see… Behold, I will stir up the Medes against them, which shall not regard silver; and *as for* gold, they shall not delight in it. *Their* bows also shall dash the young men to pieces; and they shall have no pity on the fruit of the womb; their eye shall not spare children. And Babylon, the glory of kingdoms, the beauty of the Chaldees' excellency, shall be as when God overthrew Sodom and Gomorrah. It shall never be inhabited, neither shall it be dwelt in from generation to generation: neither shall the Arabian pitch tent there; neither shall the shepherds make their fold there. But wild beasts of the desert shall lie there; and their houses shall be full of doleful creatures; and owls shall dwell there, and satyrs shall dance

Chapter 5: *The Apostasy*

> there. And the wild beasts of the islands shall cry in their desolate houses, and dragons in *their* pleasant palaces: and her time *is* near to come, and her days shall not be prolonged. (Isaiah 13:1, 17–22)

This passage foretells Babylon's downfall at the hands of the Medo-Persians, which happened in 539 BC at the Battle of Opis. The context of chapter 13, being about Babylon's downfall, is also the context of chapter 14:

> And it shall come to pass in the day that the LORD shall give thee rest from thy sorrow, and from thy fear, and from the hard bondage wherein thou wast made to serve, that thou shalt <u>take up this proverb against the king of</u>

Chapter 5: *The Apostasy*

Babylon, and say, How hath the oppressor ceased! the golden city ceased! The LORD hath broken the staff of the wicked, *and* the sceptre of the rulers. (Isaiah 14:3–5)

Isaiah 14 verse 12 says: "How art thou fallen from heaven, O Lucifer, son of the morning! *how* art thou cut down to the ground, which didst weaken the nations!" (Isaiah 14:12)

The Hebrew word translated as "Lucifer" is *helel* (הֵילֵל), which means "a shining one" or "morning star." Stars are used to symbolize world leaders (Daniel 8:10) and judgment (Matthew 24:29, Revelation 6:13). This symbolizes Nebuchadnezzar's high and exalted status.

In fact, the verse shouldn't even say "Lucifer" at all. "Lucifer" is derived from the Latin Vulgate

Chapter 5: *The Apostasy*

translation, where Jerome of Stridon replaced the Hebrew word *helel* with the Latin word "Lucifer," meaning "light-bringer" or "morning star," to make the passage sound more poetic. It should actually say something like "morning star" instead of "Lucifer."

In Daniel chapter 4, we read about Nebuchadnezzar: "It *is* thou, O king, that art grown and become strong: for thy greatness is grown, and reacheth unto heaven, and thy dominion to the end of the earth." (Daniel 4:22)

This supports the notion that Nebuchadnezzar had a star-like, exalted status.

> For thou hast said in thine heart, I will ascend into heaven, I will exalt my throne above the stars of God: I will sit also upon the mount of the congregation, in the sides of the north: I

Chapter 5: *The Apostasy*

will ascend above the heights of the clouds; I will be like the most High. (Isaiah 14:13–14)

These verses suggest that this influential figure will attempt to elevate themself to a God-like status. Does Nebuchadnezzar fit this description as well?

All this came upon the king Nebuchadnezzar. At the end of twelve months he walked in the palace of the kingdom of Babylon. The king spake, and said, Is not this the great Babylon, that I have built for the house of the kingdom by the might of my power, and for the honour of my majesty? (Daniel 4:28–30)

Once again, we see Nebuchadnezzar fitting the description of Lucifer in Isaiah chapter 14. Both credit

Chapter 5: *The Apostasy*

themselves, not God, and both take great pride in their accomplishments.

Despite this prideful mindset, Isaiah writes that Lucifer would be humbled and would be given a lowly position full of mockery and scorn:

> Yet thou shalt be brought down to hell, to the sides of the pit. They that see thee shall narrowly look upon thee, *and* consider thee, *saying, Is* this the man that made the earth to tremble, that did shake kingdoms; *that* made the world as a wilderness, and destroyed the cities thereof; *that* opened not the house of his prisoners? (Isaiah 14:15–17)

While the word *was* in the king's mouth, there fell a voice from heaven, *saying,* O king

Chapter 5: *The Apostasy*

Nebuchadnezzar, to thee it is spoken; The kingdom is departed from thee. And they shall drive thee from men, and thy dwelling *shall be* with the beasts of the field: they shall make thee to eat grass as oxen, and seven times shall pass over thee, until thou know that the most High ruleth in the kingdom of men, and giveth it to whomsoever he will. The same hour was the thing fulfilled upon Nebuchadnezzar: and he was driven from men, and did eat grass as an oxen, and his body was wet with the dew of heaven, till his hairs were grown like eagles' *feathers*, and his nails like birds' *claws*. (Daniel 4:31–33)

Chapter 5: *The Apostasy*

Here is a chart comparing the descriptions of Lucifer and Nebuchadnezzar:

Lucifer	Nebuchadnezzar
- In a prophecy concerning the king Babylon (Isaiah 14:3–5).	- Was the king of Babylon (Daniel 1:1).
- An exalted figure (Isaiah 14:12).	- An exalted figure (Daniel 4:22).
- Tried to exalt himself above God (Isaiah 14:13–14).	- Tried to exalt himself above God (Daniel 4:28–30).
- Stripped of his exalted position and made lowly (Isaiah 14:15–17).	- Stripped of his exalted position and made lowly (Daniel 4:31–33).

The description of what happens to Nebuchadnezzar in Daniel 4 fits perfectly with what Isaiah 14 says would happen to Lucifer.

Chapter 5: *The Apostasy*

To further substantiate the argument that Isaiah 14 does not refer to a fallen angel who became known as Satan or the devil, the words "angel," "Satan," and "devil" do not appear anywhere in the chapter. This is clearly a prophecy foretelling the humbling of King Nebuchadnezzar II of Babylon, which was fulfilled in Daniel chapter 4.

Satan

Let's now examine the meanings of the words devil and Satan, beginning with the latter. The word "Satan" is transliterated in both the Hebrew (Old Testament) and the Greek (New Testament). It means "adversary." It's not a title for some former angel

Chapter 5: *The Apostasy*

demon creature, but it just means adversary or opponent.

When we come across the word "Satan" in Scripture, we usually give it a negative connotation. But in fact, anyone can be a Satan or an adversary to anyone. If you prevent an alcoholic from drinking, you are being a Satan to them, even though you're doing a good thing. When someone is called Satan, that does not always mean they are sinning. For example, God is even called Satan in the parallel accounts of 2 Samuel 24 and 1 Chronicles 21:

> And again the anger of the LORD was kindled against Israel, and he moved David against them to say, Go, number Israel and Judah. (2 Samuel 24:1)

Chapter 5: *The Apostasy*

> And Satan stood up against Israel, and provoked David to number Israel. (1 Chronicles 21:1)

So God is called "Satan" here because He was being an adversary to Israel because of David's sins. God provoking David to take a census means that God was allowing David to follow his own foolish desires. David shouldn't have cared how many soldiers they had because he should have known that God was with them.

In Matthew 16, Jesus calls Peter "Satan":

> From that time forth began Jesus to shew unto his disciples, how he must go unto Jerusalem, and suffer many things of the elders and chief priests and scribes, and be killed, and be raised

Chapter 5: *The Apostasy*

again the third day. Then Peter took him, and began to rebuke him, saying, Be it far from thee, Lord: this shall not be unto thee. But he turned, and said unto Peter, <u>Get thee behind me, Satan</u>: thou art an offence unto me: for thou savourest not the things that be of God, but those that be of men. (Matthew 16:21–23)

So, since Peter refutes Jesus' claims that he would suffer, die, and then be raised after three days, Jesus calls him "Satan" due to Peter being an adversary to him.

Job was a wealthy man from the land of Uz who was considered blameless by God (Job 1:1). (This doesn't mean that Job was sinless, but that, for the most part, he walked upright in God's sight.) Then we're introduced to this Satan who proposes to God

Chapter 5: *The Apostasy*

that Job is only considered blameless and upright because of the wrong reasons.

    The identity of the Satan in the Book of Job is often speculated, so let's examine it. For the following explanation regarding the identity of this Satan, I give full credit to John A. Pople, whose methodical approach in his book *To Speak Well of God: An Exposition of the Book of Job*[36] accurately unveils the mystery surrounding the Satan's identity, at least to me. For a more detailed and well-put-together analysis, I highly recommend reading his book. (Not every single point I make in the following explanation is directly from him, though most points and the overall reasoning for who the Satan is and why is from him.)

---

[36] J. A. Pople, *To Speak Well of God: An Exposition of the Book of Job* (Raleigh, NC: Lulu.com, 2009).

Chapter 5: *The Apostasy*

Now there was a day when the sons of God came to present themselves before the LORD, and Satan came also among them. And the LORD said unto Satan, Whence comest thou? Then Satan answered the LORD, and said, From going to and fro in the earth, and from walking up and down in it. And the LORD said unto Satan, Hast thou considered my servant Job, that *there is* none like him in the earth, a perfect and an upright man, one that feareth God, and escheweth evil? Then Satan answered the LORD, and said, Doth Job fear God for nought? Hast not thou made an hedge about him, and about his house, and about all that he hath on every side? thou hast blessed the work of his hands, and his substance is increased in the land. But put forth thine hand now, and

Chapter 5: *The Apostasy*

touch all that he hath, and he will curse thee to thy face. And the LORD said unto Satan, Behold, all that he hath *is* in thy power; only upon himself put not forth thine hand. So Satan went forth from the presence of the LORD. And there was a day when his sons and daughters *were* eating and drinking wine in their eldest brother's house: and there came a messenger unto Job, and said, The oxen were plowing, and the asses feeding beside them: and the Sabeans fell *upon them*, and took them away; yea, they have slain the servants with the edge of the sword; and I only am escaped alone to tell thee. While he was yet speaking, there came also another, and said, The fire of God is fallen from heaven, and hath burned up the sheep, and the servants, and consumed them;

Chapter 5: *The Apostasy*

and I only am escaped alone to tell thee. While he was yet speaking, there came also another, and said, The Chaldeans made out three bands, and fell upon the camels, and have carried them away, yea, and slain the servants with the edge of the sword; and I only am escaped alone to tell thee. While he was yet speaking, there came also another, and said, Thy sons and thy daughters *were* eating and drinking wine in their eldest brother's house: and, behold, there came a great wind from the wilderness, and smote the four corners of the house, and it fell upon the young men, and they are dead; and I only am escaped to tell thee. Then Job arose, and rent his mantle, and shaved his head, and fell down upon the ground, and worshipped, and said, Naked came I out of my mother's

Chapter 5: *The Apostasy*

womb, and naked shall I return thither: the LORD gave, and the LORD hath taken away; blessed be the name of the LORD. In all this Job sinned not, nor charged God foolishly. (Job 1:6–22)

The phrase "sons of God" refers to human followers of God (1 John 3:1). When they came to "present themselves before the LORD" (v. 6), it means they gathered at a place to worship God (Exodus 34:1–2, Leviticus 14:11, Jude 1:24).

So we're told that followers of God came together at a religious gathering (similar to church) to worship God and an adversary was present among them. God asks the Satan where he comes from, and he says: "From going to and fro in the earth, and from walking up and down in it." (v. 7)

Chapter 5: *The Apostasy*

This implies that the Satan is an Israelite, and this takes place during Israel's 40-year journey in the wilderness when they were nomadically traveling throughout the earth. This is further proven when we're told that Job's wealth is based on his abundance of flocks, herds, and servants (Job 1:3), which was how wealth was determined during Israel's time in the wilderness.

Job was from the land of Uz. There are two people named Uz in the Bible. One was Uz, the son of Aram, the son of Shem (Genesis 10:22–23). The other was Uz, the son of Nahor, the brother of Abraham (Genesis 22:20–21), making this Uz the nephew of Abraham.

It makes more sense to believe that the land of Uz in Job 1:1 is named after Uz, Abraham's nephew. This is because later in the book, we meet someone

Chapter 5: *The Apostasy*

named Elihu, who is referred to as a Buzite (Job 32:2). Buz was the brother of Uz, the son of Nahor (Genesis 22:21). Therefore, this story must take place after the time of Abraham.

It also must take place after the Exodus because the Exodus is actually mentioned in the Book of Job: "He divideth the sea with his power, And by his understanding he smiteth through the proud. By his spirit he hath garnished the heavens; His hand hath formed the crooked serpent." (Job 26:12–13)

Here, Job mentions how God "divideth the sea with his power," just like he did during the Exodus when the Red Sea was parted (Exodus 14:21–22). It also says that God "smiteth through the proud." The Hebrew word translated as "the proud" here is *rahab* (רָהַב), which is also used as a symbolic name for Egypt (Isaiah 30:7). This further supports the idea that the

Chapter 5: *The Apostasy*

Book of Job takes place during Israel's wilderness journey since it came after the Exodus.

Notice how the Satan says he comes from the earth. Angels come from heaven, and if this is the commonly believed idea of Satan as a supernatural being who tempts us to sin, then this wouldn't make sense either because he should, therefore, come from hell, not the earth. Also, when looking at the Hebrew, it should actually say "the Satan" instead of just "Satan," which further disproves the idea of "Satan" being the name of a personal, singular being.

It's essential to establish that the Satan here is God's Satan, not Job's. God makes a claim that Job is blameless because he fears God and shuns evil (Job 1:8). The Satan then opposes that claim by saying that Job is only considered blameless because he has

Chapter 5: *The Apostasy*

everything, and if his possessions were taken away, he would then curse God (Job 1:9–11).

Now, from this alone, we can entirely rule out the possibility that the Satan is an angel. Would an angel disagree with something God says? Of course not. We're also told in 2 Peter 2 that angels do not slander (2 Peter 2:11), and the Satan very much slanders Job. The Satan in the Book of Job cannot be an angel.

So if it's not an angel and certainly not a fallen angel, then what could it be? What species would disagree with a claim God makes and think that they know better than God Himself? Humans. This Satan must be human. But who?

The Satan reappears in chapter 2 before seemingly disappearing from the book altogether.

Chapter 5: *The Apostasy*

While it's not blatantly stated, I believe Job chapter 2 introduces us to the identity of the Satan:

> Again there was a day when the sons of God came to present themselves before the LORD, and Satan came also among them to present himself before the LORD. And the LORD said unto Satan, From whence comest thou? And Satan answered the LORD, and said, From going to and fro in the earth, and from walking up and down in it. And the LORD said unto Satan, Hast thou considered my servant Job, that *there is* none like him in the earth, a perfect and an upright man, one that feareth God, and escheweth evil? and still he holdeth fast his integrity, although thou movedst me against him, to destroy him without cause. And Satan

Chapter 5: *The Apostasy*

answered the LORD, and said, Skin for skin, yea, all that a man hath will he give for his life. But put forth thine hand now, and touch his bone and his flesh, and he will curse thee to thy face. And the LORD said unto Satan, Behold, he *is* in thine hand; but save his life. So went Satan forth from the presence of the LORD, and smote Job with sore boils from the sole of his foot unto his crown. And he took him a potsherd to scrape himself withal; and he sat down among the ashes. Then said his wife unto him, Dost thou still retain thine integrity? curse God, and die. But he said unto her, Thou speakest as one of the foolish women speaketh. What? shall we receive good at the hand of God, and shall we not receive evil? In all this did not Job sin with his lips. Now when Job's

Chapter 5: *The Apostasy*

three friends heard of all this evil that was come upon him, they came every one from his own place; Eliphaz the Temanite, and Bildad the Shuhite, and Zophar the Naamathite: for they had made an appointment together to come to mourn with him and to comfort him. And when they lifted up their eyes afar off, and knew him not, they lifted up their voice, and wept; and they rent every one his mantle, and sprinkled dust upon their heads toward heaven. So they sat down with him upon the ground seven days and seven nights, and none spake a word unto him: for they saw that *his* grief was very great. (Job 2:1–13)

These first two chapters seemingly imply that the Satan is the one who brings these disasters upon

Chapter 5: *The Apostasy*

Job. God tells the Satan that Job's possessions and health are in his hands but that he must spare Job's life (Job 1:12, Job 2:6).

But we are actually told that it was, in fact, God who took away Job's possessions and children and afflicted him with painful sores (Job 1:21; Job 2:3, 9, 10; Job 42:11). This means that it wasn't the Satan who brought disaster upon Job, but God did it as a result of the Satan's slanderous accusations.

So, who is this mysterious Satan? It may seem as if it could be Job's wife since she confronts Job for not cursing God (Job 2:9), and that was what the Satan had said Job would do (Job 1:11, Job 2:5). But this wouldn't make any sense. Why would Job's wife want her husband (and thus her) to be made from rich to poor, their children to die, and her husband to be afflicted with painful sores so that he can curse the

Chapter 5: *The Apostasy*

LORD? I think we can logically rule Job's wife out of the realm of possibilities.

So, who else could it be? I'm convinced the Satan in the Book of Job is Job's three friends: Eliphaz the Temanite, Bildad the Shuhite, and Zophar the Naamathite. But how could this be the case if they comforted Job and mourned with him following his series of the most unfortunate events (Job 2:11)?

While it's true that Job's friends were truly sympathetic, this does not mean that they aren't the Satan. This is because the conversations we read between God and Satan didn't actually happen, but rather, they are used figuratively to describe the jealous thoughts of the three friends and God's response to them. The Satan is actually the jealous thoughts of the three friends.

Chapter 5: *The Apostasy*

So, these men came to present themselves before the LORD, and in their hearts was this jealousy towards Job, for he was an incredibly wealthy man who was considered blameless by God. They told themselves out of envy that if Job had certain things taken away from him, then surely he wouldn't be considered blameless by God anymore. God then takes away Job's wealth and his children and afflicts him with painful sores.

Job's three friends were shocked when they found out what had happened to him because although they may have wished it in their hearts, they didn't expect it to actually happen. Their shock naturally gave way to sympathy as they comforted their friend. However, this sympathy would eventually wear off as their jealous thoughts gradually returned.

Chapter 5: *The Apostasy*

Now, why would Job's friends harbor jealousy and resentment toward him for being considered blameless and upright? It has to do with their nationalities.

Eliphaz is a Temanite, which makes him a descendant of Esau since Teman was Esau's grandson (Genesis 36:10–11). Bildad is a Shuhite, descended from Abraham's son Shuah, whom he had with his wife Keturah (Genesis 25:1–2). Zophar is a Naamathite, probably descended from Benjamin's son Naaman (Genesis 46:21).

What do these three men have in common? They're all sons of Abraham. Was Job? No. Job was descended from Abraham's nephew Uz. He's a distant relative of Abraham but not a direct descendant.

This was the root of the jealous pride of Job's three friends. An Uzite was considered blameless and upright in God's eyes, but they, the sons of Abraham, were not.

This is the same thing that was happening in Jesus' day, with the Jewish leaders taking great pride in being Abraham's descendants and thinking it gave them a certain authority (John 8:33, 39).

The setting of the Book of Job, which takes place during Israel's wilderness journey, illustrates how three descendants of Abraham became friends with a man from the land of Uz as they wandered throughout the earth and came into contact with different peoples.

Although only Zophar was an Israelite, it makes sense for a Temanite and a Shuhite to be traveling with Israel since we're told that a mixed multitude left Egypt during the Exodus (Exodus 12:38).

Chapter 5: *The Apostasy*

After Job was afflicted with painful sores and had mourned for seven days, he began to lament about how he wishes he had never been born:

> Let the day perish wherein I was born, And the night *in which* it was said, There is a man child conceived. Let that day be darkness; Let not God regard it from above, Neither let the light shine upon it. (Job 3:3–4)

> Why died I not from the womb? *Why* did I *not* give up the ghost When I came up out of the belly? Why did the knees prevent me? or why the breasts that I should suck? For now should I have lain still and been quiet, I should have slept: then had I been at rest. (Job 3:11–13)

Chapter 5: *The Apostasy*

Why is light given to a man whose way is hid, And whom God hath hedged in? For my sighing cometh before I eat, And my roarings are poured out like the waters. For the thing which I greatly feared is come upon me, And that which I was afraid of is come unto me. I was not in safety, neither had I rest, neither was I quiet; Yet trouble came. (Job 3:23–26)

Job's friends then take turns replying to his complaints. What they say to him reveals their identity to be the Satan in the Book of Job. Eliphaz spoke first:

Remember, I pray thee, who *ever* perished, being innocent? Or where were the righteous cut off? Even as I have seen, they that plow

Chapter 5: *The Apostasy*

iniquity, And sow wickedness, reap the same. (Job 4:7–8)

What Eliphaz is saying is that Job must not be so upright in God's sight after all, or else these bad things wouldn't be happening to him. This is not true. God brings trials into people's lives, regardless of whether they are righteous or not. He brings trials into the lives of those who follow Him to build character and spiritual endurance (Deuteronomy 8:16, Psalm 66:10, Proverbs 17:3, James 1:2–4). Eliphaz gave Job completely incorrect counsel.

Then Bildad spoke:

How long wilt thou speak these *things*? And *how long shall* the words of thy mouth *be like* a strong wind? Doth God pervert judgment? Or

Chapter 5: *The Apostasy*

doth the Almighty pervert justice? If thy children have sinned against him, And he have cast them away for their transgression; If thou wouldest seek unto God betimes, And make thy supplication to the Almighty; If thou *wert* pure and upright; Surely now he would awake for thee, And make the habitation of thy righteousness prosperous… Behold, God will not cast away a perfect man, Neither will he help the evil doers. (Job 8:2–6, 20)

Bildad continues the foolish argument of Eliphaz, which is that Job must be guilty and deserving of such punishments. Notice how, in verse 6, Bildad tells Job that if he really was upright, then God would have already restored his losses. And in verse 20 when he says that if Job really is perfect, then God wouldn't

Chapter 5: *The Apostasy*

have brought any disaster on him. This is the same mentality of the Satan, who claimed that God was wrong for saying that Job is blameless and upright (Job 1:8–9, Job 2:3–4).

Then Zophar spoke to Job:

> Then answered Zophar the Naamathite, and said, Should not the multitude of words be answered? And should a man full of talk be justified? Should thy lies make men hold their peace? And when thou mockest, shall no man make thee ashamed? For thou hast said, My doctrine *is* pure, And I am clean in thine eyes. But oh that God would speak, And open his lips against thee; And that he would shew thee the secrets of wisdom, That *they are* double to that which is! Know therefore that God

Chapter 5: *The Apostasy*

> exacteth of thee *less* than thine iniquity
> *deserveth*. (Job 11:1–6)

Still, we see the same incorrect message being given to Job, that he must not be righteous after all, or else these bad things wouldn't have happened to him. Their words only made Job grow more frustrated, leading him to defend his own self-righteousness and call out God for seemingly abandoning him:

> Then Job answered and said, How long will ye vex my soul, And break me in pieces with words? These ten times have ye reproached me: Ye are not ashamed *that* ye make yourselves strange to me. And be it indeed *that* I have erred, Mine error remaineth with myself. If indeed ye will magnify *yourselves* against me,

Chapter 5: *The Apostasy*

And plead against me my reproach: Know now that God hath overthrown me, And hath compassed me with his net. Behold, I cry out of wrong, but I am not heard: I cry aloud, but *there is* no judgment. (Job 19:1–7)

This is a righteous man considered upright by God who just lost his flocks, herds, servants, children, and health, and instead of continuing to comfort him, his friends tell him that these disasters are his fault.

This back-and-forth between Job and his friends, and Job's complaints against God, continues throughout the book until God finally responds to Job. God confronts Job about his complaints by reminding him that He is the all-powerful creator of the universe:

Chapter 5: *The Apostasy*

Then the LORD answered Job out of the whirlwind, and said, Who *is* this that darkeneth counsel By words without knowledge? Gird up now thy loins like a man; For I will demand of thee, and answer thou me. Where wast thou when I laid the foundations of the earth? Declare, if thou hast understanding. Who hath laid the measures thereof, if thou knowest? Or who hath stretched the line upon it? Whereupon are the foundations thereof fastened? Or who laid the corner stone thereof; When the morning stars sang together, And all the sons of God shouted for joy? (Job 38:1–7)

Hast thou entered into the treasures of the snow? Or hast thou seen the treasures of the hail, Which I have reserved against the time of

Chapter 5: *The Apostasy*

> trouble, Against the day of battle and war? By what way is the light parted, *Which* scattereth the east wind upon the earth? (Job 38:22–24)

> Gird up thy loins now like a man: I will demand of thee, and declare thou unto me. Wilt thou also disannul my judgment? Wilt thou condemn me, that thou mayest be righteous? Hast thou an arm like God? Or canst thou thunder with a voice like him? (Job 40:7–9)

After this, Job repents (Job 42:1–6), and then this play-like book comes to a fitting conclusion:

> And it was *so*, that after the LORD had spoken these words unto Job, the LORD said to Eliphaz the Temanite, My wrath is kindled

Chapter 5: *The Apostasy*

against thee, and against thy two friends: for ye have not spoken of me *the thing that is* right, as my servant Job *hath*. Therefore take unto you now seven bullocks and seven rams, and go to my servant Job, and offer up for yourselves a burnt offering; and my servant Job shall pray for you: for him will I accept: lest I deal with you *after your* folly, in that ye have not spoken of me *the thing which is* right, like my servant Job. So Eliphaz the Temanite and Bildad the Shuhite *and* Zophar the Naamathite went, and did according as the LORD commanded them: the LORD also accepted Job. (Job 42:7–9)

A common theme surrounding Satans in Scripture is that God will reveal a truth, the Satan will oppose that truth, and then the Satan will be rebuked.

Chapter 5: *The Apostasy*

For example, in Genesis, God tells Adam and Eve that if they eat from the Tree of Knowledge of Good and Evil, they will die (Genesis 2:17). The serpent, who was acting as a Satan, opposes this by telling Eve that she will not die if she eats from the forbidden tree (Genesis 3:4). Then the serpent is rebuked by God for its adversarial deception (Genesis 3:14–15). This is also found elsewhere in Scripture (Ezra 1:4, Zechariah 3, Matthew 16:21–23).

The Book of Job is no different. God presents a truth that Job is blameless and upright (Job 1:8, Job 2:3). Eliphaz, Bildad, and Zophar refute this claim in their hearts (Job 1:9–11, Job 2:4–5). And God rebukes them (Job 42:7–8).

The Satan in the Book of Job is the jealous, prideful thoughts of Job's three friends: Eliphaz the

Chapter 5: *The Apostasy*

Temanite, Bildad the Shuhite, and Zophar the Naamathite, not a fallen angel who tempts us to sin.

The Devil

The word "devil" appears only in the New Testament. It comes from the Greek word *diabolos* (διάβολος), which means "accuser" or "slanderer," very similar to the meaning of the word "Satan." This term is used to describe the sinful nature of mankind.

Look at how *diabolos* is used in 1 Timothy 3: "Even so *must their* wives *be* grave, not <u>slanderers</u> [*diabolos*], sober, faithful in all things." (1 Timothy 3:11)

Diabolos is translated as "slanderers" when speaking of how women should not slander. This

Chapter 5: *The Apostasy*

provides no implication of there being a personal devil who tempts us to sin.

Jesus conquered death (2 Timothy 1:10) by dying on the cross as a sinless man (Hebrews 4:15) and thus was resurrected because death could not hold him (Acts 2:24) since the punishment of sin is death (Romans 6:23). So it is sin that leads to death (1 Corinthians 15:56). Hebrews chapter 2 tells us more about this:

> Forasmuch then as the children are partakers of flesh and blood, he also himself likewise took part of the same; that through death he might destroy him that had the power of death, that is, the devil. (Hebrews 2:14)

Chapter 5: *The Apostasy*

This verse tells us that "the devil" has the power of death. If this were speaking of a supernatural being who holds the power over death and is God's adversary, then it would contradict a basic Bible teaching, which is that God has the power over life and death, not any other force:

> See now that I, *even* I, *am* he, And *there is* no god with me: <u>I kill, and I make alive; I wound, and I heal</u>: Neither *is there any* that can deliver out of my hand. (Deuteronomy 32:39)

> The LORD killeth, and maketh alive: He bringeth down to the grave, and bringeth up. (1 Samuel 2:6)

Chapter 5: *The Apostasy*

So Hebrews 2:14 must be using "the devil" as a metaphor for sin.

> And the great dragon was cast out, that old serpent, called the Devil, and Satan, which deceiveth the whole world: he was cast out into the earth, and his angels were cast out with him. (Revelation 12:9)

This verse has been used to equate the devil and Satan and to prove that he is a fallen angel who was also the serpent in the Garden of Eden who deceived Eve. This verse, along with many others in Revelation, is not to be taken literally; instead, it is used figuratively to foretell the final judgment, where sin will be destroyed. The adversarial ("Satan"), sinful ("the Devil") mindset has existed since the serpent's

Chapter 5: *The Apostasy*

deception of Eve in Genesis chapter 3 and will eventually be gone for good (Revelation 21:4). Just look at what the next verse says:

> And I heard a loud voice saying in heaven, Now is come salvation, and strength, and the kingdom of our God, and the power of his Christ: for the accuser of our brethren is cast down, which accused them before our God day and night. (Revelation 12:10)

In Matthew chapter 4, we're told that Jesus was tempted by the devil:

> Then was Jesus led up of the Spirit into the wilderness to be tempted of the devil. And when he had fasted forty days and forty nights,

Chapter 5: *The Apostasy*

he was afterward an hungred. And when the tempter came to him, he said, If thou be the Son of God, command that these stones be made bread. But he answered and said, It is written, Man shall not live by bread alone, but by every word that proceedeth out of the mouth of God. Then the devil taketh him up into the holy city, and setteth him on a pinnacle of the temple, and saith unto him, If thou be the Son of God, cast thyself down: for it is written, He shall give his angels charge concerning thee: And in *their* hands they shall bear thee up, Lest at any time thou dash thy foot against a stone. Jesus said unto him, It is written again, Thou shalt not tempt the Lord thy God. Again, the devil taketh him up into an exceeding high mountain, and sheweth him all the kingdoms of

Chapter 5: *The Apostasy*

the world, and the glory of them; and saith unto him, All these things will I give thee, if thou wilt fall down and worship me. Then saith Jesus unto him, Get thee hence, Satan: for it is written, Thou shalt worship the Lord thy God, and him only shalt thou serve. Then the devil leaveth him, and, behold, angels came and ministered unto him. (Matthew 4:1–11)

Here, we have a similar situation to the one we encountered in identifying the Satan in the Book of Job, and that is identifying the devil in Matthew chapter 4.

The devil in this passage isn't a separate being but is actually Jesus himself. As we've been over, the word "devil" is used to represent the tempting, sinful nature of mankind. Jesus, being a man, shared this

Chapter 5: *The Apostasy*

nature. Even though he never gave into the temptations he faced, he: "was in all points tempted like as we are, yet without sin." (Hebrews 4:15)

The devil here refers to Jesus' own temptations to sin that he overcame. Being the Son of God, he was given power from God to perform miracles (Matthew 4:24, Matthew 14:19–20, John 9:6–7, John 11:43–44, etc.). So when he became hungry from fasting for forty days and forty nights, he was tempted to use his God-given power to turn rocks into bread so he could satisfy his hunger. He overcame this temptation by referencing Deuteronomy 8:3, which teaches how God's Word outweighs worldly food.

It's essential to remember that Jesus was fasting at this time. He had told his disciples that when they fast, do it alone:

Chapter 5: *The Apostasy*

> But thou, when thou fastest, anoint thine head, and wash thy face; that thou may appear not unto men to fast, but unto thy Father which is in secret: and thy Father, which seeth in secret, shall reward thee openly. (Matthew 6:17–18)

It would have been unlikely and even hypocritical of Jesus to have been in the company of anyone but himself during this period of spiritual cleansing.

The devil then tempts Jesus to jump off the temple, quoting Psalm 91:11–12 for proof as to why he wouldn't die if he did so. This helps to further identify Jesus as his own devil here because he often quoted Scripture (Matthew 27:46, Mark 12:30–31, Luke 4:18–19, etc.). Jesus quotes Deuteronomy 6:6 in the next verse to overcome this temptation.

Chapter 5: *The Apostasy*

Then, the devil offers Jesus all the kingdoms of the earth to rule over if he bows down and worships him. This was Jesus being tempted to achieve earthly dominion through worldly means instead of following God's plan, which was for him to be crucified and resurrected. The devil telling Jesus to bow down and worship him refers to Jesus' desire to embrace his sinful, ambitious temptations. No one on earth besides Jesus could have offered him this other than himself. Jesus overcomes this temptation by saying: "Get thee hence, Satan: for it is written, Thou shalt worship the Lord thy God, and him only shalt thou serve." (Matthew 4:10)

He rebukes his sinful thoughts by calling them "Satan" due to them being adversarial to himself and to God's will.

The passage concludes by stating that the devil left him, and then angels came to comfort him. The devil leaving him refers to his tempting thoughts going away as his mental and spiritual strength was restored.

The reason why this passage personifies the devil is to poetically portray the drama of Jesus' inner war with himself, powerfully setting the example for us on how to overcome our temptations.

There is no supernatural figure called the devil or Satan, but rather, they are words used to describe sin and adversaries.

Demons

Another common biblical misinterpretation is the existence of demons.

Chapter 5: *The Apostasy*

When he arrived at the other side in the region of the Gadarenes, two demon-possessed men coming from the tombs met him. They were so violent that no one could pass that way. "What do you want with us, Son of God?" they shouted. "Have you come here to torture us before the appointed time?" Some distance from them a large herd of pigs was feeding. The demons begged Jesus, "If you drive us out, send us into the herd of pigs." He said to them, "Go!" So they came out and went into the pigs, and the whole herd rushed down the steep bank into the lake and died in the water. Those tending the pigs ran off, went into the town and reported all this, including what had happened to the demon-possessed men. Then the whole town went out to meet Jesus. And when they

Chapter 5: *The Apostasy*

saw him, they pleaded with him to leave their region. (Matthew 8:28–34, NIV)

The King James Version uses the phrase "possessed by devils" instead of "demon-possessed" for the Greek word *daimonizomai* (δαιμονίζομαι). This word can be related to the Hebrew word *shed* (שֵׁד), which refers to "demons" or "evil spirits," which were commonly believed in by Ancient Israelites. *Shed* is used in two verses in Scripture:

> They sacrificed unto <u>devils</u> [*shed*], not to God; To gods whom they knew not, To new *gods that* came newly up, Whom your fathers feared not. (Deuteronomy 32:17)

Chapter 5: *The Apostasy*

Yea, they sacrificed their sons and their daughters unto <u>devils</u> [*shed*]. (Psalm 106:37)

The Hebrew word for "devils" or "demons" is used in just these two verses to describe false gods and idols.

Let's look at a verse in the New Testament that uses the same Greek word that is used in Matthew 8 for demons: "But I *say*, that the things which the Gentiles sacrifice to <u>devils</u> [*daimonion*], and not to God: and I would not that ye should have fellowship with <u>devils</u> [*daimonion*]." (1 Corinthians 10:20)

Clearly, this also is equating "devils" or "demons" with false gods and idols. So since the Greek word for "demon," which is *daimonion* (δαιμόνιον), and the Greek word for "demon-possessed," which is *daimonizomai*, both

Chapter 5: *The Apostasy*

relate to false gods and idols that Scripture establishes are not real (Exodus 20:2–6, Psalm 115:4–8, Isaiah 45:5, 1 Corinthians 8:6, etc.), then it's safe to conclude that demons are also not real.

Well, then, how do we explain Jesus' interaction with these "demon-possessed" people? Well, the word "demon" wasn't just used for false gods and idols, but it was also used for evil spirits, which many in Israel believed in.

Evil spirits cannot be real because all power comes from God (Deuteronomy 32:39). Yet many in Jesus' time believed in evil spirits because of their lack of understanding surrounding mental illness. We barely understand mental illness now, so how would they have understood it back then?

So when they came across those with a mental illness, the superstitious mind of mankind assumed

Chapter 5: *The Apostasy*

they were "possessed" by something paranormal. In fact, many ancient peoples believed in demons or evil spirits, not just the Israelites.

This may help explain why the Israelites believed this, as they were often influenced by the nations around them (Numbers 25:1–18, Judges 2:11–23, 1 Samuel 8:20, etc.).

Now, let's look back at Jesus' interaction with those mentally ill men in Matthew chapter 8. Verse 28 tells us that these men were violent and erratic, possibly showing signs of schizophrenia or bipolar disorder. In verse 29, they confront Jesus and ask him what he wants from them. Despite them being mentally unwell, they do acknowledge Jesus as the Son of God, highlighting Christ's authority over suffering.

Verse 30 mentions that a large group of pigs was nearby. Then, in verse 31, it says that the demons

Chapter 5: *The Apostasy*

begged Jesus to be sent into the pigs and out of the men. This may seem as if demons are actually talking to Jesus, proving their existence, but that is not the case.

There are two parallel accounts of this passage: one is found in Mark 5:1–20 and the other in Luke 8:26–39. Let's compare the passage in Luke with the passage in Mark. In these accounts, one of the mentally ill men is identified as "Legion." Notice what it says:

> Jesus asked him, "What is your name?" "Legion," he replied, because many demons had gone into him. And they begged Jesus repeatedly not to order them to go into the Abyss. (Luke 8:30–31, NIV)

Chapter 5: *The Apostasy*

This makes it seem as if the demons are begging Jesus not to make them go down to the grave ("Abyss"), personifying them. Let's now look at what the parallel account in Mark has to say:

> Then Jesus asked him, "What is your name?" "My name is Legion," he replied, "for we are many." <u>And he begged Jesus</u> again and again not to send them out of the area. (Mark 5:9–10, NIV)

Mark 5 parallels "he" (Legion) with "them" (demons) in Luke 8:31. This proves that it was not the demons that were speaking, but it was Legion himself.

So, the word "demons" is used as a synonym for the mentally ill because that was what people who lived in that period believed. When it says in Matthew

Chapter 5: *The Apostasy*

8 that the demons asked Jesus to be sent into the pigs, and he did it, it is using the language of the day since people back then understood mental illness being cured as demons departing from the person. It wouldn't have made sense to them if Jesus had said something like: "Schizophrenia, be gone from this man and go into the pigs." The Scriptures personify demons so that the people back then would not be too confused.

We see more of this in Luke chapter 11: "Jesus was driving out a demon that was mute. When the demon left, the man who had been mute spoke, and the crowd was amazed." (Luke 11:14, NIV)

This verse refers to a mute person as a demon.

Demons are not real but are used in Scripture to either refer to false gods and idols or to people who suffer from mental illness.

Chapter 5: *The Apostasy*

Heaven

The large majority of Christians today believe that the hope of salvation is in heaven after we die. They believe that when we die, our "soul" either ascends into heaven, where there is eternal paradise, or down to hell, where there is eternal punishment.

Well, what is heaven? First of all, there are the heavens, which can refer to the sky or space (Genesis 1:1, Genesis 15:5, Judges 5:20, Jeremiah 8:2, etc.). Then there's the other heaven, which is known as God's dwelling place, where His symbolic throne is (Deuteronomy 26:15, 1 Kings 8:30, Psalm 11:4, Isaiah 66:1, Matthew 5:34, Matthew 6:9, Acts 7:49, etc.). This heaven isn't necessarily in the sky, but rather in another dimension, which is home to God, the angels (Matthew 18:10), and now Jesus Christ (Luke 24:51).

Chapter 5: *The Apostasy*

Since Jesus is a man, does this mean that humans go to heaven when we die? No, it does not.

Jesus is the only human who has gone to heaven, and he didn't go up as an immortal soul. He died (Matthew 27:50), was dead for three days (Matthew 12:40), was resurrected by God (Matthew 28:6) and given immortality (2 Timothy 1:10), and stayed on earth for about forty more days before being taken up into heaven (Acts 1:1–3) where he is now and where he will eventually return from (Acts 1:11).

Well, what about Enoch and Elijah? Scripture says they escaped death by being taken up into heaven. Let's see what it actually says concerning these two, beginning with Enoch:

> And Enoch lived sixty and five years, and begat Methuselah: and Enoch walked with God after

Chapter 5: *The Apostasy*

he begat Methuselah three hundred years, and begat sons and daughters: and all the days of Enoch were three hundred sixty and five years: and Enoch walked with God: <u>and he *was* not; for God took him</u>. (Genesis 5:21–24)

First of all, before Jesus ascended into heaven, he had said: "And no man hath ascended up to heaven…" (John 3:13) So Enoch, being a man who lived before Jesus, could therefore not have been taken into heaven, God's dwelling place.

It's important to note that the Bible does, in fact, tell us that Enoch died. In Hebrews 11, multiple people of great faith are mentioned, including Enoch: "By faith Enoch was translated that he should not see death; and was not found, because God had translated

Chapter 5: *The Apostasy*

him: for before his translation he had this testimony, that he pleased God." (Hebrews 11:5)

The chapter mentions other faithful people (Abel, Noah, Abraham, Sarah, etc.) before we're brought to verse 13 which reads: "<u>These all died in faith</u>, not having received the promises, but having seen them afar off, and were persuaded of *them*, and embraced *them*, and confessed that they were strangers and pilgrims on the earth." (Hebrews 11:13) We're told that all of these faithful people, including Enoch, died.

Now, let's try to make sense of these verses that mention him seemingly escaping death. Going back to Genesis 5:24, it says that Enoch "was not; for God took him." What does this phrase "was not" mean?

It appears later in Genesis when Joseph's brothers came to Egypt during a famine and were telling Joseph who they were without realizing that

Chapter 5: *The Apostasy*

they were speaking to their brother, whom they had sold into slavery years ago: "And they said, Thy servants *are* twelve brethren, the sons of one man in the land of Canaan; and, behold, the youngest *is* this day with our father, <u>and one *is* not</u>." (Genesis 42:13)

Joseph's brothers, when speaking about him, say that he "is not." Now, they're not saying that one of their brothers is not with their father, unlike the youngest of them, which is what it may seem like. Ten of them were not with their father because they were in Egypt; so, they're not saying that Joseph is not with their father, but that he "is not," much like what is said about Enoch. Well, what could this mean then?

They had assumed Joseph was dead, but since his dead body was never found and there was no grave to prove it, they couldn't know for sure. They couldn't really say that Joseph was dead because they didn't

Chapter 5: *The Apostasy*

know he was, so they just said that he "is not." This must be the same case as Enoch. It was assumed that Enoch had died, but no one knew for sure "for God took him." (Genesis 5:24)

Now, what does it mean when it says that God "took" Enoch? The Hebrew word used for "took" in Genesis 5:24 is the word *laqach* (לָקַח). *Laqach* could refer to the act of physically moving (Genesis 2:15, Genesis 24:10, Exodus 4:20, Ezekiel 37:16, etc.).

The Greek word used for "translated" in Hebrews 11:5 is *metatithemi* (μετατίθημι), which can mean changing the physical location of something. This essentially means that God changed the physical location of Enoch so that he was not found.

Enoch's dead body was never seen ("he was not") because God moved him to a different location where he couldn't be found ("for God took him," "God

Chapter 5: *The Apostasy*

had translated him") up until his death. We can be assured that Enoch is most certainly dead, not in heaven.

Now let's see what Scripture has to say concerning Elijah:

> And it came to pass, as they still went on, and talked, that, behold, *there appeared* a chariot of fire, and horses of fire, and parted them both asunder; and Elijah went up by a whirlwind into heaven. (2 Kings 2:11)

This verse seems to clearly suggest that Elijah was taken up into heaven. However, this cannot be the case since as we've already been over, Jesus who lived after Elijah said: "And no man hath ascended up to heaven…" (John 3:13) When you read John 3:13 in

Chapter 5: *The Apostasy*

context, it becomes pretty evident that Jesus is referring to God's dwelling place, heaven, not the sky or space, which heaven could also refer to.

When we're told in 2 Kings 2:11 that Elijah went up into heaven, it must be referring to the sky or the atmosphere. It can't mean space because it wouldn't make any sense why Elijah would be taken there.

Elijah was taken up into the atmosphere and moved to a different location, much like Enoch. The purpose of this was because it was time for Elisha to take over Elijah's prophetic role (2 Kings 2:15).

What's the proof that Elijah was still on the earth after being taken up into "heaven"? When we read further in 2 Kings, we come to chapter 8, which tells us that Jehoram, son of Jehoshaphat, ascended the

Chapter 5: *The Apostasy*

throne in Judah (2 Kings 8:16). So Jehoram became king after Elijah's ascension.

Later, in 2 Chronicles 21, King Jehoram receives a letter from Elijah (2 Chronicles 21:12). This would strongly suggest that Elijah was, in fact, still alive on the earth after his temporary ascension into the atmosphere.

A great example of a righteous man being moved by God to another location comes in Acts chapter 8 concerning Philip:

> And when they were come up out of the water, the Spirit of the Lord caught away Philip, that the eunuch saw him no more: and he went on his way rejoicing. But Philip was found at Azotus: and passing through he preached in all

Chapter 5: *The Apostasy*

the cities, till he came to Caesarea. (Acts 8:39–40)

Enoch and Elijah both died and returned to dust, having never ascended to God's dwelling place. Residence in God's holy dwelling place is reserved only for God, the angels, and for now, the Lord Jesus Christ.

Chapter 6: The Future

So if we don't go to heaven when we die but are just dead, then what is the hope of salvation?

Salvation begins with the return of the Lord Jesus Christ to the earth, which could happen at any moment. Jesus currently resides in heaven, and Scripture teaches that he will eventually return from heaven back to the earth:

> And while they looked steadfastly toward heaven as he went up, behold, two men stood by them in white apparel; which also said, Ye men of Galilee, why stand ye gazing up into heaven? this same Jesus, which is taken up

Chapter 6: *The Future*

from you into heaven, shall so come in like manner as ye have seen him go into heaven. (Acts 1:10–11)

And, behold, I come quickly; and my reward *is* with me, to give every man according as his work shall be. (Revelation 22:12)

For as the lightning cometh out of the east, and shineth even unto the west; so shall also the coming of the Son of man be. (Matthew 24:27)

The return of Jesus will come when we least expect it, so we are warned to make ourselves ready and not get caught up in the ways of the world:

Chapter 6: *The Future*

And take heed to yourselves, lest at any time your hearts be overcharged with surfeiting, and drunkenness, and cares of this life, and *so* that day come upon you unawares. (Luke 21:34)

Therefore be ye also ready: for in such an hour as ye think not the Son of man cometh. (Matthew 24:44)

Behold, I come as a thief. Blessed *is* he that watcheth, and keepeth his garments, lest he walk naked, and they see his shame. (Revelation 16:15)

Chapter 6: *The Future*

Resurrection

So, what will Jesus do when he returns? The first thing he will do is raise the dead:

> For the Lord himself shall descend from heaven with a shout, with the voice of the archangel, and with the trump of God: and the dead in Christ shall rise first. (1 Thessalonians 4:16)

> And many of them that sleep in the dust of the earth shall awake, some to everlasting life, and some to shame *and* everlasting contempt. (Daniel 12:2)

> Marvel not at this: for the hour is coming, in the which all that are in the graves shall hear

Chapter 6: *The Future*

his voice, and shall come forth; they that have done good, unto the resurrection of life; and they that have done evil, unto the resurrection of damnation. (John 5:28–29)

It's important to note that not every single person who has ever died will be raised. This verse in Isaiah tells us that there will be people who will remain in their graves forever: "*They are* dead, they shall not live; *they are* deceased, <u>they shall not rise</u>: therefore hast thou visited and destroyed them, and made all their memory to perish." (Isaiah 26:14)

Also, look back at Daniel 12:2. It says <u>many</u> who are dead shall arise, not all who are dead shall arise. So, who will be the ones who get raised?

I believe it's fair to say that those who are responsible for answering the call will be raised. In other words, those who have heard the gospel will be held accountable for accepting it (Luke 12:47–48, John 12:46–48, Romans 2:12–16). Why would someone who's never heard the gospel message be held responsible and gathered to judgment?

Judgment

Jesus' return and the consequences for those who fall astray are foreshadowed in Exodus chapter 32. In this chapter, the Israelites grow impatient while waiting for Moses to return from Mount Sinai, where he had been receiving commandments from God. So, they asked Moses' brother, Aaron, to build them an idol they could worship. Aaron used the gold earrings given to him to forge a golden calf. The people then

Chapter 6: *The Future*

offered sacrifices to it and engaged in revelry. God then instructed Moses to return and see how far the people had strayed. When Moses returned, he destroyed the idol and unleashed God's judgment on them:

> And when Moses saw that the people *were* naked; (for Aaron had made them naked unto *their* shame among their enemies:) then Moses stood in the gate of the camp, and said, Who *is* on the LORD's side? *let him come* unto me. And all the sons of Levi gathered themselves together unto him. And he said unto them, Thus saith the LORD God of Israel, Put every man his sword by his side, *and* go in and out from gate to gate throughout the camp, and slay every man his neighbour. And the children of

Chapter 6: *The Future*

Levi did according to the word of Moses: and there fell of the people that day about three thousand men. (Exodus 32:25–28)

Moses' ascent to Mount Sinai represents Jesus' ascension into heaven. Moses coming down from Mount Sinai represents Jesus' future descent from heaven. The Israelites growing impatient and building and worshipping an idol represents those who will grow impatient with Jesus' return and pursue their worldly desires (2 Peter 3:4). The Levites killing 3,000 men represents the judgment of the ungodly that is to come.

God showed no mercy to those who stopped worshipping Him and instead worshipped the golden calf. We must not do the same. What are our golden calves? What are we idolizing in our lives? We must

Chapter 6: *The Future*

try our best to follow the LORD wholeheartedly because the judgment that is coming will also be merciless, and we will be given no second chances.

Well, what is the judgment that is to come? After Jesus raises the dead who are responsible for accepting the call, they, along with the alive who are also accountable, will be gathered together and judged by Jesus, having been given that authority by God:

> For we must all appear before the judgment seat of Christ; that every one may receive the things *done* in *his* body, according to that he hath done, whether *it be* good or bad. (2 Corinthians 5:10)

> And I saw the dead, small and great, stand before God; and the books were opened: and

Chapter 6: *The Future*

another book was opened, which is *the book* of life: and the dead were judged out of those things which were written in the books, according to their works. (Revelation 20:12)

But I say unto you, That every idle word that men shall speak, they shall give account thereof in the day of judgment. (Matthew 12:36)

But why dost thou judge thy brother? or why dost thou set at nought thy brother? for we shall all stand before the judgment seat of Christ. For it is written, *As* I live, saith the Lord, every knee shall bow to me, And every tongue shall confess to God. So then every one of us shall give account of himself to God. (Romans 14:10–12)

Chapter 6: *The Future*

I charge *thee* therefore before God, and the Lord Jesus Christ, who shall judge the quick and the dead at his appearing and his kingdom. (2 Timothy 4:1)

For the Father judgeth no man, but hath committed all judgment unto the Son… and hath given him authority to execute judgment also, because he is the Son of man. (John 5:22, 27)

After the responsible give an account before Christ and are judged, the accepted will be granted immortality and incorruptibility, and the rejected will be sentenced to eternal death:

Chapter 6: *The Future*

Now this I say, brethren, that flesh and blood cannot inherit the kingdom of God; neither doth corruption inherit incorruption. Behold, I shew you a mystery; We shall not all sleep, but we shall all be changed, in a moment, in the twinkling of an eye, at the last trump: for the trumpet shall sound, and the dead shall be raised incorruptible, and we shall be changed. For this corruptible must put on incorruption, and this mortal *must* put on immortality. So when this corruptible shall have put on incorruption, and this mortal shall have put on immortality, then shall be brought to pass the saying that is written, Death is swallowed up in victory. O death, where *is* thy sting? O grave, where *is* thy victory? (1 Corinthians 15:50–55)

Chapter 6: *The Future*

Who will render to every man according to his deeds: to them who by patient continuance in well doing seek for glory and honour and immortality, eternal life. (Romans 2:6–7)

And Jesus answering said unto them, The children of this world marry, and are given in marriage: but they which shall be accounted worthy to obtain that world, and the resurrection from the dead, neither marry, nor are given in marriage: neither can they die any more: for they are equal unto the angels; and are the children of God, being the children of the resurrection. (Luke 20:34–36)

Chapter 6: *The Future*

For the wages of sin *is* death; but the gift of God *is* eternal life through Jesus Christ our Lord. (Romans 6:23)

Enter ye in at the strait gate: for wide *is* the gate, and broad *is* the way, that leadeth to destruction, and many there be which go there at. (Matthew 7:13)

And to you who are troubled rest with us, when the Lord Jesus shall be revealed from heaven with his mighty angels, in flaming fire taking vengeance on them that know not God, and that obey not the gospel of our Lord Jesus Christ: who shall be punished with everlasting destruction from the presence of the Lord, and

Chapter 6: *The Future*

from the glory of his power. (2 Thessalonians 1:7–9)

But the fearful, and unbelieving, and the abominable, and murderers, and whoremongers, and sorcerers, and idolaters, and all liars, shall have their part in the lake which burneth with fire and brimstone: which is the second death. (Revelation 21:8)

Marriage Supper of the Lamb

After Jesus returns and raises, gathers, and judges the responsible, there will be this celebration known as the Marriage Supper of the Lamb. This will be to celebrate the spiritual marriage between Christ

Chapter 6: *The Future*

and the faithful believers. The faithful believers are called the bride of Christ in Scripture (John 3:29, 2 Corinthians 11:2, Ephesians 5:25–27).

The phrase "marriage supper of the Lamb" appears in Revelation chapter 19:

> Let us be glad and rejoice, and give honour to him: for the marriage of the Lamb is come, and his wife hath made herself ready. And to her was granted that she should be arrayed in fine linen, clean and white: for the fine linen is the righteousness of saints. And he saith unto me, Write, Blessed *are* they which are called unto the <u>marriage supper of the Lamb</u>. And he saith unto me, These are the true sayings of God. (Revelation 19:7–9)

Chapter 6: *The Future*

The Marriage Supper of the Lamb is for the glorification of the redeemed saints and their union with Christ following the judgment. Jesus spoke about this glorious event and of the consequences concerning those who reject the wedding invitation in the parable of the wedding feast (Matthew 22:2–14) and in the parable of the ten virgins (Matthew 25:1–13):

> The kingdom of heaven is like unto a certain king, which made a marriage for his son, and sent forth his servants to call them that were bidden to the wedding: and they would not come. (Matthew 22:2–3)

> And when the king came in to see the guests, he saw there a man which had not on a wedding garment: and he saith unto him,

Chapter 6: *The Future*

Friend, how camest thou in hither not having a wedding garment? And he was speechless. Then said the king to the servants, Bind him hand and foot, and take him away, and cast *him* into outer darkness; there shall be weeping and gnashing of teeth. For many are called but few *are* chosen. (Matthew 22:11–14)

Then shall the kingdom of heaven be likened unto ten virgins, which took their lamps, and went forth to meet the bridegroom. And five of them were wise, and five *were* foolish. They that *were* foolish took their lamps, and took no oil with them: but the wise took oil in their vessels with their lamps. (Matthew 25:1–4)

Chapter 6: *The Future*

And while they went to buy, the bridegroom came; and they that were ready went in with him to the marriage: and the door was shut. Afterward came also the other virgins, saying, Lord, Lord, open to us. But he answered and said, Verily I say unto you, I know you not. Watch therefore, for ye know neither the day nor the hour wherein the Son of man cometh. (Matthew 25:10–13)

The invitation to the Marriage Supper of the Lamb is available to all. We must put on our garments and light our lamps if we want to take part in it.

Chapter 6: *The Future*

Elijah's Mission

One of the more mysterious passages in the Bible is found in Malachi chapter 4. This is when God is speaking about the period following the resurrection and judgment but before the final battle (which we'll discuss in the next section):

> Behold, I will send you Elijah the prophet before the coming of the great and dreadful day of the LORD: and he shall turn the heart of the fathers to the children, and the heart of the children to their fathers, lest I come and smite the earth with a curse. (Malachi 4:5–6)

So God says that before the future great and terrible day of battle, He will send a prophet known as

Chapter 6: *The Future*

Elijah who will help turn the hearts of the Israelites back to Him and prepare them for their Messiah.

Some people believe this Elijah prophet will be the resurrected prophet Elijah, whom we read about in the First and Second Kings. While this could be true, I don't believe it is. Jesus says in Matthew 11 that John the Baptist could have been this Elijah if the Jewish people accepted him: "For all the prophets and the law prophesied until John. And if ye will receive *it*, this is Elias [Elijah], which was for to come." (Matthew 11:13–14)

They ultimately did not receive John as Elijah, so the prophecy will be fulfilled at the second coming of Christ rather than the first. And since John's name isn't Elijah, it's evident that this latter-day prophet will be called Elijah as a title instead of it being their given name.

Chapter 6: *The Future*

Still, it could be a reference to the prophet Elijah from the Old Testament in that this prophet will possess a similar spirit to Elijah, just as Jesus is sometimes called David due to being of the same spirit and genealogy as David (Jeremiah 30:9, Ezekiel 34:23–24, Ezekiel 37:24–25, Hosea 3:5). The name Elijah means "My God is Yahweh," highlighting the devoted faith of this prophet that is to come.

So, after the Marriage Supper of the Lamb, God will send a prophet called Elijah, a devout follower of the LORD, who will try to prepare Israel for the coming of their long-awaited Messiah.

Chapter 6: *The Future*

Armageddon

Following the Marriage Supper of the Lamb and the period of fellowship spent between Christ, the angels, and the saints, which may last one year (Deuteronomy 24:5), a great battle known as Armageddon will ensue. The word "Armageddon" appears only once in the Bible, and it's found in Revelation 16, which is a chapter concerning God's righteous judgments upon the corrupt nations of the world:

> And the sixth angel poured out his vial upon the great river Euphrates; and the water thereof was dried up, that the way of the kings of the east might be prepared. And I saw three unclean spirits like frogs *come* out of the mouth

Chapter 6: *The Future*

of the dragon, and out of the mouth of the beast, and out of the mouth of the false prophet. For they are the spirits of devils, working miracles, *which* go forth unto the kings of the earth and of the whole world, to gather them to the battle of that great day of God Almighty. Behold, I come as a thief. Blessed *is* he that watcheth, and keepeth his garments, lest he walk naked, and they see his shame. <u>And he gathered them together into a place called in the Hebrew tongue Armageddon</u>. (Revelation 16:12–16)

From previous chapters in Revelation, we can infer that "the dragon," "the beast," and "the false prophet" refer to the powers of the world (nations that mirror/emerged from the Roman papacy). This passage

Chapter 6: *The Future*

in Revelation 16 tells us that three frog-like spirits will emerge from the mouths of the dragon, the beast, and the false prophet and will gather the nations to a great battle after Jesus' return to the earth.

These three frog-like spirits represent the ideals that emerged from the French Revolution (which is prophesied about earlier in chapter 16). These ideals are liberty, equality, and fraternity, which became the official motto of France. They also more broadly represent secularism, humanism, and religious deception. These ideals have had a significant impact on the nations of the world today and will continue to do so up until the Battle of Armageddon.

Now, what's the meaning of the word "Armageddón"? The Greek word transliterated as "Armageddon" in Revelation 16:16 is the word *Harmagedón* (Ἁρμαγεδών), which many believe is

Chapter 6: *The Future*

derived from the Hebrew words *har* (הַר) and *Mgiddown* (מְגִדּוֹן), meaning "Mountain of Megiddo."

Megiddo was an ancient city situated in the Jezreel Valley of northern Israel. Many battles have been fought there, including the first recorded battle in history (the Battle of Megiddo in 1457 BC). This would seem to suggest that Revelation 16:16 indicates that the Battle of Armageddon will take place at Megiddo.

However, there is a problem with this theory. If the Greek word for "Armageddon" is derived from the Hebrew words meaning "Mountain of Megiddo," then there must be a mountain in Megiddo. But there isn't. Now, when you see pictures of Megiddo, it looks as if it's on a hill, and the Hebrew word *har* can also refer to hills, not just mountains.

Chapter 6: *The Future*

However, it isn't actually a natural hill, but rather a tel, a mound formed by the accumulation of ancient debris from people living there for thousands of years. Megiddo appears elevated due to a lack of further excavation done on the site and is not naturally raised.

So what else could the word "Armageddon" mean? It can also be broken down into three Hebrew words: *aremah-gay-din*. *Aremah* (עֲרֵם) means a heap of sheaves (as on a threshing floor), *gay* (גַּיְא) means a valley(s), and *din* (דִּין) means judgment. So, a more reasonable explanation for the meaning of "Armageddon" is "a heap of sheaves in a valley for judgment."

So, what valley could this be referring to? Fortunately, there are other passages in Scripture that provide us with more information concerning this great battle of God Almighty. Joel chapter 3 is a great example:

> For, behold, in those days, and in that time, when I shall bring again the captivity of Judah and Jerusalem, I will also gather all nations, and will bring them down into <u>the valley of Jehoshaphat</u>, and will plead with them there for my people and *for* my heritage Israel, whom they have scattered among the nations, and parted my land. (Joel 3:1–2)

We know this passage is referring to the future Battle of Armageddon because it describes all nations being brought to judgment in a valley, which aligns with Revelation 16:12–16.

Chapter 6: *The Future*

We also know that this is yet to happen because it must be after the time of Israel's restoration in 1948 ("in that time, when I shall bring again the captivity of Judah and Jerusalem").

There's even a reference to the two-state solution ("and parted my land"). No major war with all nations being brought against Israel has happened since this time.

God says in verse 2 that He will gather the nations to the "valley of Jehoshaphat." This is not a known location and is likely symbolic of a valley where God will unleash His judgment, as the name "Jehoshaphat" means "the LORD judges."

When we read further into Joel 3, we're given more clues that could lead us to identify which valley Armageddon refers to.

Chapter 6: *The Future*

Multitudes, multitudes in <u>the valley of decision</u>: for the day of the LORD *is* near in <u>the valley of decision</u>. The sun and the moon shall be darkened, and the stars shall withdraw their shining. The LORD also shall roar out of <u>Zion</u>, and utter his voice from <u>Jerusalem</u>; and the heavens and the earth shall shake: but the LORD *will be* the hope of his people, and the strength of the children of Israel. (Joel 3:14–16)

The valley is given another name here, which is "the valley of decision." Now, what does this mean? The Hebrew word translated as "decision" is the word *charuwts* (חָרוּץ) which can refer to threshing. This also helps to link Joel 3 with Armageddon, as Armageddon likely means "a heap of sheaves in a valley for judgment." Heaps of sheaves get threshed.

Chapter 6: *The Future*

We're also given the general area of this valley: Jerusalem. This further disproves the idea that Armageddon will take place at Megiddo, as Megiddo is located in northern Israel, not Jerusalem. Now, we have to find out which valley in Jerusalem this end-time prophecy is referring to.

Jerusalem has three main valleys: the Kidron, the Hinnom, and the Tyropoeon. Out of these three, the Kidron seems the most likely. It is the closest valley to the Mount of Olives, and we're told in Zechariah 14 that Jesus will reveal himself to the rest of the world when he appears on the Mount of Olives to fight against the nations attacking Israel. However, this very passage in Zechariah may actually lead us to a new conclusion:

Chapter 6: *The Future*

> And his feet shall stand in that day upon the mount of Olives, which *is* before Jerusalem on the east, and the mount of Olives shall cleave in the midst thereof toward the east and toward the west, *and there shall be* a very great valley; and half of the mountain shall remove toward the north, and half of it toward the south. (Zechariah 14:4)

When Jesus stands on the Mount of Olives before the nations, a great earthquake will occur, splitting the mountain in two and creating a large valley. Since we're told that the valley will form during this future battle against Israel, I believe Armageddon, the Valley of Jehoshaphat, and the Valley of Decision all refer to this future valley that will be formed when the Mount of Olives splits.

Chapter 6: *The Future*

Ezekiel

At the end of the day, knowing the exact location of this battle doesn't really matter. What is important is knowing that it will take place in Jerusalem.

Let's now further analyze the passages that detail this future battle, starting with Ezekiel chapters 38 and 39. In these chapters, God tells the prophet Ezekiel more about the who, where, when, and why of Armageddon.

> And the word of the LORD came unto me, saying, Son of man, set thy face against Gog, the land of Magog, the chief prince of Meshech and Tubal, and prophesy against him, and say, Thus saith the Lord GOD; Behold, I *am* against

Chapter 6: *The Future*

thee, O Gog, the chief prince of Meshech and Tubal. (Ezekiel 38:1–3)

So here we're given the "who." The antagonist is called Gog from the land of Magog, and he is the "chief prince" of Meshech and Tubal. Let's find out what these names refer to.

The Hebrew word for "Gog" comes from an uncertain derivation, but it's most likely a symbolic name for a ruler.

The Hebrew actually says: "prince of <u>Rosh</u>, Meshech, and Tubal," implying Rosh is a place or a people. This "Gog" is apparently the ruler of Rosh, Magog, Meshech, and Tubal. Where are these places today?

When speaking of a people called the Rus, the Byzantine Emperor Constantine VII Porphyrogenitus

Chapter 6: *The Future*

refers to them as the "Ros" (Ρως): "The people called the Ros (Ρως) live beyond the sea to the north. They are a people of Varangian origin who settled among the Slavs."[37]

The linguistic similarity between the terms "Rus," "Ros," and "Rosh" has led many to suggest that these names share a connection, possibly referring to the same people and region.

Assuming "Rosh" is another name for the Rus people, we need to determine who the Rus are and where they originated.

The Arab Muslim explorer Ahmad ibn Fadlan mentions an encounter with the Rus when out

---

[37] Constantine VII Porphyrogenitus, *De Administrando Imperio*, trans. and ed. G. R. Herrin (Washington, D.C.: Dumbarton Oaks Center for Byzantine Studies, 1967), 145–147.

Chapter 6: *The Future*

exploring: "I saw the Rus' arrive on their merchant expeditions and encamp on the banks of the Volga."[38]

So, we're told that the Rus dwelled near the Volga River. The Volga River is located in modern-day Russia. The word "Russia" also linguistically matches well with the terms "Rus," "Ros," and "Rosh."

Nestor the Chronicler (AD 1056–1114) writes in his book *The Primary Chronicle*: "The Slavs went overseas to the Varangians, to the Rus', and said to them: 'Our land is great and rich, but there is no order in it. Come to rule and reign over us.'"[39]

This suggests that the Rus people integrated into the Slavic people, providing further evidence that

---

[38] Ahmad ibn Fadlan, *Ahmad ibn Fadlan and the Rus' Embassy: 921–922 A.D.*, trans. and ed. James E. Montgomery (Cambridge, MA: The Medieval Academy of America, 2012), 45–46.
[39] Nestor the Chronicler, *The Russian Primary Chronicle: Laurentian Text*, trans. and ed. Samuel Hazzard Cross and Olgerd P. Sherbowitz-Wetzor (Cambridge, MA: The Mediaeval Academy of America, 1953), 52–53.

Chapter 6: *The Future*

Rus can be considered a precursor to Russia, as Russia is recognized as a Slavic nation today.

Here are a few more quotes that link Rosh/Rus with Russia:

> Rhos is the most ancient form under which history records the name of Russia. From Rhos and Meshech—referred to as the Rhossi and Moschi by historians and as mentioned by Ezekiel—descended the Russians and Muscovites, nations renowned throughout European Scythia.[40]

> The name Russia is derived from Rus, the name of the people who settled in the region, and this

---

[40] Samuel Bochart, *Geographia Sacra seu Phaleg et Canaan* (Paris: Typographia Regia, 1646), 11.

Chapter 6: *The Future*

in turn probably from the Norse term for the rowing men.[41]

Now that we've identified Rosh as Russia, let's now find out where the land of Magog is. Luckily, the Jewish historian Josephus gives us a significant clue: "Magog founded those that from him were named Magogites, but who are by the Greeks called Scythians."[42]

According to Josephus, the land of Magog is where a people known as the Scythians resided. Well, who were the Scythians?

The Greek historian Herodotus (484–425 BC) wrote this about the eight rivers of Scythia:

---

[41] *Encyclopaedia Britannica*, 11th ed. (Cambridge: Cambridge University Press, 1911), 23:433–435.
[42] Josephus, *Antiquities of the Jews*, trans. William Whiston (London: William Bowyer, 1737), 1.6.1.

Chapter 6: *The Future*

The country of the Scythians is of vast extent, and has no mountains, but is entirely flat and grassy. Many rivers flow through it... These are the names of the rivers: the Ister, the Tyras, the Hypanis, the Borysthenes, the Panticapes, the Hypacyris, the Gerrhus, and the Tanaïs.[43]

Some of these ancient river names have been linked to modern-day rivers. The Ister is the Danube, the Tyras is the Dniester, the Hypanis is the Southern Buh, the Borysthenes is the Dnieper, and the Tanaïs is the Don. The Panticapas may be Samara, and the Hypacuris or the Gerrhus may be the Molochna. These rivers indicate that the land of the Scythians, and thus the land of Magog, is located above the Black Sea in the Ukraine and southern Russia region.

---

[43] Herodotus, *The Histories*, trans. George Rawlinson (London: John Murray, 1862), book 4, secs. 46–47.

Chapter 6: *The Future*

This is validated by Professor Nicholas V. Riasanovsky, a Russian historian who said: "They [the Scyths] ruled southern Russia from the seventh to the end of the third century B.C."[44]

Now, let's find out where the lands of Meshech and Tubal are. The historians tell us that Meshech and Tubal refer to the Caucasus Mountains, and the people of Meshech were known as the "Moschi":

> Thobel [Tubal] founded the Thobelites, who are now called Iberes.[45]

---

[44] Nicholas V. Riasanovsky, *A History of Russia*, 3rd ed. (New York: Oxford University Press, 1977), 7.
[45] Flavius Josephus, *Antiquities of the Jews*, trans. William Whiston (Peabody, MA: Hendrickson Publishers, 1987), book 1, chap. 6, sec. 1 (1.124), 36.

Chapter 6: *The Future*

Meshech, proper name of a barbarous people inhabiting the Moschian mountains between Iberia, Armenia, and Colchis.[46]

Tubal: [Tubal], proper name of the Tibareni, a nation of Asia Minor, dwelling by the Euxine Sea [Black Sea], to the west of the Moschi.[47]

...After the Heniochi the Colchian country, which lies at the foot of the Caucasian, or Moschian, Mountains.[48]

Meshech has even been linked to Moscow:

---

[46] Wilhelm Gesenius, *Hebrew and Chaldee Lexicon to the Old Testament Scriptures*, trans. Samuel Prideaux Tregelles (London: Samuel Bagster and Sons, 1847), 487.
[47] George A. Morrish, *Concise Bible Dictionary* (Chicago, IL: Bible Truth Publishers, 1890), 365.
[48] Strabo, *The Geography of Strabo*, vol. 5, trans. H. L. Jones, Loeb Classical Library No. 211 (Cambridge, MA: Harvard University Press, 1928), 191.

Chapter 6: *The Future*

During the ascendancy of the Babylonians and Persians in Western Asia, the Moschi were subdued; but it seems probable that a large number of them crossed the Caucasus range and spread over the northern steppes, mingling with the Scythians. There they became known as Muscovs, and gave that name to the Russian nation and its ancient capital by which they are still generally known throughout the East.[49]

The Caucasus Mountains are located within the countries of Russia, Georgia, Azerbaijan, Armenia, and Iran, which is quite consistent with our identified locations of Rosh and Magog.

So now we have the "where." This Gogian leader is the ruler of Russia, who will also have control

---

[49] M. G. Easton, *Easton's Bible Dictionary* (New York: Thomas Nelson, 1897), 487.

Chapter 6: *The Future*

over certain nearby nations. Now let's see what God has to say concerning this ruler:

> And I will turn thee back, and put hooks into thy jaws, and I will bring thee forth, and all thine army, horses and horsemen, all of them clothed with all sorts *of armor, even* a great company *with* bucklers and shields, all of them handling swords: Persia, Ethiopia, and Libya with them; all of them with shield and helmet: Gomer, and all his bands; the house of Togarmah of the north quarters, and all his bands: *and* many people with thee. Be thou prepared, and prepare for thyself, thou, and all thy company that are assembled unto thee, and be thou a guard unto them. (Ezekiel 38:4–7)

Chapter 6: *The Future*

God is saying here that He will bring Gog to battle along with nations called Persia, Ethiopia, Libya, Gomer, and Togarmah. The Hebrew word in verse 7, translated as "guard," is *mishmar* (מִשְׁמָר), which refers to guarding a place of confinement, such as a prison guard. This would imply that these nations that will fight alongside Russia will do so because Russia will essentially force them to obey out of fear, like how a prison guard keeps watch over his prisoners.

Let's now look at which nations these ancient names refer to. Ethiopia and Libya are fittingly still referred to as such, two countries located in the east and north of Africa. It's also well known that modern-day Persia is the country of Iran. But what about Gomer and Togarmah?

Chapter 6: *The Future*

Josephus writes about Gomer: "Gomer founded those whom the Greeks now call Galatians, but were then called Gomerites."[50]

Josephus tells us that the Gomerites later became known as Galatians. Diodorus Siculus (c. 90 BC–c. 30 BC), a Greek historian from Italy, tells us some critical information about the Galatians: "Becoming renowned for his bravery, he called his subjects Galatae or Gauls after himself, and these in turn gave their name to all of Galatia or Gaul."[51]

Siculus tells us that Galatia is Gaul. This would also equate Gomer to Gaul. Tacitus tells us which modern-day nation was once called Gaul: "The province of Gaul, now called France, was once

---

[50] Josephus, *Antiquities of the Jews* (Peabody, MA: Hendrickson Publishers, 1987), 1.6.1.
[51] Diodorus Siculus, *Library of History*, trans. C. H. Oldfather, Loeb Classical Library (Cambridge, MA: Harvard University Press, 1933), 5.24.3.

Chapter 6: *The Future*

inhabited by various Celtic tribes before becoming part of the Roman Empire."⁵²

Gaul is modern-day France, which identifies France as the land of Gomer in Ezekiel 38:6.

Josephus also helps us identify the land of Togarmah: "Thrugramma [Togarmah], the father of the Thrugrammeans, who are by the Greeks called Phrygians."⁵³

According to Josephus, the people of Togarmah were known as the Phrygians.

Strabo said that Armenians are descended from the Phrygians: "The Armenians are descendants of the Phrygians and other peoples who migrated and mixed in that region."⁵⁴

---

⁵² Tacitus, *The Annals of Imperial Rome*, trans. M. Hutton (New York: Macmillan, 1931), book 12, chap. 30, 257.
⁵³ Josephus, *Antiquities of the Jews*, trans. William Whiston (Peabody, MA: Hendrickson Publishers, 1987), 31.
⁵⁴ Strabo, *Geography*, trans. H. C. Hamilton and W. Falconer (Cambridge, MA: Harvard University Press, 1917), 11.14.

Chapter 6: *The Future*

But what's interesting is Ezekiel 38:6 says "the house of Togarmah" instead of just saying the name "Togarmah," as it does for the other nations. Well, what does the house of Togarmah or the house of Armenia mean?

It is likely a reference to Turkey, which lies west of Armenia, as Armenians and Turks have historically had a strong connection with each other. Perhaps the house of Togarmah can, therefore, be more broadly referred to as encompassing Turkey as well as Armenia.

Now, we are given the "where" concerning the aggressors in the Battle of Armageddon. A Russian leader will be brought by God to battle with many nations alongside him, such as Iran, Ethiopia, Libya, Armenia, and Turkey. Now, where will they go to battle?

Chapter 6: *The Future*

After many days thou shalt be visited: in the latter years thou shalt come into the land *that is* brought back from the sword, *and is* gathered out of many people, against the mountains of Israel, which have been always waste: but it is brought forth out of the nations, and they shall dwell safely all of them. Thou shalt ascend and come like a storm, thou shalt be like a cloud to cover the land, thou, and all thy bands, and many people with thee. (Ezekiel 38:8–9)

These verses confirm what we already know about Armageddon: that it will take place in Israel. But why?

Thus saith the Lord God; It shall also come to pass, *that* at the same time shall things come

Chapter 6: *The Future*

into thy mind, and thou shalt think an evil thought: and thou shalt say, I will go up to the land of unwalled villages; I will go to them that are at rest, that dwell safely, all of them dwelling without walls, and having neither bars nor gates, to take a spoil, and to take a prey; to turn thine hand upon the desolate places *that are now* inhabited, and upon the people *that are* gathered out of the nations, which have gotten cattle and goods, that dwell in the midst of the land. Sheba, Dedan, and the merchants of Tarshish, with all the young lions thereof, shall say unto thee, Art thou come to take a spoil? hast thou gathered thy company to take a prey? to carry away silver and gold, to take away cattle and goods, to take a great spoil? (Ezekiel 38:10–13)

Chapter 6: *The Future*

So God says that when Israel feels as if they are dwelling safely, this Russian-led army will come down and invade to plunder their resources. This makes sense since Israel, although one of the smallest countries, is also one of the wealthiest, as it has an abundance of desirable resources. This is the first part of the "why" of Armageddon.

We're also told that "Sheba, Dedan, and the merchants of Tarshish" will oppose this invasion and will call out Russia for coming to take a great spoil of resources. Now which modern nations are Sheba, Dedan, and Tarshish?

Now Raamah had two sons, the one of whom was Sheba, and the other Dedan. These inhabited the country that reaches from the Euphrates to the Red Sea. Now the name of one

Chapter 6: *The Future*

of the sons of Joktan was Sheba; these are the Sabians, and they dwelt at the remotest parts of Arabia Felix.[55]

This quote from Josephus tells us that Sheba and Dedan refer to Arabia. Sheba would probably refer to Southern Arabia, such as Yemen, and Dedan would likely refer to Saudi Arabia and, by extension, the Arab Gulf Nations. Several of these nations are allies with Israel, so it would make sense for them to oppose the nations invading it. Or maybe this Russian invasion of Israel will spark jealousy in their hearts over wanting to plunder Israel's resources for themselves.

When it comes to the identity of Tarshish, many believe it to be Spain; however, upon examining

---

[55] Josephus, *Antiquities of the Jews* (Peabody, MA: Hendrickson Publishers, 1987), 1.6.2.

Chapter 6: *The Future*

what the Bible says about Tarshish, one nation stands out in particular.

Tarshish was a trading power, as evidenced in Ezekiel 38:13, which says "the <u>merchants</u> of Tarshish" rather than simply "Tarshish." This is supported by other scriptural mentions of Tarshish, which note their prominent seafaring presence (1 Kings 10:22, Psalm 48:7, Isaiah 60:9, etc.).

Knowing that Tarshish was a significant trading power, we can narrow down the list of nations to which it could be identified. What really reveals the identity of the nation of Tarshish is what we're told they were known for trading: "Tarshish *was* thy merchant by reason of the multitude of all *kind of* riches; with silver, iron, <u>tin</u>, and lead, they traded in thy fairs." (Ezekiel 27:12)

Chapter 6: *The Future*

We're told that Tarshish traded tin to other nations. The primary source of tin was mined in the regions of Cornwall and Devon in the United Kingdom. Other nations, such as Spain, did not produce as much tin. They even found tin in Israel and linked it back, saying it was originally mined in Cornwall, England.[56] Tarshish is Britain.

Now notice how it says: "the merchants of Tarshish, <u>with all the young lions thereof</u>." (Ezekiel 38:13) This is saying how Tarshish's allies will also call out Russia for their invasion of Israel. And notice how the term "young lions" is used for Tarshish's allies, and Britain's national animal just so happens to be a lion.

So which nations are Britain's "young lions"? These would be the nations who are strongly aligned

---

[56] D. Berger, L. Smith, and R. Cohen, *Ancient Trade Routes and the Biblical World* (London: Heritage Press, 2019), 142–144.

Chapter 6: *The Future*

with Britain, whose influence helped shape them. These nations include the United States, Canada, Australia, and New Zealand. These nations all speak English, which originated in Britain, and they were all founded by British colonists; hence, their nickname the "young lions," since they are essentially the offspring of Britain.

So far, in Ezekiel 38, God has set the stage for this battle. The aggressors are Russia, who will be followed by certain nations such as Iran, Ethiopia, Libya, France, and Turkey. They will invade Israel for their abundance of valuable resources. In response, nations such as Britain, the United States, Canada, and Saudi Arabia will oppose the Gogian Confederacy and will stand in support of Israel.

Chapter 6: *The Future*

Therefore, son of man, prophesy and say unto Gog, Thus saith the Lord GOD; In that day when my people of Israel dwelleth safely, shalt thou not know *it*? And thou shalt come from thy place out of the north parts, thou, and many people with thee, all of them riding upon horses, a great company, and a mighty army: and thou shalt come up against my people of Israel, as a cloud to cover the land; it shall be in the latter days, and I will bring thee against my land, that the heathen may know me, when I shall be sanctified in thee, O Gog, before their eyes. (Ezekiel 38:14–16)

So now we're given the "when." This invasion will take place "in the latter days" (v. 16). This confirms that the Battle of Armageddon will occur

Chapter 6: *The Future*

during the final period preceding the establishment of God's Kingdom on earth.

Now, as we go through the rest of Ezekiel 38, we will learn the second part of the "why" of Armageddon.

> Thus saith the Lord GOD; *Art* thou he of whom I have spoken in old time by my servants the prophets of Israel, which prophesied in those days *many* years that I would bring thee against them? And it shall come to pass at the same time when Gog shall come against the land of Israel, saith the Lord GOD, *that* my fury shall come up in my face. For in my jealousy *and* in the fire of my wrath have I spoken, Surely in that day there shall be a great shaking in the land of Israel; so that the fishes of the sea, and

Chapter 6: *The Future*

the fowls of the heaven, and the beasts of the field, and all creeping things that creep upon the earth, and all men that *are* upon the face of the earth, shall be thrown down, and the steep places shall fall, and every wall shall fall to the ground. And I will call for a sword against him throughout all my mountains, saith the Lord GOD: every man's sword shall be against his brother. And I will plead against him with pestilence and with blood; and I will rain upon him, and upon his bands, and upon the many people that *are* with him, an overflowing rain, and great hailstones, fire, and brimstone. This will I magnify myself, and sanctify myself; and I will be known in the eyes of many nations, and they shall know that I *am* the LORD. (Ezekiel 38:17–23)

Chapter 6: *The Future*

God says that when the Gogian Confederacy invades Israel, He will send a great earthquake as well as rain, hail, and fire on them, saving His people Israel so that all nations will know that He is the LORD.

This is the second part of the "why" of Armageddon. It's so God can be glorified, for despite Israel being outnumbered and overwhelmed, God will save them through divine force, showcasing His power to the world. After this, no one will doubt the existence of Yahweh. Chapter 39 summarizes it perfectly:

> Therefore, thou son of man, prophesy against Gog, and say, Thus saith the Lord GOD; Behold, I *am* against thee, O Gog, the chief prince of Meshech and Tubal: and I will turn thee back, and leave but the sixth part of thee, and will cause thee to come up from the north

Chapter 6: *The Future*

parts, and will bring thee upon the mountains of Israel: and I will smite thy bow out of thy left hand, and will cause thine arrows to fall out of thy right hand. Thou shalt fall upon the mountains of Israel, thou, and all thy bands, and the people that *is* with thee: I will give thee unto the ravenous birds of every sort, and *to* the beasts of the field to be devoured. Thou shalt fall upon the open field: for I have spoken *it*, saith the Lord GOD. And I will send a fire on Magog, and among them that dwell carelessly in the isles: and they shall know that I *am* the Lord. So will I make my holy name known in the midst of my people Israel; and I will not *let them* pollute my holy name any more: and the heathen shall know that I *am* the LORD, the Holy One in Israel. Behold, it is come, and it is done, saith the Lord GOD; this *is* the day whereof I have spoken. (Ezekiel 39:1–8)

And I will set my glory among the heathen, and all the heathen shall see my judgment that I have executed, and my hand that I have laid upon them. So the house of Israel shall know that I *am* the Lord their God from that day and forward. (Ezekiel 39:21–22)

Daniel

At the end of the third chapter of this book titled "Divine Inspiration," I said we would go over Daniel 11:40–45 in a future chapter. This is the chapter, as this passage provides details concerning the Battle of Armageddon.

Chapter 6: *The Future*

As we discussed in chapter 3, Daniel 11 describes the hostility between the Seleucid Kingdom ("king of the north") and the Ptolemaic Kingdom ("king of the south"). Verses 40–45 provide another prophecy concerning the king of the north versus the king of the south, but this time, it is not referring to the Seleucid and Ptolemaic conflicts.

> And at that time of the end shall the king of the south push at him: and the king of the north shall come against him like a whirlwind, with chariots, and with horsemen, and with many ships; and he shall enter into the countries, and shall overflow and pass over. He shall enter also into the glorious land, and many *countries* shall be overthrown: but these shall escape out of his hand, *even* Edom, and Moab, and the

chief of the children of Ammon. (Daniel 11:40–41)

So, how do we know that this prophecy refers to the Battle of Armageddon? Well, we're told here that a northern nation will come down and invade Israel ("the glorious land," see Daniel 8:9) with chariots, horsemen, and ships like a whirlwind.

Is this not the same type of language we read about in Ezekiel 38? In that chapter, we're told of a nation from the far north (Ezekiel 38:6, "king of the north," Russia is the utmost north of Israel) who will come against Israel (Ezekiel 38:8) with a great army (Ezekiel 38:4–6) like a cloud covering the land (Ezekiel 38:9).

Chapter 6: *The Future*

And when will this take place? "In the latter days" (Ezekiel 38:16) "And at that time of the end" (Daniel 11:40)

All clues point to Daniel 11:40–45 and Ezekiel 38 referencing the same future battle. In the Daniel 11 passage, Russia has inherited the title of the "king of the north" from the Seleucids.

Verse 40 tells us that Gog's ambitions will extend past Israel and he will first conquer other nations, but Edom, Moab, and Ammon "shall escape out of his hand" (v. 41)

These regions (Edom, Moab, and Ammon) are located in modern-day Jordan. So when Russia comes down to conquer nations, Scripture tells us that Jordan will avoid their wrath. So, which nations will Russia succeed in invading?

Chapter 6: *The Future*

He shall stretch forth his hand against upon the countries: and the land of Egypt shall not escape. But he shall have power over the treasures of gold and of silver, and over all the precious things of Egypt: and the Libyans and the Ethiopians *shall be* at his steps. (Daniel 11:42–43)

Here, we're told that this large army spearheaded by Russia will invade Egypt and gain control over its resources. It also tells us how Libya and Ethiopia will submit to this northern invader.

We're told in Ezekiel 38:5 that Libya and Ethiopia will align themselves with Russia against Israel. This would imply that when Russia conquers Egypt, Libya and Ethiopia (two countries close to

Chapter 6: *The Future*

Egypt) will then join the Russian Confederacy out of fear.

> But tidings out of the east and out of the north shall trouble him: therefore he shall go forth with great fury to destroy, and utterly to make away many. And he shall plant the tabernacles of his palace between the seas in the glorious holy mountain; yet he shall come to his end, and none shall help him. (Daniel 11:44–45)

These last two verses of Daniel 11 tell us that when Gog is in Egypt, troubling news from the north and the east will lead him in that direction to conquer. What's directly northeast of Egypt? Israel.

It goes on to say that he will establish a military/political presence ("plant the tabernacles of his palace") in Israel ("glorious holy mountain"), which is between the Dead Sea and the Mediterranean Sea ("between the seas"). The chapter concludes by mentioning the eventual defeat of the Gogian host ("none shall help him").

To summarize, Daniel 11:40–45 teaches us that Russia will invade multiple nations as they come down. After they conquer Egypt, they will head up northeast towards the land of Israel, where they will be ultimately defeated by God's divine hand.

Joel

The next Armageddon passages we'll be examining are Joel chapters 2 and 3.

Chapter 6: *The Future*

Blow ye the trumpet in Zion, and sound an alarm in my holy mountain: let all the inhabitants of the land tremble: for the day of the LORD cometh, for *it is* nigh at hand; a day of darkness and of gloominess, a day of clouds and of thick darkness, as the morning spread upon the mountains: a great people and a strong; there hath not been even the like, neither shall be any more after it, *even* to the years of many generations. (Joel 2:1–2)

The first two verses of Joel chapter 2 already indicate that this is about Armageddon. It warns the inhabitants of Israel (also called Zion) to be prepared for battle. It's even referred to as God's holy mountain, just like in Daniel 11:45.

Chapter 6: *The Future*

We're told that there will be a mighty army coming against Israel unlike an army anyone has ever seen, which matches with Ezekiel 38:4–6 and Daniel 11:40. This horde is also compared to a storm with dark clouds, matching with Ezekiel 38:9. As we read further into the chapter, we see the theme of Armageddon becoming more and more apparent:

> A fire devoureth before them; and behind them a flame burneth: the land *is* as the garden of Eden before them, and behind them a desolate wilderness; yea, and nothing shall escape them. The appearance of them *is* as the appearance of horses; and as horsemen, so shall they run. Like the noise of chariots on the tops of mountains shall they leap, like the noise of a flame of fire

Chapter 6: *The Future*

that devoureth the stubble, as a strong people set in battle array. (Joel 2:3–5)

These verses describe the destructive, fire-like force the army will have. Verse 5 describes them as chariots who will jump over mountains. This is strange, considering chariots cannot jump over mountains. This could possibly be a reference to warplanes that make a great noise, and are likened to "a flame of fire."

> The earth shall quake before them, the heavens shall tremble: the sun and the moon shall be dark, and the stars shall withdraw their shining: and the LORD shall utter his voice before his army: for his camp *is* very great: for *he is* strong that executeth his word: for the day of

Chapter 6: *The Future*

the LORD *is* great and very terrible; and who can abide it? (Joel 1:10–11)

These verses parallel Ezekiel 38:19–23, which also speak of God's mighty judgment against the Gogian host, involving an earthquake.

Therefore also now, saith the LORD, turn ye *even* to me with all your heart, and with fasting, and with weeping, and with mourning: and rend your heart, and not your garments, and turn unto the LORD your God: for he *is* gracious and merciful, slow to anger, and of great kindness, and repenteth him of the evil. Who knoweth *if* he will return and repent, and leave a blessing behind him; *even* a meat offering and a drink offering unto the LORD

Chapter 6: *The Future*

your God? Blow the trumpet in Zion, sanctify a fast, call a solemn assembly: gather the people, sanctify the congregation, assemble the elders, gather the children, and those that suck the breasts: let the bridegroom go forth of his chamber, and the bride out of her closet. Let the priests, the ministers of the LORD, weep between the porch and the altar, and let them say, Spare thy people, O LORD, and give not thine heritage to reproach, that the heathen should rule over them: wherefore should they say among the people, Where *is* their God? (Joel 2:12–17)

This passage reveals more about why God is sending a vast host of nations against His people, Israel. It's a judgment against the Israelites for forgetting Him, and He's using it to turn their hearts back to Him.

We're told something very interesting in verse 16: "let the bridegroom go forth of his chamber, and the bride out of her closet." (Joel 2:16)

Who do the bridegroom and the bride refer to? It's Jesus (the bridegroom) and the saints (the bride) (Matthew 25, John 3:29, 2 Corinthians 11:2, Ephesians 5:25–27, Revelation 19:7–9, etc.).

So what verse 16 is telling us is that during the battle, when Israel is crying out to God for help, Jesus and the saints, after leaving the period of fellowship with each other following the Marriage Supper of the Lamb ("chamber," "closet"), will join the battle and come to Israel's defense.

Chapter 6: *The Future*

Then will the LORD be jealous for his land, and pity his people. Yea, the LORD will answer and say unto his people, Behold, I will send you corn, and wine, and oil, and ye shall be satisfied therewith: and I will no more make you a reproach among the heathen: but I will remove far off from you the northern *army*, and will drive him into a land barren and desolate, with his face toward the east sea, and his hinder part toward the utmost sea, and his stink shall come up, and his ill savour shall come up, because he hath done great things. (Joel 2:18–20)

God will hear the cries for help from among His people and will drive out the "northern *army*" (v. 20) and destroy it. We're once again told that this army

Chapter 6: *The Future*

that will attack Israel will be from the north. Russia is the most northern nation from Israel.

> And it shall come to pass afterward, *that* I will pour out my spirit upon all flesh; and your sons and your daughters shall prophesy, your old men shall dream dreams, your young men shall see visions: and also upon the servants and upon the handmaids in those days will I pour out my spirit. (Joel 2:28–29)

In these verses, God states that the gifts of the Holy Spirit will be restored when the Kingdom of God is established (which we'll go over later).

> And I will shew wonders in the heavens and in the earth, blood, and fire, and pillars of smoke.

Chapter 6: *The Future*

The sun shall be turned into darkness, and the moon into blood, before the great and terrible day of the LORD come. And it shall come to pass, *that* whosoever shall call on the name of the LORD shall be delivered: for in mount Zion and in Jerusalem shall be deliverance, as the LORD hath said, and in the remnant whom the LORD shall call. (Joel 2:30–32)

The sun being turned to darkness and the moon being turned to blood represent God's judgment on the nations of the world.

Verse 32 speaks of a remnant in Israel following the battle, which tells us that many Israelites will die in Armageddon, but there will be those who survive who will be saved.

Now let's look at chapter 3:

Chapter 6: *The Future*

> For behold, in those days, and in that time, when I shall bring again the captivity of Judah and Jerusalem, I will also gather all nations, and will bring them down into the valley of Jehoshaphat, and I will plead with them there *for* my heritage Israel, whom they have scattered among the nations, and parted my land. (Joel 3:1–2)

As we've discussed, if the Valley of Jehoshaphat is literal and not symbolic, I believe it to be the valley that will be formed when Jesus stands on the Mount of Olives (Zechariah 14:4); however, that is not particularly important. What is important is how God will bring judgment upon the nations for scattering His people and for parting their land.

Chapter 6: *The Future*

The parting of the land must refer to Palestine's occupation of the Gaza Strip and the West Bank, land which God says belongs to Israel (Genesis 17:8, Leviticus 25:38, Numbers 13:2, 1 Chronicles 16:14–18, Psalm 105:11). All land is God's land and He can give it to whomever He wishes.

> Yea, and what have ye to do with me, O Tyre, and Zidon, and all the coasts of Palestine? will ye render me a recompence? and if ye recompense me, swiftly *and* speedily will I return your recompence upon your own head; because ye have taken my silver and my gold, and have carried into your temples my goodly pleasant things. (Joel 3:4–5)

Chapter 6: *The Future*

In these verses, God calls out "Tyre, and Zidon, and all the coasts of Palestine" for opposing Israel. God is saying He will turn their aggression against them.

"The coasts of Palestine" fittingly refers to the nation of Palestine (also called "Philistia" in some translations). Tyre and Zidon were cities in modern-day Lebanon.

So what we're being told is before Armageddon takes place, there will be a conflict with Israel on one side and Lebanon and Palestine on the other. Israel will be ultimately victorious in this battle due to God being with them.

This could very well be a reference to the terrorist groups Hamas (which is based in Palestine) and Hezbollah (which is based in Lebanon). These groups launched attacks on Israel in 2023, and both

Chapter 6: *The Future*

seek to wipe Israel off the map entirely. This could also possibly be the war that Israel will be recovering from when Russia invades (Ezekiel 38:8).

Notice what the next verse in Joel 3 says: "The children also of Judah and the children of Jerusalem have ye sold unto the Grecians, that ye might remove them far from their border." (Joel 3:6)

So what we're being told here is that Tyre, Zidon, and Palestine sold Jews to Greece ("the Grecians"). This implies that the conflict between these nations and Israel is historical as well as present and futural. This selling of Jews to Greece likely refers to Jewish captives being sold as slaves to Greek regions by the Phoenicians (Tyre and Zidon) and the Philistines (Palestine).

We're told in Amos 1:6–10 that Gaza (Palestine) and Tyre will be judged for selling captives.

Chapter 6: *The Future*

Ezekiel 27:13 mentions Tyre trading humans to Greece ("Javan"), providing further proof for this historical interpretation.

But since we're told of this in a chapter concerning the Battle of Armageddon, then this judgment against Tyre, Zidon, and Palestine can also be applied to the present day and the future. This conflict will take place before Armageddon, setting the stage for that most anticipated day of God's wrath.

This is what God says He will do to these hostile neighboring nations attacking Israel:

> Behold, I will raise them out of the place whither ye have sold them, and will return your recompence upon your own head: and I will sell your sons and your daughters into the hand of the children of Judah, and they shall sell

Chapter 6: *The Future*

them to the Sabeans, to a people far off: for the LORD hath spoken *it*. (Joel 3:7–8)

So, just as the Jews were sold to the Greeks, those in Lebanon and Palestine who seek Israel's destruction will be scattered to the land of the Sabeans (modern-day Yemen), putting the people of Israel out of their reach.

After Tyre, Zidon, and Palestine are dealt with, the chapter focuses back to Armageddon:

> Proclaim ye this among the Gentiles; Prepare war, wake up the mighty men, let all the men of war draw near; let them come up: beat your plowshares into swords, and your pruninghooks into spears: let the weak say, I *am* strong. Assemble yourselves, and come, all ye heathen,

Chapter 6: *The Future*

and gather yourselves together round about: thither cause thy mighty ones to come down, O LORD. Let the heathen be wakened, and come up to the valley of Jehoshaphat: for there will I sit to judge all the heathen round about. (Joel 3:9–12)

Here, God is essentially challenging the Gentile nations to come to battle against Israel, where His mighty power will be displayed against them.

Put ye in the sickle, for the harvest is ripe: come, get you down; for the press is full, the fats overflow; for their wickedness *is* great. Multitudes, multitudes in the valley of decision: for the day of the LORD *is* near in the valley of decision. The sun and moon shall be darkened,

Chapter 6: *The Future*

and the stars shall withdraw their shining. The LORD also shall roar out of Zion, and utter his voice from Jerusalem; and the heavens and the earth shall shake: but the LORD *will be* the hope of his people, and the strength of the children of Israel. (Joel 3:13–16)

These verses significantly enhance the drama of this battle. There will be multitudes of soldiers gathered in the land of Israel who will become victims of God's wrath.

Verse 15 says that the "sun and moon shall be darkened, and the stars shall withdraw their shining." (Joel 3:15) This is not literal, but it's symbolic of the overthrow of worldly powers. The sun, moon, and stars are often used in Scripture as symbols of the worldly

Chapter 6: *The Future*

nations, rulers, and authorities (Isaiah 13:9–10, Ezekiel 32:7–8, Daniel 8:10, Revelation 6:12–13).

Verse 16 tells us that despite all the chaos that will be unleashed in Israel, God will protect His people, which shows His loving nature.

> So shall ye know that I *am* the LORD your God dwelling in Zion, my holy mountain: then shall Jerusalem be holy, and there shall no strangers pass through her any more. And it shall come to pass in that day, *that* the mountains shall drop down new wine, and the hills shall flow with milk, and all the rivers of Judah shall flow with waters, and a fountain shall come forth of the house of the LORD, and shall water the valley of Shittim. Egypt shall be a desolation, and Edom shall be a desolate wilderness, for

Chapter 6: *The Future*

the violence *against* the children of Judah, because they have shed innocent blood in their land. But Judah shall dwell for ever, and Jerusalem from generation to generation. For I will cleanse their blood *that* I have not cleansed: for the LORD dwelleth in Zion. (Joel 3:17–21)

These verses offer a brief glimpse into what God's Kingdom will be like. No longer will blood be shed, and no longer will the people of Israel suffer, but an age of peace and of praising God will be established with Jerusalem at the center of it.

Chapter 6: *The Future*

Zechariah

Now, we're going to go over the Armageddon prophecies in the Book of Zechariah, specifically chapters 12 to 14.

> Behold, I will make Jerusalem a cup of trembling unto all the people round about, when they shall be in the siege both against Judah *and* against Jerusalem. And in that day will I make Jerusalem a burdensome stone for all people: all that burden themselves with it shall be cut in pieces, though all the people of the earth be gathered together against it. In that day, saith the LORD, I will smite every horse with astonishment, and his rider with madness: and I will open mine eyes upon the house of

Chapter 6: *The Future*

> Judah, and will smite every horse of the people with blindness. And the governors of Judah shall say in their heart, The inhabitants of Jerusalem *shall be* my strength in the LORD of hosts their God. (Zechariah 12:2–5)

God says that all nations will be gathered against Israel, and He will defend His people from them so that they will know He is their God. This is a clear reference to Armageddon.

> In that day shall the LORD defend the inhabitants of Jerusalem; and he that is feeble among them at that day shall be as David; and the house of David *shall be* as God, as the angel of the LORD before them. And it shall come to pass in that day, *that* I will seek to

destroy all the nations that come against Jerusalem. (Zechariah 12:8–9)

In verse 8, God says that after Israel's enemies are destroyed, the house of David will be like God, like the angel that will go before them. This is a reference to the Lord Jesus Christ, who is a direct descendant of David (Matthew 1:1).

This is also a reference to the accepted saints, as we're told that the angel of the LORD is also like God. And we're told in the Book of Luke that the saints will be made equal unto the angels (Luke 20:36). The house of David in this passage refers to the saints with Christ at the head.

And I will pour upon the house of David, and upon the inhabitants of Jerusalem, the spirit of

Chapter 6: *The Future*

grace and of supplications: and they shall look upon me whom they have pierced, and they shall mourn for him, as one mourneth for *his* only *son*, and shall be in bitterness for him, as one that is in bitterness for *his* firstborn. In that day shall there be a great mourning in Jerusalem, as the mourning of Hadadrimmon in the valley of Megiddon. (Zechariah 12:10–11)

So after the nations who will attack Israel are defeated, the Jewish survivors will look on "whom they have pierced" and bitterly mourn for him. Their mourning is compared to the lamenting over King Josiah's death, which took place in Megiddo (2 Chronicles 35:22–25).

This must be a reference to Jesus, whom the Jews reject as the Messiah. When he reveals himself to

Chapter 6: *The Future*

them following Armageddon, they will look upon the one they have pierced and deeply repent over rejecting him.

> Awake, O sword, against my shepherd, and against the man *that is* my fellow, saith the LORD of hosts: smite the shepherd, and the sheep shall be scattered: and I will turn mine hand upon the little ones. And it shall come to pass, *that* in all the land, saith the LORD, two parts therein shall be cut off *and* die; but the third shall be left therein. And I will bring the third part through the fire, and will refine them as silver is refined, and will try them as gold is tried: they shall call on my name, and I will hear them: I will say, It *is* my people: and they

Chapter 6: *The Future*

shall say, The LORD *is* my God. (Zechariah 13:7–9)

God says that two-thirds of Israel will die at Armageddon, but one-third will survive. This remnant, having experienced trial, suffering, and ultimately salvation, will be purified so they may become faithful, devoted members of God's Kingdom, that even the feeblest among them will be like David (Zechariah 12:8).

> Behold, the day of the LORD cometh, and thy spoil shall be divided in the midst of thee. For I will gather all nations against Jerusalem to battle; and the city shall be taken, and the houses rifled, and the women ravished; and half of the city shall go forth into captivity, and the

Chapter 6: *The Future*

residue of the people shall not be cut off from the city. Then shall the LORD go forth, and fight against those nations, as when he fought in the day of battle. And his feet shall stand in that day upon the mount of Olives, which *is* before Jerusalem on the east, and the mount of Olives shall cleave in the midst thereof toward the east and toward the west, *and there shall be* a very great valley; and half of the mountain shall remove toward the north, and half of it toward the south. And ye shall flee *to* the valley of the mountains; for the valley of the mountains shall reach unto Azal: yea, ye shall flee, like as ye fled from before the earthquake in the days of Uzziah king of Judah: and the LORD my God shall come, *and* all the saints with thee. (Zechariah 14:1–5)

Chapter 6: *The Future*

Much of Israel will be made desolate from the battle until God steps in to defend His people. We're told: "And his feet shall stand in that day upon the mount of Olives" (v. 4). This seemingly implies that God Himself will physically stand on the Mount of Olives. However, this is actually a reference to Jesus, who is subordinate to God (John 14:28). But how is this about Jesus when in verse 3, the one being spoken of is the LORD (Yahweh)?

God Himself will not stand on the Mount of Olives because He cannot be seen by anyone (Exodus 33:20, 1 Timothy 6:16). The last place Jesus was on earth before he ascended into heaven was the Mount of Olives (Acts 1:11–12). It makes perfect sense why the Mount of Olives would be where Jesus reveals himself to the rest of the world.

Chapter 6: *The Future*

Although Jesus and God are not the same, Jesus can still take on God's name at times as His righteous representative, just as the angels can (Genesis 22:11–12, Genesis 31:11–13, Exodus 23:20–21, Judges 2:1, etc.). Surely, since Jesus was made greater than the angels (Hebrews 1:4), he can also take on the name of the LORD. So, when Jesus reveals himself to the world on the Mount of Olives, the mount will split, the Jewish remnant will flee to "the valley of the mountains," and then the saints and angels, led by Jesus, will attack and mightily defeat the invaders.

So now, let's summarize the future Battle of Armageddon. After Jesus has returned to the earth, raised, gathered, and judged the responsible, during the period of fellowship between Christ, the angels, and the saints, a large Eurasian army headed by a Russian leader known as "Gog" will come down to conquer

Chapter 6: *The Future*

many nations (Ezekiel 38:2–6). They will invade the land of Egypt, which will force the submission of Libya and Ethiopia (Daniel 11:40–43). After hearing alarming reports from the northeast, Gog will set his sights on the land of Israel and attack it with many nations behind him (Daniel 11:44–45).

In response to this, certain Arabian countries, alongside Britain and nations founded by British colonists, will call out Gog for coming to plunder resources (Ezekiel 38:13). The army will be too overwhelming for Israel to handle and two-thirds of Israel will perish (Zechariah 13:8).

During the battle, Jesus will reveal himself to the world with the saints and angels by his side (Joel 2:16) by standing on the Mount of Olives. There will then be a great earthquake, and the mount will split, creating a massive valley (Zechariah 14:4–5). The

Chapter 6: *The Future*

one-third of Israel that will remain will flee to a mountainous region (Zechariah 14:5).

Jesus, the saints, and the angels, with rain, fire, and brimstone sent by God, will then utterly destroy the Gogian host and save Israel from destruction (Ezekiel 38:22, Joel 3:16, Zechariah 14:13). The Jews will then look upon Jesus whom they have pierced and deeply lament and mourn over rejecting him as the Messiah (Zechariah 12:10). They will then become spiritually purified (Zechariah 13:1).

March of the Rainbow Angel

Following Armageddon, there will be something occasionally referred to as the March of the

Chapter 6: *The Future*

Rainbow Angel. This phrase was coined from Revelation chapter 10:

> And I saw another mighty angel come down from heaven, clothed with a cloud: and a rainbow *was* upon his head, and his face *was* as it were the sun, and his feet as pillars of fire. (Revelation 10:1)

The mighty angel that descends from heaven clothed with a cloud, with a rainbow over his head, and his face and feet resembling the sun and fire, must represent the Lord Jesus in his glorified state. This mighty angel descends from heaven, which is what Jesus will do (Acts 1:11).

Each part of his described appearance symbolizes something. Clouds represent divine presence and are also used to describe Jesus' return (Exodus 13:21, Daniel 7:13, Revelation 1:7). Additionally, clouds are representative of the saints (Hebrews 12:1, Revelation 1:7). Therefore, this angel represents the glorified Jesus with the saints by his side.

The rainbow represents God's covenant (Genesis 9:13). Jesus is the mediator of the new covenant (Hebrews 9:15). His face like the sun represents Jesus' transfigured, illuminated form (Matthew 17:2, Revelation 1:16). His feet resembling pillars of fire further represents Jesus' glorified state (Revelation 1:15) as well as representing judgment (Isaiah 66:15–16, Malachi 4:1, 2 Thessalonians 1:7–8, Revelation 20:14–15). Jesus will be the judge (Acts 17:31). The angel in Revelation 10, often referred to as

Chapter 6: *The Future*

the rainbow angel, must be representative of Jesus Christ.

> And he had in his hand a little book open: and he set his right foot upon the sea, and *his* left *foot* on the earth. (Revelation 10:2)

The "little book" represents the remaining prophecies of God's purpose. Jesus placing his right foot on the sea and his left foot on the land represents his dominion over the Gentile nations and Israel. The Gentile nations are represented by the sea in Scripture (Psalm 65:7, Isaiah 17:12–13, Daniel 7:2–3, Revelation 17:15), and Israel is represented by land (Genesis 15:18, Ezekiel 20:38, Daniel 8:9, Zechariah 2:12).

Chapter 6: *The Future*

This must be what this chapter is speaking of: the subduing of nations under Christ's rule. After Jesus, the saints, and the angels save Israel and destroy the Gogian forces, many nations will refuse to accept his claim as king over the earth, so they will be subdued.

> And cried with a loud voice, as *when* a lion roareth: and when he had cried, seven thunders uttered their voices. And when the seven thunders had uttered their voices, I was about to write: and I heard a voice from heaven saying unto me, Seal up those things which the seven thunders uttered, and write them not. And the angel which I saw stand upon the sea and upon the earth lifted up his hand to heaven, and swore by him that liveth for ever and ever, who

Chapter 6: *The Future*

created heaven, and the things that therein are, and the earth, and the things that therein are, and the sea, and the things which are therein, that there should be time no longer. (Revelation 10:3–6)

Verse 3 tells us that when the mighty angel cried out, it sounded like a lion's roar, further identifying this angel as symbolic of Jesus, who is described as the lion of Judah (Revelation 5:5). The seven thunders represent God's complete and final judgments because the number seven represents completeness (Genesis 2:2) and thunder represents judgment (Psalm 29:3–5). These must refer to God's final judgments upon the nations of the world.

John being told to seal up what the seven thunders said and not write them down means they

Chapter 6: *The Future*

were not to be revealed yet. The angel saying: "there should be time no longer" (v. 6) refers to when God's purpose will come to its appointed end.

> But in the days of the voice of the seventh angel, when he shall begin to sound, the mystery of God should be finished, as he hath declared to his servants the prophets.
> (Revelation 10:7)

This verse speaks of the time when the seventh angel begins to sound. What does this refer to? When we look at the next chapter, we find the answer:

> And the seventh angel sounded; and there were great voices in heaven, saying, The kingdoms of this world are become *the kingdoms* of our

Chapter 6: *The Future*

Lord, and of his Christ; and he shall reign for ever and ever. (Revelation 11:15)

So when the seventh angel sounds, all the nations of the world will become subjugated to Christ's rule.

And the voice which I heard from heaven spake unto me again, and said, Go *and* take the little book which is open in the hand of the angel which standeth upon the sea and upon the earth. And I went unto the angel, and said unto him, Give me the little book. And he said unto me, Take *it*, and eat it up; and it shall make thy belly bitter, but it shall be in thy mouth sweet as honey. And I took the little book out of the angel's hand, and ate it up; and it was in my

Chapter 6: *The Future*

mouth sweet as honey: and as soon as I had eaten it, my belly was bitter. And he said unto me, Thou must prophesy again before many peoples, and nations, and tongues, and kings. (Revelation 10:8–11)

In this vision, John eats the scroll, which probably contains God's judgments upon the nations, and the taste is both bitter and sweet. John, being the one who eats the scroll, means he will take part in carrying out these judgments, which means he must rise again. This same invitation is also extended to us, as we too can be part of the body of the saints.

The scroll tasting bitter symbolizes the sorrow that will come with these judgments (death). The scroll tasting sweet symbolizes the joy of fulfilling God's plan righteously. Verse 11 speaks about the mission

Chapter 6: *The Future*

that John and the rest of the saints will be given: to spread God's word throughout the whole earth.

Revelation 10:7 says that this is what God "declared to his servants the prophets." Now, let's look further back into the Scriptures to see if we can find passages where the prophets wrote about the forced subjugation of nations in the end times:

> I will declare the decree: the LORD hath said unto me, Thou *art* my Son; this day have I begotten thee. Ask of me, and I shall give *thee* the heathen *for* thine inheritance, and the uttermost parts of the earth *for* thy possession. Thou shalt break them with a rod of iron; thou shalt dash them in pieces like a potter's vessel. (Psalm 2:7–9)

Chapter 6: *The Future*

This passage in Psalm 2 starts out by making a Messianic prophecy about the Lord Jesus Christ being the Son of God. The idea of this being about Jesus is reinforced in Acts 13:33, where God states that He will give Jesus all the nations of the earth as an everlasting possession.

Then, verse 9 says that the Messiah will have to break these nations "with a rod of iron," indicating that some nations will submit to Jesus' rule through force. The nations being conquered are compared to pottery getting shattered into numerous pieces. This connects to another Old Testament prophecy concerning the subjugation of the nations, which is found in the Book of Daniel:

> And in the days of these kings shall the God of heaven set up a kingdom, which shall never be

Chapter 6: *The Future*

> destroyed: and the kingdom shall not be left to other people, *but* it shall break in pieces and consume all these kingdoms, and it shall stand for ever. Forasmuch as thou sawest that the stone was cut out of the mountain without hands, and that it brake in pieces the iron, the brass, the clay, the silver, and the gold; the great God hath made known to the king what shall come to pass hereafter: and the dream *is* certain, and the interpretation thereof sure. (Daniel 2:44–45)

These verses are part of Daniel's explanation of Nebuchadnezzar's dream, in which the stone that represents Jesus strikes the statue made of gold, silver, brass, iron, and clay, which represents the nations or mighty empires of the world, and it shatters into

Chapter 6: *The Future*

nothing. The stone ends up becoming a mountain and fills the whole earth (Daniel 2:35). This is clear visual symbolism of the nations being overthrown and submitting to Jesus.

> And there shall come forth a rod out of the stem of Jesse, and a Branch shall grow out of his roots: and the Spirit of the LORD shall rest upon him, the spirit of wisdom and understanding, the spirit of counsel and might, the spirit of knowledge and of the fear of the LORD; and shall make him of quick understanding in the fear of the LORD: and he shall not judge after the sight of his eyes, neither reprove after the hearing of his ears. (Isaiah 11:1–3)

Chapter 6: *The Future*

Verse 1 of Isaiah 11 alone shows that this is a Messianic prophecy. Jesse was the father of David (1 Samuel 17:12), who is the father (direct ancestor) of Jesus, the Messiah (Matthew 1:1). Jesus is the Branch out of Jesse.

> But with righteousness shall he judge the poor, and reprove with equity for the meek of the earth: and he shall smite the earth with the rod of his mouth, and with the breath of his lips shall he slay the wicked. (Isaiah 11:4)

Here, we find the same imagery in Psalm 2:9, where Jesus is depicted striking the nations with a rod and destroying those who oppose his righteous rule. These passages may seem confusing to those who've labeled Jesus as this purely peaceful man. He was a

Chapter 6: *The Future*

lamb his first time on earth (John 1:29) but he will return the second time as a lion (Revelation 5:5).

> I saw in the night visions, and, behold, *one* like the Son of man came with the clouds of heaven, and came to the Ancient of days, and they brought him near before him. And there was given him dominion, and glory, and a kingdom, that all people, nations, and languages, should serve him: his dominion *is* an everlasting dominion, which shall not pass away, and his kingdom *that* which shall not be destroyed. (Daniel 7:13–14)

This passage in Daniel provides a perfect conclusion to the March of the Rainbow Angel and

Chapter 6: *The Future*

serves as a smooth transition into our next topic: the Kingdom of God.

The Kingdom

After the nations that oppose Christ are subdued, God's Kingdom will be established over the whole earth. This was God's plan and purpose ever since creation, revealed to us through His prophets Isaiah and Habakkuk:

> They shall not hurt or destroy in all my holy mountain; for the earth shall be full of the knowledge of the glory of the LORD, as the waters cover the sea. (Isaiah 11:9)

Chapter 6: *The Future*

> For the earth shall be filled with the knowledge of the glory of the LORD, as the waters cover the sea. (Habakkuk 2:14)

God's plan is for His glory to fill the earth forever, not for the earth to be destroyed or for us to reside in heaven, as many believe.

A misinterpretation found commonly within mainstream Christianity is the doctrine of the rapture—the belief that faithful believers will be brought up into heaven following Jesus' return and the resurrection of the dead. This passage in 1 Thessalonians chapter 4 is mainly used to support this idea:

> For the Lord himself shall descend from heaven with a shout, with the voice of the archangel,

Chapter 6: *The Future*

and with the trump of God: and the dead in Christ shall rise first: then we which are alive *and* remain shall be caught up together with them in the clouds, to meet the Lord in the air: and so shall we ever be with the Lord. (1 Thessalonians 4:16–17)

This passage can be confusing, especially since, if taken literally, it contradicts the very clear passages in Scripture that tell us that the earth is where the faithful will reside. That's because this passage isn't meant to be taken entirely literally, and when we interpret it symbolically, we see how it aligns with the rest of Scripture.

The Greek word translated as "caught up" in verse 17 is *harpazó* (ἁρπάζω), which means to be suddenly taken away. It does not mean to be carried

Chapter 6: *The Future*

upwards, which we see in John 10:12, which speaks of how a wolf "catcheth" (*harpazó*) sheep. A wolf attacking a sheep would obviously not imply that the sheep ascended into the sky, but that it was suddenly taken away.

Verse 17 of 1 Thessalonians 4 goes on to say that the living believers will be "caught up" (*harpazó*) with the resurrected believers "...in the clouds, to meet the Lord in the air..." This is oddly specific. Why does it need to say "in the air" after saying "in the clouds"? Wouldn't one assume that clouds are already in the air? Since the Bible does not waste words, this must be symbolic.

Clouds are used in Scripture to represent the saints (Hebrews 12:1, Revelation 1:7, Revelation 10:1). The Greek word used for "air" is *aér* (ἀήρ),

Chapter 6: *The Future*

which refers to the lower air that we breathe here on earth.

So, with our newfound understanding of this passage, what it could also say is:

> For the Lord himself shall descend from heaven with a shout, with the voice of the archangel, and with the trump of God: and the dead in Christ shall rise first: then we which are alive *and* remain shall be brought together with them as a body of believers, to meet the Lord on the earth: and so shall we ever be with the Lord. (cf. 1 Thessalonians 4:16–17, with paraphrased portion)

The earth is the everlasting inheritance of the saints. So, where does this idea of an everlasting

Chapter 6: *The Future*

Kingdom on earth come from? It's a recurring prophecy found throughout Scripture. Looking back at Daniel 2:44, the promise of an everlasting Kingdom is clear:

> And in the days of these kings shall the God of heaven set up a kingdom which shall never be destroyed: and the kingdom shall not be left to other people, *but* it shall break in pieces and consume all these kingdoms, and it shall stand for ever. (Daniel 2:44)

This coming Kingdom will replace all the kingdoms of the world and will last forever.

> Blessed *are* the meek: for they shall inherit the earth. (Matthew 5:5)

Chapter 6: *The Future*

These are the words of Jesus himself, in which he tells us that it is the earth that will be inhabited by the faithful believers, highlighting meekness as a key quality they will possess.

> After this manner therefore pray ye: Our Father which art in heaven, Hallowed be thy name. <u>Thy kingdom come. Thy will be done in earth,</u> as *it is* in heaven. (Matthew 6:9–10)

This is the beginning of what is known as the Lord's Prayer. Jesus tells his followers that God's Kingdom is coming and that His will shall be done on earth as it is already done in heaven.

Well, what is God's will with the earth? That it be filled with His glory (Isaiah 11:9, Habakkuk 2:14).

Chapter 6: *The Future*

Is the earth currently filled with the glory of God? Certainly not. The earth is currently filled with corruption and immorality (2 Timothy 3:1–5). God's will shall be done on earth when His "kingdom come."

Here are some other noteworthy verses which speak of the earth as the everlasting possession of the righteous:

> The righteous shall inherit the land, And dwell therein for ever. (Psalm 37:29)

> *One* generation passeth away, and *another* generation cometh: but the earth abideth forever. (Ecclesiastes 1:4)

> For thus saith the LORD that created the heavens; God himself that formed the earth and

Chapter 6: *The Future*

made it; he hath established it, he created it not in vain, he formed it to be inhabited: I *am* the LORD; and *there is* none else. (Isaiah 45:18)

The Bible clearly teaches that the earth will not pass away but will be inhabited by the faithful forever, filled with the glory of the LORD.

So, what will the Kingdom of God be like? Scripture tells us that Jesus will be the king and Jerusalem will be the capital. This goes back to God's promise to David that he would see his descendant sit on his throne in Jerusalem forever:

> And when thy days be fulfilled, and thou sleep with thy fathers, I will set up thy seed after thee, which shall proceed out of thy bowels, and I will establish his kingdom. He shall build

Chapter 6: *The Future*

an house for my name, and I will stablish the throne of his kingdom for ever. I will be his father, and he shall be my son. If he commit iniquity, I will chasten him with the rod of men, and with the stripes of the children of men: but my mercy shall not depart away from him, as I took *it* from Saul, whom I put away before thee. And thine house and thy kingdom shall be established for ever before thee: thy throne shall be established for ever. (2 Samuel 7:12–16)

This prophecy partially refers to David's son Solomon (1 Chronicles 22:9–10) and is ultimately fulfilled by David's descendant Jesus. Solomon succeeded David on the throne of Israel, and his reign was one of peace and prosperity (1 Kings 4:20–25), a

Chapter 6: *The Future*

state that would not be seen again until Jesus reigns (though Jesus' reign will be incomparably greater than Solomon's).

Solomon built the physical temple in Jerusalem ("an house for my name", 1 Kings 6), whereas Jesus built the spiritual temple of believers (Ephesians 2:19–22). The Davidic throne will be established "for ever." The Hebrew word translated as "ever" is *olam* (עוֹלָם), which can also refer to a long, indefinite time, not always literally forever (Exodus 40:15, Jonah 2:6, Hebrews 7:12). The future new order of the earth will last forever, but Jesus will not actually be king forever, which we'll go over later.

Solomon (1 Chronicles 22:9–10) and, especially, Jesus (Matthew 3:17; Matthew 16:16; Luke 1:32, 35; Hebrews 1:5; etc.) are referred to as the sons of God.

Chapter 6: *The Future*

Verse 14 of 2 Samuel 7, in which God says He will punish him with a rod when he does wrong, is about God's disciplining judgments upon Solomon and his descendants for their sins (Psalm 89:30–33). It's also a reference to Jesus' sacrificial crucifixion, for he was: "wounded for our transgressions, *he was* bruised for our iniquities: the chastisement of our peace *was* upon him; and with his stripes we are healed." (Isaiah 53:5)

In verse 16 of 2 Samuel 7, God finishes by telling David that his kingdom will endure forever before him. David died not seeing this, which means it applies to when Jesus returns and raises David from the dead; then the immortal, incorruptible David will see his descendant sit on his throne "for ever."

Chapter 6: *The Future*

Let's continue to look at more passages that teach that Jesus will be king over David's throne in Jerusalem:

> And, behold, thou shalt conceive in thy womb, and bring forth a son, and shalt call his name JESUS. He shall be great, and shall be called the Son of the Highest: and the Lord God shall give unto him the throne of his father David: and he shall reign over the house of Jacob for ever; and of his kingdom there shall be no end. (Luke 1:31–33)

This fully confirms that the promises God made to David in 2 Samuel 7 are ultimately about the Lord Jesus Christ.

Chapter 6: *The Future*

Jesus answered, My kingdom is not of this world: if my kingdom were of this world, then would my servants fight, that I should not be delivered to the Jews: but now is my kingdom not from hence. Pilate therefore said unto him, Art thou a king then? Jesus answered, <u>Thou sayest that I am a king. To this end was I born</u>, and for this cause came I into the world, that I should bear witness unto the truth. Every one that is of the truth heareth my voice. (John 18:36–37)

When Jesus says that his kingdom isn't of this world, he isn't referring to the physical earth, but rather to how his kingdom isn't part of the existing world system ruled by mortal sinners. Jesus is telling

Chapter 6: *The Future*

Pilate, as well as us, that his purpose is to become king.

We're also told of how significant Jerusalem will be as the capital of the world:

> And it shall come to pass in the last days, *that* the mountain of the LORD's house shall be established in the top of the mountains, and shall be exalted above the hills; and all nations shall flow unto it. And many people shall go and say, Come ye, and let us go up to the mountain of the LORD, to the house of the God of Jacob; and he will teach us of his ways, and we will walk in his paths: for out of Zion shall go forth the law, and the word of the LORD from Jerusalem. And he shall judge among the nations, and shall rebuke many people: and

Chapter 6: *The Future*

they shall beat their swords into plowshares, and their spears into pruninghooks: nation shall not lift up sword against nation, neither shall they learn war any more. (Isaiah 2:2–4)

At that time they shall call Jerusalem the throne of the LORD; and all the nations shall be gathered unto it, to the name of the LORD, to Jerusalem: neither shall they walk any more after the imagination of their evil heart. (Jeremiah 3:17)

And it shall come to pass, *that* every one that is left of all the nations which came against Jerusalem shall even go up from year to year to worship the King, the LORD of hosts, and to keep the feast of tabernacles. And it shall be,

Chapter 6: *The Future*

that whoso will not come up of *all* the families of the earth unto Jerusalem to worship the King, the LORD of hosts, even upon them shall be no rain. (Zechariah 14:16–17)

This worldwide Kingdom will be one of righteousness and peace, with Jesus ruling from Jerusalem, God's chosen city (Psalm 132:13–14). All people around the earth will go to Jerusalem to seek counsel and to worship.

Well, who will be the inhabitants of this Kingdom? Jesus will rule with the angels and saints by his side (Revelation 5:10). But since Jesus, the angels, and the saints are/will be immortal and incorruptible, then there has to be a population of mortals who are still prone to sin, or else there would be no need for a king and thus a Kingdom.

Chapter 6: *The Future*

We're told that there will be those in the Kingdom who will be taught the truth (Isaiah 2:3–4). We're also told that whoever doesn't go to Jerusalem to worship will be punished with a drought (Zechariah 14:17). A drought would have zero effect on immortals, so this is concrete proof that despite the Kingdom being mostly filled with righteousness, there will still be a population of sinful, flawed mortals.

Well, who will these people be? They must be the people who are alive when Jesus returns but are not considered responsible for knowledge and obedience to the gospel; therefore, they are not brought to the judgment seat.

This is why there will even be a Kingdom—because what's the point of there being a permanently righteous king ruling over everyone if everyone is permanently righteous anyway? Jesus will

Chapter 6: *The Future*

be king, so those who were unable to be granted salvation at his return may be given it at the second resurrection and judgment if they're found worthy.

As I've previously mentioned, although Jesus, the angels, and the saints will, in fact, live on earth forever in harmony, the actual Kingdom itself will not last forever and will last only 1,000 years. This comes from Revelation chapter 20:

> And I saw thrones, and they sat upon them, and judgment was given unto them: and *I saw* the souls of them that were beheaded for the witness of Jesus, and for the word of God, and which had not worshipped the beast, neither his image, neither had received *his* mark upon their foreheads, or in their hands; and they lived and reigned with Christ a thousand years. But the

Chapter 6: *The Future*

rest of the dead lived not again until the thousand years were finished. This *is* the first resurrection. Blessed and holy *is* he that hath part in the first resurrection: on such the second death hath no power, but they shall be priests of God and of Christ, and shall reign with him a thousand years. (Revelation 20:4–6)

What this is telling us is that those responsible for the knowledge and obedience of the gospel when Jesus returns will be judged and, if accepted, will be granted immortality and incorruptibility, as we've previously discussed. These people (the saints) will reign as priests alongside Christ for 1,000 years.

The people who are alive at Christ's return but are not responsible will not be brought to the judgment seat. Instead, they will live out their mortal lives in the

Chapter 6: *The Future*

1,000-year reign of Christ, as will their offspring. They will be taught the truth and expected to accept and follow it.

At the end of the 1,000 years, there will be a second resurrection and judgment. The mortals who died during the 1,000-year reign of Christ will be raised and judged, and those who answered the call will also be given immortality and incorruptibility. Those who did not answer the call will die forever, the same fate as those who didn't answer the call at the first judgment. After this, Jesus will give all the power back to God, and the earth will be filled with the glory of the LORD forever, just as He always intended:

> Then *cometh* the end, when he shall have delivered up the kingdom to God, even the Father; when he shall have put down all rule

Chapter 6: *The Future*

and all authority and power. For he must reign, till he hath put all enemies under his feet. The last enemy *that* shall be destroyed *is* death. For he hath put all things under his feet. But when he saith all things are put under *him, it is* manifest that he is expected, which did put all things under him. And when all things shall be subdued unto him, then shall the Son also himself be subject unto him, that God may be all in all. (1 Corinthians 15:24–28)

This period of eternal peace, righteousness, joy, and praise will be so incomprehensibly amazing that even the best moments of this life will not compare with the worst moments of the everlasting life that is to come. Let's conclude this chapter by looking at some passages which detail this perfected Age of Eternity:

Chapter 6: *The Future*

The wolf also shall dwell with the lamb, and the leopard shall lie down with the kid; and the calf and the young lion and the fatling together; and a little child shall lead them. And the cow and the bear shall feed; their young ones shall lie down together: and the lion shall eat straw like the ox. And the sucking child shall play on the hole of the asp, and the weaned child shall put his hand on the cockatrice' den. They shall not hurt nor destroy in all my holy mountain: for the earth shall be full of the knowledge of the LORD, as the waters cover the sea. (Isaiah 11:6–9)

Then the eyes of the blind shall be opened, and the ears of the deaf shall be unstopped. Then shall the lame *man* leap as an hart, and the

Chapter 6: *The Future*

tongue of the dumb sing: for in the wilderness shall waters break out, and streams in the desert. And the parched ground shall become a pool, and the thirsty land springs of water: in the habitation of dragons, where each lay, *shall be* grass with reeds and rushes. And an highway shall be there, and a way, and it shall be called The way of holiness; the unclean shall not pass over it; but it *shall be* for those: the wayfaring men, though fools, shall not err *therein*. No lion shall be there, nor *any* ravenous beast shall go up thereon, it shall not be found there; but the redeemed shall walk there: And the ransomed of the LORD shall return, and come to Zion with songs and everlasting joy upon their heads: they shall

Chapter 6: *The Future*

obtain joy and gladness, and sorrow and sighing shall flee away. (Isaiah 35:5–10)

And I saw a new heaven and a new earth: for the first heaven and the first earth were passed away; and there was no more sea. And I John saw the holy city, new Jerusalem, coming down from God out of heaven, prepared as a bride adorned for her husband. And I heard a great voice out of heaven saying, Behold, the tabernacle of God *is* with men, and he will dwell with them, and they shall be his people, and God himself shall be with them, *and be* their God. And God shall wipe away all tears from their eyes; and there shall be no more death, neither sorrow, nor crying, neither shall

Chapter 6: *The Future*

there be any more pain: for the former things are passed away. (Revelation 21:1–4)

Chapter 7: Righteousness

Now that we've gone over what salvation entails, the question becomes how do we achieve salvation? How do we get accepted into the Kingdom by Jesus when he returns? We must strive for righteousness by following Jesus' example: "And he said to *them* all, If any *man* will come after me, let him deny himself, and take up his cross daily, and follow me." (Luke 9:23)

Well, how are we to live by Jesus' example? He was the only man who died without sinning. He conquered his temptations and thus conquered death (Acts 2:24). We sin all the time. Every day is a constant battle against sin. But that is what we must

Chapter 7: *Righteousness*

do. We must continue to fight our sinful desires every day instead of embracing them like the world does. God understands our nature (Psalm 103:13–14), and so does Jesus, our judge, who experienced the temptations of mankind firsthand (Hebrews 4:15). God doesn't expect us to be perfect, like Jesus, but He expects us to try.

Just think about David. He was called a man after God's own heart (1 Samuel 13:14), yet he committed lust, adultery, and murder (2 Samuel 11). When the prophet Nathan told David that God was angry with him, David repented, and God immediately forgave him (2 Samuel 12:13). God still punished him (2 Samuel 12:14), as a father disciplines his son. Still, He forgave him because He understands our nature. When we genuinely repent of our sins, God will forgive us (1 John 1:9).

Chapter 7: *Righteousness*

So what exactly is righteousness? Paul sums up for us in Galatians the behaviors we're supposed to avoid and the behaviors we're supposed to strive for:

> Now the works of the flesh are manifest, which are *these*; <u>Adultery, fornication, uncleanness, lasciviousness, idolatry, witchcraft, hatred, variance, emulations, wrath, strife, seditions, heresies, envyings, murders, drunkenness, revellings, and such like</u>: of the which I tell you before, as I have also told *you* in time past, that they which do such things shall not inherit the kingdom of God. But the fruit of the Spirit is <u>love, joy, peace, longsuffering, gentleness, goodness, faith, meekness, temperance</u>: against such there is no law. And they that are Christ's have crucified the flesh with the affections and

lusts. If we live in the Spirit, let us also walk in the Spirit. Let us not be desirous of vain glory, provoking one another, envying one another. (Galatians 5:19–26)

We must strive daily to shun the works of the flesh and embrace the fruit of the Spirit. In the Old Testament, God often instructed the Israelites to avoid or destroy the surrounding nations (Exodus 23:32–33, Numbers 33:52–53, Deuteronomy 7:2–4). This was to prevent His people from being influenced by their sinful practices, so they could remain holy (Leviticus 20:26). We must also remove worldly influences from our lives and stay separate from the world.

Chapter 7: *Righteousness*

Forgiveness

Since God forgives us of our sins when we repent, we must also forgive others when they sin against us: "For if ye forgive men their tresspasses, your heavenly Father will also forgive you: but if ye forgive not men their trespasses, neither will your Father forgive your trespasses." (Matthew 6:14–15)

We cannot expect to be forgiven by the all-righteous God when our flawed selves become too proud to forgive each other.

Faith

To be granted salvation, we must also have faith which is: "the substance of things hoped for, the evidence of things not seen." (Hebrews 11:1)

Chapter 7: *Righteousness*

We must believe in God and what He has revealed to us in the Bible, even though we can't physically see Him. Luckily for us, God has provided us with plenty of irrefutable evidence of His existence and of His inspiration of the Scriptures.

In Ephesians 2, Paul writes: "For by grace are ye saved through faith; and that not of yourselves: *it is* the gift of God: not of works, lest any man should boast." (Ephesians 2:8–9)

This passage has commonly been misinterpreted to mean that as long as we have faith, regardless of our works, we will be saved. This has led people to have the mentality of: "If I just say that I believe in Jesus Christ, I will be saved." They try to convince themselves of this so they may feel free to pursue their worldly desires while still believing they'll be given eternal life.

Chapter 7: *Righteousness*

While faith is absolutely essential for salvation, we must also perform good works to demonstrate our faith. Just look at the very next verse of the same chapter, which reads: "For we are his workmanship, created in Christ Jesus unto good works, which God hath before ordained that we should walk in them." (Ephesians 2:10)

And just in case anyone were to still doubt the importance of good works, James, the half-brother of Jesus, gives us a very straightforward answer: "For as the body without the spirit is dead, so <u>faith without works is dead</u> also." (James 2:26)

Faith without works is dead! To be true servants of God and of His son, the Lord Jesus Christ, we cannot have faith without works, nor can we have works without faith. Also, if we have faith, why

Chapter 7: *Righteousness*

wouldn't we show it through good works? The two must be united.

Works

Well, what are some examples of good works? God loves those who give to the poor and provide for the sick (Deuteronomy 15:7–8, Proverbs 19:17, Isaiah 58:6–7, Matthew 25:35–36, Luke 14:13–14, James 2:15–16). When people were asking John the Baptist how they were to live righteously, he answered: "He that hath two coats, let him impart to him that hath none; and he that hath meat, let him do likewise." (Luke 3:11)

To put in perspective how much God hates it when we don't give to the poor and are greedy, just look at Sodom and Gomorrah. Sodom and Gomorrah

Chapter 7: *Righteousness*

were two cities that were sinning greatly against the LORD, so God rained down fire and sulfur and completely destroyed them (Genesis 19). In the Book of Ezekiel, God mentions the wickedness of the Sodomites in more detail:

> Behold, this was the iniquity of thy sister Sodom, pride, fulness of bread, and abundance of idleness was in her and in her daughters, <u>neither did she strengthen the hand of the poor and needy</u>. And they were haughty, and committed abomination before me: <u>therefore I took them away as I saw *good*</u>. (Ezekiel 16:49–50)

Chapter 7: *Righteousness*

May the fate of Sodom and Gomorrah be a reminder to us of what the consequences are of refusing to help the poor and the needy.

> Every man according as he purposeth in his heart, *so let him give*; not grudgingly, or of necessity: for God loveth a cheerful giver. (2 Corinthians 9:7)

We're also called to preach the gospel and spread God's word:

> And he said unto them, Go ye into all the world, and preach the gospel to every creature. (Mark 16:15)

Chapter 7: *Righteousness*

How then shall they call on him in whom they have not believed? and how shall they hear without a preacher? And how shall they preach, except they be sent? as it is written, How beautiful are the feet of them that preach the gospel of peace, and bring glad tidings of good things! (Romans 10:14–15)

The importance of preaching isn't to show everyone how right we think we are, but rather to spread the truth so that we can help as many people as possible find their way towards eternal life. One of my personal favorite Bible passages comes in Philippians chapter 1, which reads:

For me to live *is* Christ, and to die *is* gain. But if I live in the flesh, this *is* the fruit of my

Chapter 7: *Righteousness*

labour: yet what I shall choose I wot not. For I am in a strait betwixt two, having a desire to depart, and to be with Christ; which is far better: nevertheless to abide in the flesh *is* more needful for you. And having this confidence, I know that I shall abide and continue with you all for your furtherance and joy of faith; that your rejoicing may be more abundant in Jesus Christ for me by my coming to you again. (Philippians 1:21–26)

In this passage, Paul is writing to the Christians at Philippi, and he says that he wants to die so he can be with Christ. However, he also knows that his preaching efforts are beneficial for their spiritual well-being, so for their sake, he will dedicate his life to continuing to spread the gospel message. We must

Chapter 7: *Righteousness*

show the same devotion and embrace the role of being "fishers of men" (Matthew 4:19).

We must also remember the importance of prayer:

> Rejoice evermore. Pray without ceasing. In every thing give thanks: for this is the will of God in Christ Jesus concerning you. (1 Thessalonians 5:16–18)

> Be careful for nothing; but in every thing by prayer and supplication with thanksgiving let your requests be made known unto God. (Philippians 4:6)

When we pray, we cannot doubt or our prayers are meaningless (James 1:6). We also cannot be

Chapter 7: *Righteousness*

praying for selfish outcomes (James 4:3). These are some things we're told to pray for: God's Kingdom to come soon, for each other, for forgiveness, for guidance, for our enemies, for the sick and needy, for the spreading of the gospel, and for our daily needs (Psalm 51:10, Matthew 5:44, Matthew 6:9–13, Matthew 9:37–38, 1 Timothy 2:1, James 5:14, 1 John 1:9, etc.).

Jesus tells us that we are to pray humbly before God:

> And when thou prayest, thou shalt not be as the hypocrites *are*: for they love to pray standing in the synagogues and in the corners of the streets, that they may be seen of men. Verily I say unto you, They have their reward. But thou, when thou prayest, enter into thy closet, and when

Chapter 7: *Righteousness*

thou hast shut thy door, pray to thy Father which is in secret; and thy Father which seeth in secret shall reward thee openly. (Matthew 6:5–6)

Even though God knows what we need before we ask, we must still pray because it's a way of acknowledging God's authority so He may be given the glory when He provides for us.

We must also read and meditate upon the Scriptures daily (Joshua 1:8, Psalm 1:2, Psalm 119:105, Colossians 3:16, etc.). Not everyone in biblical and even post-biblical times had access to the Scriptures. Today, you can read the entire Bible online for free. We mustn't take this great blessing for granted.

Chapter 7: *Righteousness*

Solomon, on his quest for finding the meaning of life in the Book of Ecclesiastes, comes to this conclusion:

> Let us hear the conclusion of the whole matter: Fear God, and keep his commandments: for this *is* the whole *duty* of man. For God shall bring every work into judgment, with every secret thing, whether *it be* good, or whether *it be* evil. (Ecclesiastes 12:13–14)

Baptism

Now let's get into the topic of baptism. The word for "baptism" or "baptize" in the Greek is *baptizó* (βαπτίζω), which refers to a complete immersion in

Chapter 7: *Righteousness*

water: "And Jesus, when he was baptized, went up straightway out of the water..." (Matthew 3:16)

Jesus was fully immersed in water during his baptism. This is what baptism is, not sprinkling water on the heads of babies, but a full immersion.

We're also told that we must repent and get baptized (Acts 2:38). We cannot repent when we're babies, nor do we have any sins when we're babies, nor do we even understand the concept of sinning. The decision to get baptized must be made by the person who gets baptized as a way to signify their repentance. The decision cannot be made for them.

Why is baptism to be performed through complete immersion in water? What does it mean? Baptism represents resurrection. Going underwater represents death, and coming up out of the water represents being raised to life again. It washes away

Chapter 7: *Righteousness*

our past sins (Acts 2:38, Acts 22:16), though we will still sin again, and is a commitment to following Jesus as well as a spiritual union with him:

> The like figure whereunto *even* baptism doth also now save us (not the putting away of the filth of the flesh, but the answer of a good conscience toward God,) by the resurrection of Jesus Christ. (1 Peter 3:21)

> Know ye not, that so many of us as were baptized into Jesus Christ were baptized into his death? Therefore we are buried with him by baptism into death: that like as Christ was raised up from the dead by the glory of the Father, even so we also should walk in newness of life. For if we have been planted together in

Chapter 7: *Righteousness*

the likeness of his death, we shall be also *in the houses of his* resurrection: knowing this, that our old man is crucified with *him*, that the body of sin might be destroyed, that henceforth we should not serve sin. (Romans 6:3–6)

Many claim that baptism is not essential for salvation. Let's see what Jesus has to say about this: "He that believeth <u>and is baptized</u> shall be saved; but he that believeth not shall be damned." (Mark 16:16)

We must believe and be baptized to be saved. It doesn't say "those who believe not nor get baptized shall be damned" because why would anyone get baptized if they don't believe in the first place? Baptism is absolutely essential for salvation. But belief comes first. So once we've gained enough knowledge

Chapter 7: *Righteousness*

of the gospel message, it is our responsibility to answer the call to baptism.

A commonly misinterpreted verse surrounding baptism is found in Romans 10: "That is thou shalt confess with thy mouth the Lord Jesus, and shalt believe in thine heart that God hath raised him from the dead, thou shalt be saved." (Romans 10:9)

Many claim that this verse teaches that if you just say you believe in Jesus Christ and in his resurrection, you will be saved regardless of baptism or works. While this confession is essential, it is not the only thing we are required to do.

Confessing "Jesus is Lord" is one of the first steps towards salvation, but it is not the only step. Paul had already gone over the necessity of baptism in Romans 6:3–5. Jesus even clarifies this misconception himself: "Not everyone who saith unto me, Lord, Lord,

Chapter 7: *Righteousness*

shall enter into the kingdom of heaven; but he that doeth the will of my Father which is in heaven." (Matthew 7:21)

Jesus is literally saying here that not everyone who confesses that he is their Lord will be saved, but only those who perform God's will.

We must live by faith, demonstrate our faith through good works, and repent and get baptized in order to be on the track for salvation.

> Likewise, I say unto you, there is joy in the presence of the angels of God over one sinner that repenteth. (Luke 15:10)

Chapter 7: *Righteousness*

Careers

As servants of Christ, we must ensure that our careers do not hinder our discipleship. In this money-driven world, we must remember that we don't take our money with us to the grave, and we should strive to achieve true wealth: everlasting life in God's Kingdom.

> For the love of money is the root of all evil: which while some coveted after, they have pierced themselves with many sorrows. (1 Timothy 6:10)

This doesn't mean that having money is a sin, but it's the love and unwavering pursuit of wealth that's a sin. It's materialistic and temporary. This

Chapter 7: *Righteousness*

principle is particularly relevant to our careers, as the primary purpose of them is to earn a living.

> And the soldiers likewise demanded of him, saying, And what shall we do? And he said unto them, Do violence to no man, neither accuse *any* falsely; and <u>be content with your wages</u>. (Luke 3:14)

We are not to grow frustrated with not receiving the ideal payment. If we put our trust in God, He will provide for our needs:

> Therefore take no thought, saying, What shall we eat? or, What shall we drink? or, Wherewithal shall we be clothed? (For after all these things do the Gentiles seek:) for your

Chapter 7: *Righteousness*

heavenly Father knoweth that ye have need of all these things. But seek ye first the kingdom of God, and his righteousness; and all these things shall be added unto you. (Matthew 6:31–33)

If we prioritize righteousness and keep the Kingdom as our ultimate goal, holding on to that vision, God will surely provide for us. We need to ensure that our jobs do not require us to act against godly principles.

Careers that involve violence such as the military, law enforcement, security jobs, and so on, would force us to break the peaceful principles that Jesus taught us to live by until he returns (Matthew 5:39, Matthew 26:52, Luke 6:27–28, John 18:36). We should also avoid jobs that force us to swear oaths and

Chapter 7: *Righteousness*

be involved in disputes at court such as judges, lawyers, and prosecutors, among others (Matthew 5:34–37, 1 Corinthians 6:1–7).

Jobs that promote immoral behavior, such as gambling, alcohol, sexually explicit content, and so on, do not at all align with biblical principles (Galatians 5:19–21). Other careers that should be avoided are ones that might put you in a position to practice deceit, fraud, or exploitation (Proverbs 11:1).

Politics

As followers of God and His Son, Jesus Christ, we must also refrain from involvement in politics. This means not pursuing political careers nor voting for political candidates. Daniel writes in Daniel chapter 4:

Chapter 7: *Righteousness*

"...the most High ruleth in the kingdom of men, and giveth it to whomsoever he will." (Daniel 4:32)

God is in control of all political outcomes, and if we were to involve ourselves in the politics of this world, it would show that we don't trust God's plan and we want our will to be done, not His.

God might place certain corrupt individuals in power, not to reward them, but to bring about world events that will ultimately lead to the inevitable return of His Son. These rulers will never solve the world's problems, but Jesus certainly will.

Although we are to stay out of politics, this does not mean we are to disregard the laws of the nation we reside in. Paul writes in Romans:

> Let every soul be subject unto the higher powers. For there is no power but of God: the

Chapter 7: *Righteousness*

powers that be are ordained of God. Whosoever therefore resisteth the power, resisteth the ordinance of God: and they that shall receive to themselves damnation. (Romans 13:1–2)

This same message is repeated in Titus 3:1 and 1 Peter 2:13–14. Now, if worldly rulers were to enact laws that would force us to go against godly principles, then we must not obey, and we must remember that God is the true, ultimate authority.

A great example of this is found in Daniel chapter 3, where Shadrach, Meshach, and Abednego refused King Nebuchadnezzar's command to bow down to the golden statue because it conflicted with God's commands (Exodus 20:4–5). As a result, Nebuchadnezzar ordered them to be thrown into the fire. When they were, an angel of the LORD appeared, saving the three faithful men from death because they feared God more than man. We must never forget to do the same.

Relationships

Now let's move on to the topic of relationships. God's view on marriage is revealed to us in the second chapter of the Bible: "Therefore shall a man leave his father and his mother, and shall cleave unto his wife: and they shall be one flesh." (Genesis 2:24)

Marriage is supposed to be between one man and one woman. Not two men, or two women, or one man and multiple women, or one woman and multiple men, or multiple men and multiple women, but just one man and one woman.

Chapter 7: *Righteousness*

Since a husband and wife are to be made "one flesh," it is imperative that they do not have sex with anyone but their spouse and thus become "one flesh" with multiple people, defiling themselves.

Marriage is committing yourself to your spouse, so we should not have sex before we've made that commitment through marriage. Marriage represents Jesus' relationship with the saints (Ephesians 5:22–23) as well as God's relationship with His people Israel (Isaiah 54:5, Jeremiah 3:14, Hosea 2:19–20), so it should be treated as purely as possible.

Chapter 8: Resolution

So now that we've gone over why there is a higher power, why the God of the Bible is real and is not evil, why the Bible is divinely inspired, why the Bible has authority and the Quran does not, why Jesus is the Messiah, how the beliefs of mainstream Christianity differ from what God actually says, and what the hope and path to salvation is, the question arises of which group, if any, holds these beliefs?

I believe the Christadelphians are the closest group to true first-century Christianity. The Christadelphians were founded by Dr. John Thomas (1805–1871) in 1848. Now, how can a relatively small

Chapter 8: *Resolution*

group founded in the 1800s be the closest to the Christianity taught in the Bible?

God has always worked through a small group. A prime example of this is the nation of Israel:

> The LORD did not set his love upon you, nor choose you, because ye were more in number than any people; <u>for ye *were* the fewest of all people</u>: but because the LORD loved you, and because he would keep the oath which he had sworn unto your fathers, hath the LORD brought you out with a mighty hand, and redeemed you out of the house of bondmen, from the hand of Pharaoh king of Egypt. (Deuteronomy 7:7–8)

Chapter 8: *Resolution*

When, in biblical times, did the majority ever hold the truth concerning religion? Most nations worshipped false gods and idols. Yet the outnumbered Israelites were the only group that worshipped Yahweh (and still strayed from Him several times). Other examples of the faithful being in the minority include Noah's ark (Genesis 6–9), Gideon's 300 men (Judges 7), Abraham and Sarah (Genesis 12–21), the twelve apostles (Acts 1–2), and many more. So, to make the case that the Christadelphians cannot hold the truth because they are a relatively small group completely contradicts a common biblical theme.

Christadelphians believe that their true founder is Jesus Christ. Still, due to the apostasy, which Scripture warns us about, there wasn't an official established group that held the truth fully since Jesus' time until Dr. Thomas refounded it. That's not to say

Chapter 8: *Resolution*

that there weren't true believers before the Christadelphian movement. Many groups throughout history have held very similar beliefs to the Christadelphians, studying the Bible as the sole authority and rejecting many false doctrines that contradict the Scriptures.

Some of these groups include the Ebionites, Arian Christians, Paulicans, Waldensians, Socinians, and the Polish Brethren. Although Christadelphians do not claim that any of these groups fully held the truth, it shows that certain correct scriptural teachings were preserved throughout history before John Thomas systematized them.

Dr. Thomas coined the name "Christadelphian" from the Greek words *Christos* (Χριστός) and *adelphoi* (ἀδελφοί), meaning "brothers and sisters in Christ," which is found in Colossians 1:2.

Chapter 8: *Resolution*

After surviving a storm while traveling to America aboard the ship *Marquis of Wellesley* in 1832, Dr. Thomas devoted himself to finding the truth. Through his studies, he discovered that what most so-called Christians believed was not in line with the teachings of the Bible. These teachings include the Trinity, the immortality of the soul, and a personal devil, among others.

Through his writings, debates, and personal evangelism, Dr. Thomas attracted numerous people who agreed with his understanding of the doctrines he had discovered through thorough, logical, and unbiased Bible study.

Christadelphians do not claim that John Thomas was a prophet, but rather that he was a man who studied the Bible, sought the truth, and found it (Matthew 7:7–8). Through his studies, Dr. Thomas

Chapter 8: *Resolution*

made several correct predictions surrounding world events through the lens of Bible prophecy. Let's take a look at some:

> There is, then, a restoration of the Jews before the manifestation, which is to serve as a nucleus, or basis, of future operations in the restoration of the rest of the tribes after he has appeared in the kingdom.[57]

Based on the prophecy in Ezekiel 37, John Thomas correctly predicted Israel's reestablishment 100 years before it happened.

> The sixth vial is therefore preparing the way for the advent of Christ. It is drying up the

---

[57] John Thomas, *Elpis Israel* (London: Benj. L. Green, 1848), 441–42.

Chapter 8: *Resolution*

dominion of the "Turkish power," or the "Ottoman Empire," to make room for the reappearance of the Jews upon the stage of history as the subjects of God's kingdom.[58]

Here, Dr. Thomas correctly predicted the fall of the Ottoman Empire and its significance in the reestablishment of Israel. He wrote this 74 years before the Ottoman Empire fell in 1922.

The future movements of Russia are notable signs of the times, because they are predicted in the Scriptures of Truth.[59]

---

[58] John Thomas, *Elpis Israel* (1848; reprint, Birmingham, England: Christadelphian Printing and Publishing Association, 1973), Part III, Chapter 1.
[59] John Thomas, *Elpis Israel* (London: Benj. L. Green, 1848), Preface.

Chapter 8: *Resolution*

Dr. Thomas predicted Russia would be a significant world power in the end times, as we can clearly see today.

> Britain cannot be included among them.[60]

In this quote, Dr. Thomas predicted that Britain must leave the European Union for Ezekiel 38:13 to make sense. Britain officially left the European Union in 2020, an event commonly referred to as "Brexit." John Thomas predicted this about 170 years before it happened because he studied his Bible.

Christadelphian beliefs generally encompass what we've already covered in the previous chapters: God is one, Jesus is the Son of God (not God the Son),

---

[60] John Thomas, *Elpis Israel* (London: Benj. L. Green, 1848), 89.

Chapter 8: *Resolution*

the resurrection, the Kingdom of God on earth, the importance of baptism, and so on.

Instead of calling them churches, Christadelphians refer to their places of meeting as "ecclesias," which comes from the Greek word *ekklésia* (ἐκκλησία), meaning a church, assembly, or congregation. They don't call them churches to avoid being associated with mainstream Christianity.

Christadelphians have no hierarchy within their ecclesias; no priests, no pastors, and certainly no pope. This is based on how the early Christians operated in the New Testament, characterized by collective decision-making and shared responsibilities.

Christadelphians gather for a memorial service on Sunday (Acts 20:7), where they partake in the bread and wine to remember Jesus' sacrifice (1 Corinthians 11:23–26), sing hymns (Colossians 3:16), and listen to

Chapter 8: *Resolution*

a scripturally-based exhortation given by a baptized brother (Acts 20:7, Hebrews 10:24–25).

The baptized sisters are not permitted to speak during the memorial service (1 Corinthians 14:34–35). This is not because women aren't as good Bible students as men, because that's not true. Women remaining silent in the ecclesia reflects how our relationship with Christ will be in the Kingdom (1 Corinthians 11:3), where we will all be submissive to his teachings. Paul explains to us why it is the men who are to speak and not the women:

> Let the women learn in silence with all subjection. But I suffer not a woman to teach, nor to usurp authority over the man, but to be in silence. <u>For Adam was first formed, then Eve. And Adam was not deceived, but the woman</u>

Chapter 8: *Resolution*

<u>being deceived was in the transgression</u>. Notwithstanding she shall be saved in childbearing, if they continue in faith and charity and holiness with sobriety. (1 Timothy 2:11–15)

Women are not permitted to speak within the ecclesia because Eve was deceived by the serpent and Adam was not (even though they both sinned).

Verse 15 says that women "shall be saved in childbearing." This refers to a woman's role, which is to nurture children and raise them in the faith.

Women are also to cover their heads during meeting and when praying and prophesying (1 Corinthians 11:5). The role of faithful women is summed up by the Apostle Paul in Titus chapter 2:

Chapter 8: *Resolution*

> The aged women likewise, that *they be* in behaviour as becometh holiness, not false accusers, not given to much wine, teachers of good things; that they may teach the young women to be sober, to love their husbands, to love their children, *to be* discreet, chaste, keepers at home, good, obedient to their own husbands, that the word of God be not blasphemed. (Titus 2:3–5)

These gender roles are only temporary, and in the Kingdom, we will all be equally yoked in servitude to God our creator and to Jesus Christ our king:

> For ye are all the children of God by faith in Christ Jesus. For as many of you as have been baptized into Christ have put on Christ. There

Chapter 8: *Resolution*

is neither Jew nor Greek, there is neither bond nor free, <u>there is neither male nor female: for ye are all one in Christ Jesus</u>. And if ye *be* Christ's, then are ye Abraham's seed, and heirs according to the promise. (Galatians 3:26–29)

There are no mandatory payments that brothers and sisters must pay to the ecclesia, but it's purely voluntary. The payments go towards maintaining the places of meeting (ecclesias), Bible schools, charity, preaching efforts, and other related expenses.

Since we are all sinful beings, there is not always perfect harmony within the ecclesias. When certain disputes arise, they are resolved through scripturally-based discussions.

Despite this, Christadelphia is overall a very loving community focused on emulating the early

Chapter 8: *Resolution*

Christian church as closely as possible in its beliefs, practices, and structure. It is the closest group to the true first-century Christianity taught in the Scriptures, and unlike many other religious groups, it just makes sense. However, making sure that we understand God's principles and striving to live by them daily is more important than specifically becoming a Christadelphian.

May we take these principles to heart, meditating on them daily so we might have confidence on the day of judgment (1 John 4:17) and be given a small and humble place in the coming Kingdom, so we can help to fill the earth with God's glory, praising His name with joy, peace, gladness, and servitude in our hearts forever.

Chapter 8: *Resolution*

He which testifieth these things saith, Surely I come quickly. Amen. Even so, come, Lord Jesus. The grace of our Lord Jesus Christ *be* with you all. Amen. (Revelation 22:20–21)

Bibliography

Ahmad ibn Fadlan. *Ahmad ibn Fadlan and the Rus' Embassy: 921–922 A.D.* Translated and edited by James E. Montgomery. Cambridge, MA: The Medieval Academy of America, 2012.

Aharoni, Yohanan. *The Archaeology of the Land of Israel.* Boulder: Westview Press, 1979.

Appian. *Syrian Wars.* Translated by Horace White. London: Macmillan, 1899.

Berger, D., L. Smith, and R. Cohen. *Ancient Trade Routes and the*

Biblical World. London: Heritage Press, 2019.

Biran, Avraham, and Joseph Naveh. *The Tel Dan Inscription.*

Jerusalem: Israel Exploration Society, 1995.

Bochart, Samuel. *Geographia Sacra seu Phaleg et Canaan.* Paris:

Typographia Regia, 1646.

Bradley, Walter L., Charles B. Thaxton, and Roger L. Olsen. *The*

Mystery of Life's Origin: Reassessing Current Theories. New York: Philosophical Library, 1984.

Bryce, Trevor. *Life and Society in the Hittite World.* Oxford:

Oxford University Press, 2002.

Canivet, Maria Teresa Fortuna. "The Pontius Pilate Inscription."

Israel Exploration Journal 13, no. 2 (1963): 79–84.

Catholic Church. *Catechism of the Catholic Church.* Vatican City:

Libreria Editrice Vaticana, 1994.

Charles, R. H. *The Book of Enoch.* London: SPCK, 1912.

Chrysostom, John. *Homilies on the Martyrs.* In *Patrologia Graeca,*

edited by J.-P. Migne, vol. 50. Paris: Migne, c. 347–407 AD.

Diodorus Siculus. *Library of History.* Translated by C. H.

Oldfather. Loeb Classical Library. Cambridge, MA: Harvard University Press, 1933.

Dunn, James D. G. *The Partings of the Ways: Between Christianity and Judaism and Their Significance for the Character of Christianity.* London: SCM Press, 2003.

Easton, M. G. *Easton's Bible Dictionary.* New York: Thomas Nelson, 1897.

The Episcopal Church. *The Book of Common Prayer.* New York:

Church Publishing, 1979.

Epstein, I., ed. *The Babylonian Talmud: Tractate Bava Batra.*

London: Soncino Press, 1935.

Flavius Josephus. *Antiquities of the Jews.* Translated by William

Whiston. Peabody, MA: Hendrickson Publishers, 1987.

Gesenius, Wilhelm. *Hebrew and Chaldee Lexicon to the Old*

Testament Scriptures. Translated by Samuel Prideaux Tregelles. London: Samuel Bagster and Sons, 1847.

Herodotus. *The Histories.* Translated by George Rawlinson.

London: John Murray, 1862.

Hertz, J. H. *The Pentateuch and Haftorahs: Hebrew Text, English*

Translation and Commentary. London: Soncino Press, 1936.

Hoffmeier, James K. *Israel in Egypt: The Evidence for the*

Authenticity of the Exodus Tradition. Oxford: Oxford University Press, 1997.

Justinus. *Epitome of the Philippic History of Pompeius Trogus.*

Translated by Rev. John Selby Watson. London: Henry G. Bohn, 1853.

Klein, F. A. *Discovery of the Moabite Stone.* London: Palestine Exploration Fund, 1868.

Luckenbill, Daniel D. *The Annals of Sennacherib.* Chicago: University of Chicago Press, 1926.

Luther, Martin. *Against the Roman Papacy: An Institution of the Devil.* In *Luther's Works*, vol. 41. Philadelphia: Fortress Press, 1966. Originally published 1545.

Mazar, Eilat. *The Palace of King David: Excavations at the City of*

David. Jerusalem: Shoham Academic Research and Publication, 2006.

Morrish, George A. *Concise Bible Dictionary.* Chicago, IL: Bible

Truth Publishers, 1890.

Newton, Isaac. *Memoirs of the Life, Writings, and Discoveries of*

Sir Isaac Newton. Edited by David Brewster. Edinburgh: Thomas Constable and Co., 1855.

Nestor the Chronicler. *The Russian Primary Chronicle: Laurentian*

Text. Translated and edited by Samuel Hazzard Cross and Olgerd P. Sherbowitz-Wetzor. Cambridge, MA: The Mediaeval Academy of America, 1953.

Petrie, Flinders. *Six Temples at Thebes, 1896.* London: Egypt Exploration Fund, 1897.

Pliny the Younger. *The Letters of the Younger Pliny.* Translated by Betty Radice. London: Penguin Books, 1969.

Polybius. *The Histories.* Translated by Evelyn S. Shuckburgh. London: Macmillan, 1899.

Pope Leo XIII. *Praeclara Gratulationis Publicae*. New York:

    Benziger Brothers, 1894.

Pope Pius IX (attributed). In Karl Joseph von Hefele. *History of*

    the Councils, vol. 7. Edinburgh: T. & T. Clark, 1870.

Porphyrogenitus, Constantine VII. *De Administrando Imperio*.

    Translated and edited by G. R. Herrin. Washington, D.C.: Dumbarton Oaks Center for Byzantine Studies, 1967.

Rassam, Hormuzd. *Asshur and the Land of Nimrod*. New York:

Harper & Brothers, 1885.

Riasanovsky, Nicholas V. *A History of Russia.* 3rd ed. New York:

    Oxford University Press, 1977.

Robinson, Edward. *Biblical Researches in Palestine.* Boston:

    Crocker & Brewster, 1841.

Rohl, David. *The Lost Testament: From Eden to Exile – The*

    Five-Thousand-Year History of the People of the Bible. London: Century, 2002.

Rollston, Christopher A. "The Seal Impressions of Jehucal and

Gedaliah." *Bulletin of the American Schools of Oriental Research*, no. 357 (2010): 41–51.

Schaff, Philip. *History of the Christian Church*, vol. 3, *Nicene and Post-Nicene Christianity.* New York: Charles Scribner's Sons, 1884.

———. *History of the Christian Church*, vol. 4, *Medieval Christianity.* New York: Charles Scribner's Sons, 1884.

Strabo. *Geography.* Translated by H. C. Hamilton and W. Falconer. Cambridge, MA: Harvard University Press, 1917.

———. *The Geography of Strabo,* vol. 5. Translated by H. L. Jones. Loeb Classical Library No. 211. Cambridge, MA: Harvard University Press, 1928.

Suetonius. *The Twelve Caesars.* Translated by Robert Graves.

London: Penguin Books, 2007.

Tacitus. *The Annals of Imperial Rome.* Translated by Alfred John

Church and William Jackson Brodribb. London: Macmillan, 1876.

———. *The Annals of Imperial Rome.* Translated by M. Hutton. New York: Macmillan, 1931.

Thomas, John. *Elpis Israel.* London: Benj. L. Green, 1848.

———. *Elpis Israel*. 1848. Reprint, Birmingham, England: Christadelphian Printing and Publishing Association, 1973.

Tov, Emanuel. *Textual Criticism of the Hebrew Bible*. Minneapolis: Fortress Press, 2012.

VanderKam, James C., and Peter W. Flint. *The Meaning of the Dead Sea Scrolls*. San Francisco: HarperOne, 2002.

Wylie, J. A. *The History of Protestantism*, vol. 1. London: Cassell & Company, 1878.

www.ingramcontent.com/pod-product-compliance
Lightning Source LLC
Chambersburg PA
CBHW021136160426
43194CB00007B/608